READY THEN. READY NOW.
READY ALWAYS.

MORE THAN A CENTURY OF SERVICE BY CITIZEN-SAILORS

THE UNITED STATES NAVY RESERVE

1915·2015

UNITED STATES NAVY RESERVE

USN

1915·2015

100 YEARS

THEN ★ READY NOW ★ READY ALWAYS

READY THEN. READY NOW.
READY ALWAYS.

MORE THAN A CENTURY OF SERVICE BY CITIZEN-SAILORS
★★★ THE UNITED STATES NAVY RESERVE ★★★

COMMANDER DAVID F. WINKLER
U.S. NAVY RESERVE (RETIRED)
NAVAL HISTORICAL FOUNDATION

LEAD CONTRIBUTORS

MASTER CHIEF JAMES L. LEUCI
U.S. NAVY RESERVE

CAPTAIN JOHN LYNN SHANTON
U.S. NAVY RESERVE (RETIRED)

Published by
NAVY RESERVE CENTENNIAL BOOK COMMITTEE
WASHINGTON, DC

Published by: Navy Reserve Centennial Book Committee, Washington, DC
Vice Admiral Dirk J. Debbink, U.S. Navy Reserve (Retired), Chairman

In cooperation with Navy League of the United States
2300 Wilson Boulevard, Suite 200
Arlington, VA 22201-5424
Phone: 703.528.1775

Design: See Saw Creative, Jeff Lukes, Denver, CO

Printed in the United States of America by Quad/Graphics, Sussex, WI
Book pages printed on Appleton Coated – U1X® Silk Text
Manufactured in Wisconsin with Green Power

Minimum 20% post-consumer recycled fiber, FSC ©-Forestry Stewardship
Council certified fiber, Green-e® Certified Power. Acid free, pH neutral for
archival use. Enhanced elemental chlorine free, Lacey Act compliant

ISBN: 978-0-692-32765-4

ACKNOWLEDGMENTS

This book is the result of a tremendous team effort with most of the team consisting of current and former Navy Reserve Sailors. Commander Dave Winkler is a splendid author, and it was a privilege to watch him assemble the narrative and selected illustrations in a truly masterful way. Lead contributors Captain John Lynn Shanton and Master Chief James Leuci provided invaluable assistance. Captain Shanton had a vision to publish a history book for the 90th Anniversary of the Navy Reserve, and he provided many vignettes on Navy Reserve people, places, and units from his prior effort. Master Chief Leuci, a former Navy Reserve shipmate, collected hundreds of images on the Navy Reserve and contributed several sidebars detailing unique aspects of Navy Reserve history.

Other sidebar writers who contributed to enhancing this book include retired reserve Rear Admirals Joseph Callo and F. Neale Smith; Captains Wilbur D. Jones, Jr. and Alexander "Sandy" Monroe; and Commanders Randy Grojean and Paul Stillwell. Contributors who still wear the uniform part-time include Captain Laura Wesely and Commander J. Travis Moger, and Command Master Chief Ron Naida. I also thank Captain Peter Swartz who allowed us to reuse a piece he wrote on Secretary of the Navy John Lehman for a previous Naval Historical Foundation publication.

Jeff Lukes of SeeSaw Creative in Denver is credited with the wonderful graphic design, interior layout and cover. It was amazing to watch him assemble the pieces! We were assisted by a most capable editorial board consisting of Vice Admirals Robert F. Dunn and John Totushek; Force Master Chiefs Ronney Wright and David Pennington. Thanks also to Amy Wittman, Editor in Chief at the Navy League of the United States for her counsel and assistance, and for recruiting her husband, Jack Wittman to do the copyedit work on the manuscript. Finally, Heidi Bough worked under tight timelines to produce a very useful index.

Other individuals who contributed to this project include interns Aaron McDougal and Alicia Petersen at the Naval Historical Foundation who located a number of the images we used. Navy Department librarians Glenn Helm and Allen Knechtman made many key resources available for our use, including U.S. Naval Reserve Papers that were completed for the Naval War College Center for Naval Warfare Studies in 1992. The work completed by Captain Mel Chaloupka; Commanders Rick Bigelow, James Watters, and Walt Johanson; Lieutenant Commanders Andy Rockett, L.L. Borges-DuBois, and Christopher Haskell provided a wealth of chronologic material that was accumulated from hundreds of source materials.

Our team not only consisted of individuals but of organizations. First and foremost, the Navy League of the United States deserves recognition as the primary sponsor of the project as a way to fulfill one of their core missions: To inform Congress and the American public on the importance of strong sea services. The Naval Historical Foundation generously lent the services of its historian, Dr. Dave Winkler, to the cause. In addition to these organizations, the Navy Memorial Foundation and the Association of the United States Navy, formerly the Naval Reserve Association, have agreed to take a lead role in promoting this book.

All net proceeds from the sale of this book will stay with the Navy Reserve Centennial Book Committee to be used during the Centennial of the Navy Reserve in 2015 and beyond to help inform and educate the American public of the tremendous contributions our Navy's Reserve has made to the defense and security of our nation. We gratefully acknowledge all of the individuals who helped underwrite the costs of producing this book in order to maximize funds available for this important task.

Finally and most important, we acknowledge the hundreds of thousands of Navy Reserve Sailors, Naval Reserve Sailors and naval militiaman who have unfailingly answered our nation's call to serve, often at a moment's notice and usually in harm's way. They and their loved ones wrote the chapters of this book by their deeds, actions and sacrifice over more than a century of service as Citizen-Sailors—Ready Then, Ready Now, Ready Always—and they have our eternal gratitude.

Vice Admiral Dirk J. Debbink
U.S. Navy Reserve (Retired)

TABLE OF CONTENTS

INTRODUCTION   **8**

1 FROM PRIVATEER TO NAVAL MILITIA 1775–1915   **10**

Quasi and First Barbary Wars and The Proposed Naval Militia Act	11
The War of 1812	12
The American Merchant Marine Reigns Supreme	13
The Civil War	14
Sea Power in Decline	15
Defining the Problem	15
Competing Visions	16
The Creation of Naval Militias	17
The Naval Militia Mission Debate	19
The War Against Spain	20
Recognizing the Need For A Federal Force	22
Growth of the Naval Militia	23
The Naval Militia Act	25

2 THE NAVAL RESERVE FORCE AND THE GREAT WAR 1916-1918   **26**

America Prepares For War	27
Creation of the Naval Reserve Force	29
The Recruitment of Women	31
America Declares War!	32
Mobilization and Training	33
Building the Naval Reserve Flying Corps	36
The Amalgamation	37
Winning the War	40

3 FROM THE NAVAL RESERVE FORCE TO THE NAVAL RESERVE 1919-1940   **44**

The Great Pandemic	45
The Post-War Naval Reserve Force	46
ALNAV 67	49
Reorganization	49
The Naval Reserve Act of 1925	51
NROTC	52
The Naval Reserve Gains Strength	53
Naval Reserve Aviation Takes Flight	55
The Great Depression	56
The Course to Legislative Reform	58
Naval Reserve Act of 1938	59
The Global Situation	60
The Naval Reserve Prepares For War	60
The Naval Air Cadet Program	62

4 TO DEFEND THE FREE WORLD NAVAL RESERVISTS FIGHT A GLOBAL WAR 1941-1945   **66**

Mobilization For War	68
Officer Procurement	70
The Selective Service Act	72
The V-12 Program	73
Breaking Down Barriers	75
WAVES	79
Service and Sacrifice	81

5 THE GREATEST GENERATION BECOMES THE GREATEST NAVAL RESERVE 1946-1949   **86**

Demobilization	87
Budget Struggles	89
Planning the Post-War Naval Reserve	90
Building Reserve Infrastructure	91
Women Remain	93
Return of the Draft	94

6 KOREA 1950-1953   **96**

Pulling the Fleet (and Sailors) Out of Mothballs	97
Naval Reservists Join the Fight	100
The Transition to Jet Aircraft	101
Combat Support Services	103
The Birth of OCS	104

7 THE GROWING SOVIET THREAT AND THE NAVAL RESERVE RESPONSE 1954-1962   106

Armed Forces Reserve Act of 1952	107	Readiness	112
The New Look	108	Flexible Response	113
Refocusing the Mission	110	The Berlin Crisis	115
Antisubmarine Warfare	110		

8 VIETNAM AWAITING THE CALL 1963-1968   118

The Communist Threat in Southeast Asia	119	Combat Support	122
To Mobilize Or Not to Mobilize?	120	The Soviet Threat	127
The Seizure of *Pueblo* and Tet	121	The Anti-War Movement	128
Limited Mobilization	122		

9 THE TOTAL FORCE POLICY AND TAR WARS 1969-1979   130

Advancing Careers	131	Proposed Massive Cuts	139
The Total Force Policy—One Navy Concept	135	Continuing to Serve	142
Chief of Naval Reserve Established	137	A New Administration	143
Modest Reductions in Force	138	TAR Wars	144

10 THE MARITIME STRATEGY 1980-1990   146

Rude Awakening	147	A Traditional Mission Returns	155
A New President and Navy Secretary	148	War in the Gulf	156
New Reserve Force Ships	152	Changes At the Helm	158
Naval Reserves Respond	153	The Collapse of the Soviet Empire	159

11 DESERT SHIELD & DESERT STORM THE NAVAL RESERVE MEETS THE CHALLENGE! 1990-2000   162

Mobilization For Desert Shield	163	The Paradigm Shift	174
On to Desert Storm	164	Uphold Democracy	176
War Begins	168	Reserves Take Charge	176
The Aftermath	171		

12 READY NOW, ANYTIME, ANYWHERE 2001-2015   178

Defending the Homeland and Waging War	179	Deep Change	184
Operation Iraqi Freedom	182	Side By Side	188

CONTRIBUTORS   200

LISTS, IMAGE CREDITS & BIBLIOGRAPHY   202

INDEX   204

INTRODUCTION

Vice Admiral John Totushek.

At 9:36 a.m. on September 11, 2001, Vice Admiral John Totushek sat at his desk in the E-Ring of a recently renovated section of the Pentagon. The Chief of Naval Reserve had just hosted two retired flag officers and during the cordial visit one of Totushek's staff stuck his head in and said, "You ought to turn the TV on. Something's going on up in New York." As the live feed came on with news coverage of a burning World Trade Center tower, the three men witnessed an airliner fly into the second tower. After watching the two buildings ablaze for a few minutes, the visitors dismissed themselves to allow the Naval Reserve boss to conduct some paperwork chores. Totushek will never forget when the impact hit:

> *You felt it as much as heard it. It was just a big concussion. Saw a flash of something go by—not the airplane but more the explosion, the fireball. And immediately you could tell something big had hit the building, and I pretty much knew what it was, from having watched the TV.*

The blow knocked one of his aides off his chair. Debris floated down from the overhead. Walking into the corridor, Totushek looked down about twenty feet away and saw the ceiling had all fallen in. "It was dark down there. It was hard to tell exactly what was going on." With smoke starting to billow out, Totushek saw some people down the hall. He yelled: "Come this way, come this way." More people emerged who were dazed and panicked. Totushek, his two aides, and writer calmed the survivors down and directed them to orderly move out of the building through the Corridor 3 escalator and out to the south parking lot.

Thousands of other Pentagon employees poured out of the building, crowding the parking lot. With cell phones not working, one aide said, "Well, my car's right over here." Totushek responded, "I think our best move might be to get over to the Washington Navy Yard." So the Chief of Naval Reserve and immediate staff jumped in the car, sped across the 14th Street bridge and pulled up to the Latrobe Gate, just as the Marines were closing it. The driver beeped the horn, the Marines opened the gate to allow the car in, and Totushek and his staff went into his Navy Yard residence.

A few minutes later the Marines allowed another car onto the yard—one carrying Chief of Naval Operations Admiral Vern Clark. Given the proximity of Totushek's office to the impact point of American Airlines Flight 77, the CNO was pretty sure he had lost his Chief of Naval Reserve. Clark asked his wife to call to comfort Jan Totushek. Much to her pleasant surprise, John answered the phone. "That's how they found out I was still alive."

Reflecting on what happened in the immediate aftermath, the Chief of Naval Reserve recalled:

> *The response of the Reserve was incredible, as you would expect. It always has been and always will be. People were coming on active duty without even being called. The command center, of course, was wiped out. All the reservists that weren't injured or working already came to the Pentagon, because they knew very quickly that they were going to be needed. And frankly, the Reserve Force basically stood the new command center up at the Navy Annex the following day, and they manned it, pretty nearly. The reservists we lost were primarily in the command center.*

Once again the nation was at war. Outside of St. Louis, Jeffrey Covington recalled watching the events on television with his teenage son and younger daughter. "I knew everything in my world changed completely that day." His son, remembering that his father was away for months during Operation Desert Shield/Desert Storm, watched the nonstop news coverage and realized "this was not good." Once again, his father would be donning the uniform of a Sailor of the United States Navy in the service of his country.

Both Totushek and Covington were carrying on a tradition of service that traced its roots to the American Revolution, when merchant mariners, fishermen, and others joined the fight at sea to preserve American freedom. While a centennial for any organization is an impressive milestone, the question that needs to be asked is: "Why is the Navy Reserve only 100, given the 240-year history of the U.S. Navy?" It turns out we had Navy Reservists long before we had a Navy Reserve.

1 FROM PRIVATEER
TO NAVAL MILITIA
(1775-1916)

I f the nation's third president had the support of Congress, Thomas Jefferson's grave marker could have read:

Author of the Declaration of American Independence, of the Statute of Virginia for Religious Freedom, Founder of the University of Virginia, and Father of the Navy Reserve.

Indeed, this book could have been a bicentennial history had President Jefferson's proposed 1805 Naval Militia legislation to give the Navy the ability to call up pre-identified trained sailors to service in national emergencies been approved by Congress.

As the nation's first secretary of state, Jefferson had argued that commerce would be key to building the "peace and friendship of every nation, even of that which has injured us most." Jefferson's vision resonated in a Congress that had little interest in appropriating the required funding for a large standing Army and Navy. Thus, Congress passed the Militia Act of 1792, which called for every free, able-bodied white male between the ages of 18 and 45 to enroll in their respective state militias and spelled out the circumstances for presidential call-up.

QUASI AND FIRST BARBARY WARS AND THE PROPOSED NAVAL MILITIA ACT

Thirteen years later, now-President Jefferson, having completed his first term, realized that without a strong naval force, American commercial vessels were subject to plunder. As the eighteenth century closed, Congress created a new Federal Navy to respond to French captures of American merchantmen, authorizing six

The author of the Declaration of Independence and third president of the United States, Thomas Jefferson almost added "Father of the Navy Reserve" to his list of lifetime achievements.

frigates. The new United States Navy ably met the challenge during what became known as the Quasi-War with France.

Jefferson entered office with a new maritime challenge. On May 10, 1801, the Pasha of Tripoli, hoping to extract greater payments from across the Atlantic to facilitate American trade in the Mediterranean, declared war on the United States. Instead of tribute, the pasha awoke one day to find an American squadron attempting to blockade his port. As time passed, the Americans continued to apply military pressure. With the U.S. naval presence continuing off Tripoli, the pasha finally agreed to a peace treaty on June 10, 1805.

Symbolic of the turn of fortunes for France was the capture of the French frigate *Insurgente* by *Constellation* off the island of Nevis on February 9, 1799. With greater firepower and superior shiphandling, Captain Thomas Truxtun successfully raked his French foe over the course of an hour and would report the duel concluded with *Constellation* "being athwart his stern, ready with every gun to fire when he struck his colors."

A Jeffersonian gunboat, designed as an early nineteenth century version of the Littoral Combat Ship, would have served as drilling sites for the proposed naval militia. In effect, they were the first Naval Reserve Force ships.

Below: Letter of Marque. Rather than acquire ships and crews to expand the Navy during times of war, an alternative in the days of the early republic was to authorize merchant ships to wage war against enemy commerce. Of course, with prize money awarded for captured ships and cargoes, merchant captains had incentives to act aggressively—and the toll on British commerce contributed to an eventual peace treaty.

Due to the maritime nature of these confrontations, the Navy did not have to compete with state militias to enlist sailors, but in a future war involving a land foe, Jefferson's naval manning requirements might not be met. One initiative that had its genesis in the war against Tripoli was to construct shallower draft gunboats to better navigate the waters off North Africa. The initial production of fifteen gunboats in 1804 turned into a major procurement in the immediate following years of 176 vessels at a cost of more than $1,500,000.

To crew these gunboats, Jefferson's Naval Militia bill stated that "every free, able-bodied, white, male, citizen, of the U.S. of 18 years & under 45 whose principal occupation is on the high sea, or on the tide-waters within the US. shall be of the militia for the Naval service of the US. and shall be exempt from the service of the land militia."

While Congress was more than happy to appropriate funds for gunboats that would be built in congressional districts from Massachusetts to Georgia, it balked at funding Jefferson's plan that also required six days of active training in artillery and maneuver per annum for all those subjected to the law. Perhaps Congress didn't see the need to train sailors of America's merchant marine as their skill sets were interchangeable with those in naval service.

THE WAR OF 1812

Unfortunately, Jefferson's maritime woes only worsened following the British naval triumph at Trafalgar over a combined French-Spanish fleet on October 21, 1805. The British victory off Spain meant the Royal Navy could effectively enforce its restrictions on American trade to France. Between 1803 and 1807, Britain seized some 528 ships and their cargoes. In addition, while the U.S. Congress would not formalize the drafting of American merchant sailors in wartime, the British, at war with Napoleonic France, did. During the decade, British men-of-war continuously halted, boarded, and impressed hundreds of sailors off American merchantmen, claiming they were British deserters.

On June 12, 1812, President James Madison signed a bill declaring a state of war existed between the United States and Great Britain. Measuring naval force levels, the American declaration seemed foolhardy given that the Royal Navy floated over 600 seagoing warships.

Given the small size of the Navy, the manpower pool of officers and enlisted Sailors was adequate, with many having combat experience from the Quasi-War with France and later operations in the Mediterranean. At the beginning of 1812, the Navy had 4,010 sailors. At the war's conclusion this number totaled nearly 15,000. With a dormant merchant marine, the Navy easily could fill its need. Not only were the needs of the Navy met, but there were ample bodies to crew American privateers whose owners

Left: Especially embarrassing to the young republic was the seizure of four Sailors off the U.S. frigate *Chesapeake* by the British frigate *Leopard*. On June 22, 1807, the British warship sailed alongside the American frigate off the Virginia Capes, made a demand for the repatriation of four former Royal Navy sailors, and fired into an unprepared *Chesapeake*, killing three, when the demand was not met. Helpless, *Chesapeake* struck her colors and acceded to a Royal Navy boarding party.

In areas away from the coast, such as the lakes bordering Canada and the United States, Army and militia troops were also pressed into service to perform bluejacket duties. Such was the case during the Battle of Lake Erie, where Commodore Oliver Hazard Perry augmented his flotilla with citizen-soldiers turned Sailors. In victory, they demonstrated that men from non-maritime backgrounds can step in and make a substantial contribution.

received letters of marque to capture enemy vessels. During the War of 1812, twenty-four U.S. Navy warships captured 254 vessels. American privateers captured some 1,300 British merchantmen, and this disruption of British commerce would factor into Britain's decision to end hostilities in 1814.

THE AMERICAN MERCHANT MARINE REIGNS SUPREME

The impact of the end of hostilities on American commerce was immediate. In the first year after the war the value of American goods sold overseas jumped from $7 million to $53 million. Imports increased from $13 million to $113 million. More significant for the economy, these cargoes were being carried in American-built hulls. Over the next four decades, the American merchant marine proved a dominate force on the high seas as sleek Yankee clipper tall ships sped across the Atlantic and Pacific to Asia, Europe, and the new American ports of the West Coast that opened up after the War with Mexico. By 1840, 82 percent of overseas trade was being carried in American hulls.

Below: With the American merchant marine ruling supreme on the high seas, there was a ready pool of sailors to draw upon if the nation went to war. An 1836 Board of Navy Commissioners report concluded that the merchant marine could provide the Navy 30,000 sailors should the nation go to war.

African Americans provided some 20 percent of the Navy's enlisted force during the Civil War—double that of the Army. Shown here are the crews of *Hunchback* (bottom) and *Miami* (top).

THE CIVIL WAR

The political expediency of the Militia Act of 1792 that eschewed a large standing army for state-based citizen-soldier militias had two unintended consequences. First, when the southern states chose to secede from the Union, little needed to be done to organize and train ground forces to defend the fledgling Confederate States of America against the Northern militia regiments that were mobilized to put down the insurrection. With the ability to quickly field mass armies, the Civil War would become the bloodiest conflict in American history.

The second unintended consequence would impact the Union Navy. A naval blockade of southern ports would be a key component of northern strategy. To implement the strategy, not only did new Secretary of the Navy Gideon Welles have to rapidly increase the size of his afloat force, he had to find officers and crews for these ships. His task was made all the more challenging as 259 officers resigned their naval commissions due to southern allegiances and many enlisted men also deserted to fight for the South.

To replace the departed officers and expand the officer corps, Welles recruited from the ranks of former naval officers and masters and mates from the merchant marine. Welles also claimed that the maritime trades provided the Navy with adequate trained crews. Writing two decades later, however, historian James Russell Soley argued that the Navy was challenged throughout the war as states offered bounties as an enticement to enlist with local regiments, and once a draft was put in place, "Mariners were subjected to it like other citizens, without regard to the service which they would prefer." The Navy also had to compete with the private sector. Writing from the Midwest, gunboat squadron commander Andrew H. Foote complained he had only 650 of the 1,700 men needed to crew his eight gunboats. Foote noted that civilian deckhands earned $30 a month while the Navy only offered $18 for the same work.

Finally in 1864, Congress authorized the Navy to offer incentives for enlistment and allowed for the lateral transfer of skilled mariners who had been drafted into the Army. By the time Congress acted, Welles had succeeded in putting in place an increasingly effective blockade force. To crew the offshore flotillas, Welles turned to a manpower source that had been excluded from the 1792 Militia Act and proposed 1805 militia legislation: African Americans. A silver cloud associated with the non-passage of the Jeffersonian legislation was that the Navy was never restricted from enlisting black Sailors. Because African Americans ably served in the antebellum navy, a comfort level existed in the Navy about the ability of these men to make good Sailors.

Welles expanded the Union Navy by hiring, purchasing, or contracting for "such vessels as may be deemed necessary for the temporary increase of the Navy." Under provisions of the Congressional Act passed on July 24, 1861, the crews of these ships were given naval status and additional legislation made pay comparable to the regular Navy. The officers and crews of these ships had been, in effect, a naval reserve.

Secretary of the Navy Gideon Welles decided against the previous practice of offering letters of marque to privateers to hunt down Confederate merchant ships and raiders. The Declaration of Paris of April 16, 1856, outlawed the practice. As a non-signatory to the declaration, the Union could have sent armed merchantmen to sea; however, Welles was sensitive to international concerns and also did not desire to bestow legitimacy to a Southern privateering effort.

SEA POWER IN DECLINE

The demobilization of military and naval forces following the Civil War is well-documented. Less noted was the impact on America's merchant marine. Not only was it savaged by Southern commerce raiders during the war, but Europe was given a five-year window to continue its transformation away from sail, while American technological prowess focused on the war effort. In 1860, 66.5 percent of cargo was carried in American hulls. By 1865, the percentage of cargo coming to and from abroad in American-flagged merchantmen dropped to 27.7 percent.

With no immediate threat from overseas, American naval architects could observe armored warship developments in Great Britain and France and learn from the trials and errors of others. Furthermore, given a clean slate, American naval theorists could reflect on how sea power had been used in the past and how changing technologies would affect the equation. Amidst the change, there was one constant...the need for trained crews. French Admiral de Joinville observed: "Money will not make sailors; gold will not make a well-disciplined crew nor an experienced staff of officers; and of what use are ships without the living soul to command and the ready hands to obey?"

DEFINING THE PROBLEM

Captain Stephen B. Luce used that de Joinville quotation in an article he wrote titled: "The Manning of Our Navy and Mercantile Marine" that he read at the first meeting of the United States Naval Institute in 1874. Luce argued that education and training were critical to success in any fleet. To facilitate a maritime education infrastructure, Congress that year approved legislation to create, with the support of the Navy, maritime schools throughout the nation.

With the Naval Institute publishing papers from annual gatherings in the form of *Proceedings*, the organization provided an important sounding board

In his first annual report as secretary of the Navy in 1869, George M. Robeson observed that American exporters, in contracting foreign hulls to carry American goods, were, in effect, subsidizing the training of a foreign naval reserve manpower pool that could potentially be called upon to wage war against the United States. Confronted with the demise of American commercial maritime supremacy, Robeson called for a new system to provide skilled seamen to the Navy in a time of war.

on the future of the Navy and how to find crews for an expanded wartime fleet. Several authors echoed a concern that simply drawing on a depleting merchant marine for manpower would not suffice. Not only were the numbers not there but as naval warships grew more sophisticated, skills were not as readily translatable. Lieutenant Sidney A. Staunton would observe: "Fifty years ago when a gun was a piece of cast iron with a hole in it, fired by a match and throwing a solid shot, little special training was necessary to make to make of a merchant sailor a man-of-warsman." In the ensuing half-century, weaponry had become complex.

James Russell Soley, in *The Navy in the Civil War* (1883) argued that one lesson from the Civil War was: "A trained reserve force is a greater necessity for the navy than for the army, not because one service is more important than the other, but because its ranks are less easily recruited." Soley, a commander who taught at the Naval Academy, explained that in addition to being military professionals as with soldiers, sailors have to be professional seamen. "Hence the greater necessity for the navy of a large body of trained officers; and hence, also, the greater importance of a partially-trained naval reserve."

Two years after Soley published his Civil War history, another development occurred to further the creation of a naval reserve, as now-Commodore Luce established the Naval War College along Narragansett Bay at Newport, Rhode Island. Commodore Luce was replaced a year later with Captain Alfred T. Mahan, who continued to establish the new institution as a facilitator of strategic debate. Thus, the intellectual grounding for a national maritime strategy fostered through forums provided by the Naval Institute and Naval War College began to percolate toward Capitol Hill. On February 17, 1887, Senator Washington C. Whitthorne of Tennessee sponsored a bill

Born in 1850, too young to have served in the war between the states, James Russell Soley likely benefited from the first-hand knowledge of his older brother John Codman Soley, a Harvard graduate, who served with John Worden in the ironclad *Monitor* and later with Admiral David Farragut. After the war, the elder Soley served as naval attaché to Berlin and Paris and gathered intelligence on European naval reserve structures. His report to the Office of Naval Intelligence stated the French had a naval reserve of 10,000. French merchant sailors were also required to don a naval uniform for a year of service.

In the 1880s, Congress began funding a modern steel Navy, which promoted discussions on how such ships should be crewed and deployed. Seen here, the Texas would be rated as the Navy's first battleship.

Above: A protégé of President James K. Polk, Washington C. Whitthorne was the adjutant general of Tennessee during the Civil War and served in the Confederate Army. After the war he was elected to the House of Representatives in 1870 and chaired the Naval Affairs Committee from 1875 to 1881.

Augustus P. Cooke (above left) was an admirer of the Prussian military system that rapidly integrated trained civilians into a potent armed force. In contrast, Jacob W. Miller (above right) argued for state-based organizations that would compete to provide quality units.

"to create a naval reserve of auxiliary cruisers, officers, and men from the mercantile marine of the United States." The bill aimed to maintain the nineteenth century philosophy shared by all the maritime powers that the merchant marine should continue to provide the Navy its manpower safety net.

With Whitthorne's Senate term expiring the following month, his bill failed passage. However, Whitthorne remained in Washington, having been re-elected to the House of Representatives where he had earlier served as the chairman of the Committee on Naval Affairs. On January 4, 1888, he reintroduced his legislation as a House bill. Subsequently, Secretary of the Navy William C. Whitney submitted his 1887 report to Congress. Having assigned naval attachés a mission of charting the naval reserve organizations overseas, the Office of Naval Intelligence provided Whitney with a variety of schemes. Studying the overseas models, the Navy secretary called for an organization that should resemble "that of the militia or national guard, rest upon the foundation of local interest, contemplate the employment and rapid mobilization of steamers enrolled on the auxiliary navy list, and be calculated to produce the best results upon a comparatively small national expenditure."

COMPETING VISIONS

If intellectual discussions stimulated activity in Washington, they also served to further the dialog. On February 9, 1888, the New York branch of the Naval Institute met at the Seawanhaka Corinthian Yacht Club in Manhattan. Interspersed within the standard core of active and retired officers were representatives of New York's commercial and maritime communities. What drew the crowd was a subject of "popular interest and national importance"—the establishment of a naval reserve.

With legislation pending in Washington, Captain Augustus P. Cooke presented a lengthy paper echoing calls for government support for commercial carriers to strengthen the merchant marine and diverged somewhat from the Navy secretary's position by calling for an "efficient naval reserve organized by the general government." Cooke's vision called for enrolling former Navy and other seafaring men into the nationally organized reserve. "The establishment of a Naval Reserve, if entrusted to the States alone, would surely be beset with difficulties." Cooke did not dismiss the formation of volunteer forces for coastal and harbor defense, but he saw the need for a manpower reserve to augment the afloat forces.

Jacob W. Miller led the charge for a strong state-based militia system. A graduate of Annapolis who fought in the Civil War, rising to the rank of lieutenant, Miller had done well in the commercial sector and spoke that evening as the general manager of the New York, Providence, and Boston Railroad. Miller also represented a constituency of yachtsmen and extolled their potential worth in support of the Navy. Miller warned: "In forming a National Naval Reserve, the traditions hostile to centralizing armed forces may feel outraged and the scheme may become unpopular."

Unfortunately, the enthusiasm generated in New York did not transcend Congress when it took up the Whitthorne legislation.

A month after the Naval Institute gathering, snow began to fall in the northeast—a lot of snow. The Great Blizzard of 1888, a three-day nor'easter from March 11 through 14, dumped upwards of 50 inches of snow in Connecticut and Massachusetts. The snow did not thwart John C. Soley, supported by his colleagues of the Dorchester Yacht Club, to lobby the Massachusetts legislature to establish a Massachusetts State Militia. With snow piled around the Massachusetts State House on Beacon Hill, a bill was passed on March 17, 1888, to establish a "Naval Militia of Volunteers" consisting of four companies of naval militia to form a battalion.

In the Empire State, a follow-on initiative of merchants, steamship men and members of the Board of Trade and Transportation appointed Aaron Vanderbilt to lead a

Many senior flag officers were dismissive of Captain Alfred Thayer Mahan and the Naval War College, believing that the best school for learning the art of war was the deck of a ship. Many of those perspectives would change following Mahan's publication of *The Influence of Sea Power on History* in 1890.

feasibility study for a New York naval militia. Vanderbilt wrote to Navy Secretary Whitney, who embraced the concept as part of a grander scheme that would draw reserve manpower from diverse sources during national crises. Whitney pressed Congress, pointing out how the major European powers trained, equipped, and paid for reservists, using naval auxiliary ships strategically located to serve as training ships. On June 26, 1888, Whitthorne again introduced a bill "to provide for the enrollment of naval militia and the organization of naval forces." Whitney shared the bill with Vanderbilt and portions pertaining to state militias were crafted into legislation that would eventually pass in Albany the following year.

Meanwhile, up at the Naval War College, Captain Mahan directed that one of the academic sessions be dedicated to how best to pursue the creation of a naval reserve. Titled "Naval Reserves and the Recruiting of Men for the Navy," the course was led by Lieutenant Staunton, who expressed concern that naval militia proponents simply sought to elevate their social status and would add little combat value to the Navy.

In 1890, however, the new secretary of the Navy, Benjamin Tracy, seemed content with the state militia initiatives. By appointing historian James Russell Soley to be assistant secretary of the Navy in July 1890, Tracy had a blood connection in his office with the first commander of the Massachusetts Naval Militia— Lieutenant Commander John C. Soley.

THE CREATION OF NAVAL MILITIAS

On February 28, 1890, 172 men formed up a battalion in front of the Massachusetts State House under the command of the elder Soley. Shortly thereafter, the New York Militia conducted its initial muster. Jacob W. Miller would eventually be placed in command. In addition to Massachusetts and New York, other states to authorize naval units during this period included Pennsylvania and Rhode Island in 1889, California in 1891, and Maryland, Vermont, and South Carolina in 1892. Michigan, North Carolina, and Georgia established naval militias in 1893, and during the following year, Illinois, Connecticut, Virginia, New Jersey, and Louisiana joined the growing list. Addressing Congress on December 7, 1896, President Grover Cleveland praised the naval militia for developing into "a body of enterprising young men, active and energetic in the discharge of their duties and promising great usefulness."

Squadron of Evolution—In 1891, a White Squadron consisting of the steel-hulled ships *Philadelphia, Atlanta, Chicago, Charleston, Baltimore, Boston, Vesuvius, Cushing,* and *Petrel* commenced a tour of the Great Lakes. The cruise not only showed off the Navy's technological advancements to Americans in the hinterlands, but provided training opportunities for newly formed naval militias along the Great Lake states.

Those duties and promise of usefulness would be the subject of debate throughout the decade between those who saw the naval militia providing for harbor and coastal defense and those who saw the state organizations as a manpower pool for the fleet. To assist the state organizations with training, the Navy began offering old hulls, such as *Minnesota* and *Wabash* and coastal monitors of Civil War fame. In 1891, the Navy began to embark militia companies on short summer training cruises. On March 2, 1891, Congress provided $25,000 to the Navy for the "arming and equipping of the Naval Militia." This money, distributed to the states via the Navy Department, gave the Navy some leverage. For example, in 1892 the Navy offered a $5,000 bonus to those state naval militias that drilled on a warship for four days.

Herbert L. Satterlee took a leading role in organizing the New York Naval Militia. He would go on to be a founder of the Navy League of the United States.

While the chain of command for naval militias led to the governor's office, there was a strong dotted line leading to Washington. Furthermore, there was another dotted line to other state militias that came as a result of the creation of associations. The first such organization, the Naval Reserve Association, was formed in January 1890 by a group of New York yachtsmen, including August Belmont Jr. and Herbert L. Satterlee.

The New York-based association would soon be superseded by the broader-based Association of Naval Militias of the United States. The first national convention in 1895, drawing officers from ten states, was held aboard the sloop of war *Dale* berthed at Baltimore. As part of the effort to standardize training, Lieutenant William Slayton in 1895 published the *Naval Militiamen's Handbook* that discussed how a militia unit should be organized. Two years later John H. Bernard published *The Naval Militiaman's Guide,* which served as an encyclopedia of naval terminology and deck seamanship. The book's premise was used in a similar publication that debuted in 1902 and remains in print as *The Bluejacket's Manual.*

In an article published in *Outing* magazine in 1893, Everett B. Mero wrote: "Great care is also taken to enlist only a desirable class of young men in the ranks, and most have a high social position." The pampered pedigree of the Massachusetts unit was evident at the 1896 encampment at Lovells Island in Boston Harbor, where Lieutenant Commander Soley's men

Built after the War of 1812 as one of "nine ships to rate not less than 74 guns each," the *Alabama* remained on the stocks until needed in the Civil War, when renamed and commissioned May 13, 1864, as the *New Hampshire*, to serve as a store and depot ship at Port Royal, South Carolina. Following duties as a receiving and apprentice training ship in Newport, Rhode Island, she would be decommissioned in 1892 and loaned to the New York Naval Militia as a training ship. *New Hampshire* was renamed *Granite State* on November 30, 1904, to free the name *New Hampshire* for a newly authorized battleship.

The *Illinois* shown here is a replica of an *Indiana*-class coastal battleship that was built in Lake Michigan on pilings and heavy timbers for the World's Columbian Exposition in 1893. With her hull constructed of brick, plastered with cement and superstructure, redoubts, barbettes, turrets and main and secondary guns assembled using wood framing that was covered with cement and metal lathing, the ship looked authentic. Anchors, torpedo nets, davits, railings, berthing spaces, cabins, galley, and other living spaces added to the realistic effect. Plans to use the ship as a headquarters and training platform for the Illinois Naval Militia had to be dropped given the expense of moving the ship to another location.

trained on the monitor *Passaic*. Many in the battalion brought their servants to handle menial chores. Asked why the regiment needed to hire chefs and waiters, Soley responded that his men "are not accustomed to such food [navy rations], and if it was attempted, their stomachs would be so upset that they would not be capable of doing as much work."

THE NAVAL MILITIA MISSION DEBATE

Such impressions of the naval militia being a "schoolboy movement" contributed to a consensus that they should be used for coastal and harbor defense, given the comfort level many militiamen had with small craft. Studying the reserve manpower issue in Newport, the Navy's strategic thinkers came to a similar conclusion.

However, others saw other augmentation possibilities. Secretary of the Navy Tracy envisioned the militias attracting mechanics and electricians who could serve as technical specialists on new ships joining the fleet. The Rhode Island Naval Militia, for example, focused on mastering torpedoes and trained at the Navy torpedo school at Newport. Some of the more ardent advocates for an expanded role for the naval militias were a small minority of the naval militia commanders who understood that the regular Navy needed a manpower reserve for high seas services.

The divergence of views on how to meet the afloat manpower void during war was apparent at the 1897 Naval Militia Association meeting, where proposals to pursue legislation to establish a national naval reserve to address the Navy's needs was not acted on following expressed concerns that such an entity would compete with the naval militias for personnel.

From 1891 to 1897 the numbers of officers and enlisted men in the various naval militias rose from 1,149 to 4,157. Whereas the Navy desired a pool a seafaring men for its reserve pool, what it got with the naval militia was "landsman with aquatic tastes." The summer cruise program helped inject some salt in the veins of the citizen-sailors. To further professionalize the naval militia officer corps that, for the most part, were graduates of Annapolis, Assistant Secretary of the Navy William McAdoo offered Naval War College instruction to them in 1896. His successor, Theodore Roosevelt, renewed the invitation the following year.

New York Naval Militia pose on the deck of *New Hampshire*.

Above and above right: The explosion that ripped through the *Maine* would force the Navy to confront its manpower augmentation issue by turning to naval militias.

A perplexing dilemma remained for the Navy on how to augment the afloat forces in wartime. Much of the blame has to be directed at a leadership that was bore-sighted on building a fleet for the twentieth century. How to find crews for these ships could be solved over time. Time, however, would not be so cooperative. On February 15, 1898, a massive explosion rocked the battleship *Maine* at Havana, Cuba. Accusations were made against Spain.

THE WAR AGAINST SPAIN

By mid-March Navy leaders began to prepare for a potential war with Spain. On March 23, the Navy assigned Commander Horace Elmer to organize a "mosquito flotilla" to handle coastal defense. He would identify the location of potential vessels for acquisition and conversion and figure out where the crews would come from. He also was directed to develop a coastal defense organization. Not provided a staff, Elmer worked himself to death. Ordered to prepare contracts to alter the vessels he had identified for naval use on April 19, Elmer pressed on despite contracting pneumonia. Collapsing on April 22, Elmer succumbed four days later.

As assistant secretary of the Navy and then as president of the United States, Theodore Roosevelt would be the first of three Roosevelts who would influence the future of the Naval Reserve.

Also on April 19, the U.S. Senate and House passed resolutions demanding Spain withdraw from her Cuban colony and authorized the president to use force as necessary to forge Cuban independence. Spain responded by declaring war on the United States on April 23. Two days later, the U.S. Congress declared war on Spain. By that time, U.S. naval forces had already arrived off the coast of Cuba to establish blockades of Cuban ports. Assistant Secretary of the Navy Theodore Roosevelt had already set the wheels in motion leading to the outbreak of hostilities in the Eastern Hemisphere. Meanwhile, as Admiral George Dewey's flotilla departed Hong Kong for Manila, Roosevelt continued to build naval power replicating what had been done three and a half decades earlier during the Civil War—acquiring ships to augment the fleet. In the wake of Elmer's death, on April 28 Roosevelt delegated the challenge of organizing an Auxiliary Navy Force by bringing Rear Admiral Henry Erben out of retirement.

For Roosevelt it was one of his last acts as assistant secretary of the Navy, a post for which he had penned a resignation letter three days earlier. A believer in militia forces, Roosevelt stepped down to form an Army Volunteer Calvary unit that would gain acclaim that summer as "The Rough Riders."

Erben did not wait for Congressional authorization (which eventually came) to act. Using blueprints developed by Elmer, he created eight coastal districts to overlay the territorial organization of the lighthouse service and assigned a naval militia officer to command each district. With many on the eastern seaboard concerned that the explosion of shells within their communities would serve as the first notice of the location of the Spanish Navy, the authorization by the various state governors to deploy naval militia forces to perform their coastal defense missions reassured local populations.

The naval militia responded, manning eight converted yachts, ten converted tug boats, and a side-wheel steamer. The Navy further reinforced the coastal defense force by placing ten monitors that were being preserved at Philadelphia's League Island Navy Yard back into service. The naval militia crewed these obsolete Civil War-era warships.

However, as previously noted, the Navy had manpower problems afloat. The Navy's warships needed additional Sailors, as did four merchant ships that the Navy acquired to serve as naval auxiliaries as part of an Auxiliary Naval Force. In the aftermath of Dewey's stunning triumph at Manila, on May 26, Congress authorized President William McKinley to commission officers and Secretary of the Navy John D. Long to enlist up to 3,000 Sailors as needed for the naval auxiliaries. To find those officers and recruits, the Navy turned to the naval militias. Governors allowed naval militiamen leaves of absence so they could join the Navy and fill needed billets. Former members of the state organizations in New York, Massachusetts, Michigan, and Maryland provided crews for newly commissioned auxiliaries *Yankee*, *Prairie*, *Yosemite*, and *Dixie*. Hundreds more were sent to receiving ships along the eastern seaboard down to Key West, Florida, where they received assignments to commissioned warships.

The naval militias' contribution proved significant. Two auxiliaries played important support roles. *Prairie*, which arrived off Cuba following the U.S. Navy's destruction of a Spanish Navy flotilla off Santiago on July 3, shielded the eastern seaboard, having been initially assigned to the Northern Patrol Squadron. *Dixie* arrived off Cuba in mid-June, served as an Army transport convoy escort, performed blockade force duties, and eventually landed an armed force in Puerto Rico in late July to capture the towns of Ponce and La Playa.

Militia on Guard on the monitor *Wyandotte* at the Boston Navy Yard. While the naval militiamen who deployed on the four auxiliaries attracted the media attention, those who remained behind were unsung heroes. Captain Alfred Thayer Mahan observed that "proper coast defense, the true and necessary complement of an efficient navy, releases the latter for its proper work—offensive, upon the open seas, or off the enemy's shores."

Commenting on the performance of the Michigan Naval Militiamen who served on *Yosemite*, historian John Spears observed: "If anyone had doubted the efficiency of our auxiliary cruisers manned by Naval Militia, the work off San Juan in June dispelled it entirely."

The other two auxiliaries did fire their guns in anger. *Yosemite* arrived in Cuban waters in early June and steamed on to Puerto Rico, where she withstood the barrage of Spanish shore batteries and gunboat attacks to engage and destroy the blockade runner *Antonio Lopez*. *Yosemite* remained on blockade duty off San Juan until the cessation of hostilities.

Yankee, crewed by New York Naval Militiamen, joined the blockade force off Santiago in early June. Combat activities included dueling Spanish shore batteries in the vicinity of Santiago, supporting a cable-cutting mission within Guantanamo Bay, fending off Spanish gunboats as the cruiser *St. Louis* dragged the channel to cut communication lines, silencing a Spanish Fort at Caimanera, engaging suspected Spanish blockade runners and gunboats at the port of Casida; and capturing and destroying Spanish fishing vessels before heading to Key West to refuel and north to New York to take on ammunition for the blockading force. She returned to distribute the ammunition following the cessation of hostilities.

RECOGNIZING THE NEED FOR A FEDERAL FORCE

During the war, the Navy operated with a total force of 24,123 enlisted. Of these, 4,224 were provided to the Navy from the militias, of which 2,600 enlisted directly into the Navy and the remaining state sailors serving in harbor and coastal defense assignments—overall constituting approximately 17.5 percent of the Navy's enlisted strength. The naval militias also provided 267 officers to receive temporary naval officer commissions to serve with the fleet during the war. Commenting on the performance of the naval militia Sailors who augmented the regular Navy, the secretary of the Navy's 1898 annual report concluded: "Considering their lack of [seafaring] experience, the services rendered by them were so valuable that the country has been amply repaid for the money expended in their instruction and training."

Praise for the naval militias was loud, yet not without some reservations. Writing after the war, author H.W. Wilson noted that the militiamen could not be expected to do the work of trained seamen: "At best they were makeshift, and the necessity of a national naval reserve to supplement the active force is one of the first lessons of the war." In his State of the State address, Theodore Roosevelt, having ridden his Rough Rider fame to be elected governor of the Empire State, praised his state's naval militia for what it had accomplished, but argued a federally controlled reserve was still needed.

Sensing the imminent creation of a federal naval reserve, leaders in the naval militias conducted a preemptive strike by working with friends on Capitol Hill to introduce H.R. 11535, which aimed to create a naval reserve with naval militias forming "The first nucleus of the Reserve." That the Navy would be forced to administer its reservists within the boundaries of the forty-five states was among the provisions the department found distasteful. Instead, the Navy preferred a regional administrative approach, which was reflected in H.R. 12126, a detailed piece of legislation that contained many elements of operation

NAVAL WAR COLLEGE CONFERENCE OF 1900

To evaluate the lessons of the recent war and the failure in Congress to establish a national naval reserve, the Naval War College convened a conference on August 20, 1900, to include leaders of various state naval militias and representatives from the Navy Department.

In the wake of America's resounding victory and newly elevated status as a world power, the discourse at the Newport gathering was hardly magnanimously celebratory. The president, Captain Charles H. Stockton, opened his remarks with an appeal for the need of a national naval reserve and turned the floor to one of his instructors, Lieutenant J. M. Ellicott, who shared with the attendees the Navy Department's vision. For naval militia officers such as Captains Miller and Satterlee of New York, the vision may have played out as a nightmare. In Ellicott's detailed presentation, Miller saw no role whatsoever being assigned to the naval militia in the nation's defense. Over the remainder of the day there would be some serious discussions. While all attending were unanimous that a national naval reserve was needed, naval militia officers insisted that such a force not be created to the detriment of their organizations.

Summarizing the conference, historian Harold T. Wieand would write:

> *It foundered on the reef of unsettled relationship between a national naval reserve and the Naval Militia.*

He further observed:

> *The strength of the Naval Militia was mostly in the fact of their organized existence. In other words, they already were. They had performed creditably during the War with Spain and had a status that could not be easily obliterated. And what is more they had access to their state representatives in Washington and they knew how to behave politically.*

Growing in Strength: New York Naval Militia musters in Brooklyn on May 24, 1908.

and organization that would have been recognizable to twenty-first century reservists. For example, reservists would be expected to train for a period of four weeks divided over convenient periods and have the opportunity to participate in a two-week cruise.

Both pieces of legislation died in the 56th Congress.

With Theodore Roosevelt now the commander in chief, Congress again considered legislation that year to elevate the status of the naval militia to match that of what the National Guard achieved through passage of the Dick Act, which broadened the powers of the president to call state army militias into federal service. Another bill was introduced to create a federal naval reserve that had been developed by the Navy's General Board, which was headed by Admiral Dewey. Both bills failed.

With this setback, the Navy once again reintroduced the General Board-drafted proposals in 1906, as did the naval militia with their effort to attain National Guard-like status. Both failed. The chairman of the House Naval Affairs Committee again introduced the Naval Militia legislation 1907. The bill was vigorously supported by Assistant Navy Secretary Truman H. Newberry. As a former Michigan Naval Militiaman who served in the *Yosemite* during the Spanish-American War, Newberry was the ultimate insider. One of his first actions in 1905 was to bring the naval militias under the direct control of his office.

Newberry, who would eventually serve as Theodore Roosevelt's last secretary of the Navy, could not overcome opposition in Congress. After the huzzahs of the glorious victory over Spain, the United States became a colonial power and confronted an insurrection in the Philippines. This turn of events did not sit well with many Americans, considering the nation's roots in fighting a revolution to free itself of the shackles of colonial rule. The views of a growing anti-imperialist movement were clearly reflected in Congress, which opposed legislation to enhance the military's ability to project power overseas. A strong naval reserve would do just that. In 1909 and 1910, the Navy's attempts to have Congress enact its national naval reserve again failed.

GROWTH OF THE NAVAL MILITIA

Despite the reservations of several in Congress, the performance of the Navy as a component of peacetime diplomacy enhanced the service's popularity with the American public. In 1903, Roosevelt's interjected the Navy to resolve a crisis involving Germany and Venezuela and to support Panamanian rebels in their bid for independence from Colombia. In 1904, the Navy helped to stabilize the debt dispute situation in Santo Domingo. Following incidents on the West Coast concerning the treatment of Japanese workers, Roosevelt sent the Navy on a round-the-world cruise beginning in December 1907 on a most successful show-of-power and fence-mending mission. Arriving off Yokohama on October 18, 1908, the "Great White Fleet" was escorted into Tokyo Bay by three Japanese cruisers. Dudley W. Knox wrote: "For a week the Americans remained, to be feted and given the most enthusiastic greetings by great crowds of people, as well by officials from the Emperor down."

The naval militias both contributed to the Navy's popularity and benefited from the high public acclaim. From 1906 to 1912 the overall size of the naval militias increased from 4,477 to 7,320. In 1912, 23 states had militia organizations, giving the Navy a presence and a community outreach capability well beyond its stations on the coasts.

Left: Lieutenant (j.g.) Frank Bailey of the New York Naval Militia.

Above: Naval Militia boarding the battleship *Alabama* for their annual training.

Hawk was a converted yacht built as *Hermione* by Fleming & Ferguson of Paisley, Scotland, in 1891 and was acquired by the Navy to serve in the Spanish American War with the North Atlantic Squadron in blockading Cuba. Decommissioned on September 14, 1898, she was recommissioned in 1900 and loaned to the Ohio Naval Militia, which transferred her to the New York Naval Militia in 1909. She was decommissioned again on May 21, 1919, only to be brought back on April 16, 1922, and assigned to the 9th Naval District. She was operated on the Great Lakes as a Naval Reserve training ship until she was decommissioned one final time on February 14, 1940.

An example of the naval militia growth was the creation of a Third Division of the New York Naval Militia at Buffalo on July 27, 1907. A Stanford graduate in civil engineering and active member of the Buffalo Yacht Club, thirty-two-year-old Frank J. Bailey signed on as a seaman and became one of the division's forty-two plank owners. Within six months he had risen to the rank of boatswain's mate first class. In 1908,

he joined fellow naval militiamen on a training cruise in the auxiliary cruiser *Prairie* of Spanish-American War fame. The transfer of the *Hawk* from the Ohio Naval Militia on August 3, 1909, presented Bailey with another opportunity as the converted yacht needed to operate on the Great Lakes with a member holding a master and first-class pilot license. Bailey had both and after passing his officer exams, received his commission as an ensign. For the next seven years Bailey spent much underway time on Lake Erie as well as developing a good set of sea legs on cruises in the battleships *Nebraska*, *Utah*, *Alabama*, *Kearsarge,* and *New Jersey*. For his day job, Bailey had latched on with the Buffalo-based Pierce Arrow automobile company and had a reputation as an expert salesman of these luxury cars.

To sustain the Buffalo Division and other naval militia units the annual federal appropriation had risen to $125,000. To administer the naval militias the organization evolved out of the assistant secretary's office to an Office of Naval Militia that was established in 1911 and that eventually was placed into the Bureau of Navigation. That Bailey found himself conducting cruises on battleships for his annual training made sense, given that the growth of the battle fleet had outpaced recruiting, and the Navy decided to fully crew the newer battleships and place older battleships "in commission in reserve" with partial crews to be augmented by naval militiamen.

THE NAVAL MILITIA ACT

The Navy finally began to crack the legislative roadblock in 1912 with the passage of an act on August 22 to establish a Medical Reserve Corps. On March 4, 1913, Congress authorized the establishment of a Dental Reserve Corps. Then on February 16, 1914, Congress passed the Naval Militia Act.

An important piece of legislation, the act finally put in place a legal structure that formalized Navy supervision of the state militias and gave the president the authority to call them into federal service in a time of war or national emergency—similar to the authority he had with the National Guard. Furthermore, the bill provided compensation for training. Unfortunately, the act did not override provisions of the Constitution allowing for overseas deployment. The legislation also addressed issues related to rank and precedence between naval militia and regular Navy officers. The Office of Naval Militia was abolished to be elevated to the Division of Naval Militia—still ensconced in the Bureau of Navigation. Commander Frederic B. Bassett Jr. served as the first officer in charge.

Commander Frederic B. Bassett Jr. served as the first officer in charge of the Division of Naval Militia.

The three successive acts proved timely, given emerging world events. On June 28, 1914, Austrian Archduke Franz Ferdinand was assassinated in Sarajevo, Serbia. When Serbia failed to meet Austrian-Hungarian demands following the murder, Austria-Hungary declared war on July 28. With Russia allied with Serbia and Germany allied with Austria-Hungary, the war quickly escalated to most of Europe. With a quick onslaught through Belgium, Germany hoped to knock France out of the war. Supported by the British, the French stopped the German advance and the war on the Western Front would turn into a bloody stalemate.

The passage of the Naval Militia Act combined with ominous events overseas spurred the creation of new naval militia divisions as well as new recruits to established units. To support the infrastructure a permanent appropriation of $200,000 was provided. The Navy also made plans to assign regular Navy officers to oversee the instruction of the militia under the title inspector-in-structors. In addition, funds were made available to enable ample at-sea opportunities for the naval militiamen. Unfortunately, the feedback from the fleet was not all positive. Commanding officers observed that the units were top heavy with officers, both in rank and in number. Many holding enlisted ratings hardly seemed qualified to perform their jobs. At the December 1914 Naval Militia Association meeting, with officers from seventeen of twenty-three militias, the attendees received a laundry list from Navy officials of issues and carelessness problems to include "failure to fill vessels loaned to the Naval Militia with coal before leaving on a cruise."

With modern battleships such as *Pennsylvania* and *Arizona* featuring a main armament of twelve fourteen-inch guns on the building ways, the Navy still desired a more capable reserve manpower pool to fully crew such ships during time of war—especially given the circumstances abroad. Coinciding with the Naval Militia Association meeting, the Naval Affairs Committee held hearings to discuss naval appropriations and heard from Captain Victor Blue, then the chief of the Bureau of Navigation. Blue argued for a reserve built around ex-enlisted men who could be recalled to active duty. Secretary of the Navy Josephus Daniels and Assistant Secretary Franklin D. Roosevelt threw their full support behind the new concept that relied on a pool of former Sailors rather than drawing men away from the merchant marine.

The testimony impressed the Naval Affairs Committee to forward legislation authorizing monetary incentives to recruit former Sailors into a new national naval reserve prorated on time in service and also on the separation period from service. Introduced in Congress in early 1915, the bill that incorporated language to create a naval reserve was hardly debated. The bill also had provisions impacting other aspects of the Navy, in particular the creation of the office of the Chief of Naval Operations. The act was passed on March 3, 1915—the date the Navy Reserve has established as its birthday.

The future president of the United States, Franklin D. Roosevelt, successfully pushed for the creation of the Naval Reserve in his position as assistant secretary of the Navy.

2
THE NAVAL RESERVE FORCE
AND THE GREAT WAR
(1916-1918)

On May 7, 1915, two months after Congress approved legislation leading to the creation of a naval reserve, the German submarine U-20 fired a torpedo that struck the RMS *Lusitania* beneath the wheelhouse on her starboard side. The ship had departed New York a week earlier carrying 1,959 passengers and crew, and was due to berth at Liverpool on the day she was struck. The blow, followed by a secondary explosion, doomed the passenger liner. As the hull rapidly filled with cold seawater, a severe list prevented the launch of most of the lifeboats. Within twenty minutes the ocean liner had succumbed to the Irish Sea. Drowning and hypothermia claimed the lives of most of the 1,195 lost that day, of which 128 were Americans.

The German need to resort to U-boats to wage war at sea was, in effect, an unanticipated consequence of Great Britain's successful mobilization of its naval reserve. Numbering some 51,900 by 1912, the Royal Navy Volunteer Reserve enabled front line fleet units to be fully manned by providing manning for second-line older combatants that could be put to sea within two to thirty days. The swift manning and deployment of these ships to the North Sea with the Grand Fleet following events in Sarajevo in June 1914 clearly deterred the German High Seas Fleet from attempting an early engagement to wrest control of the seas.

AMERICA PREPARES FOR WAR

With the loss of *Lusitania* serving as a blunt reminder of the horrors of warfare, Americans became more supportive of military preparedness. On February 1, 1915, Commander Bassett sent a circular challenging the various state militias to consider establishing an "aeronautical reserve." Only four years earlier, Captain Washington Chambers, on May 8, 1911, prepared requisitions for two Curtiss biplanes. This rather routine administrative event is celebrated today as the birth of naval aviation. In the four subsequent years, the Navy's fledgling aeroplane branch had made some significant strides, including the first use of aircraft in combat, supporting operations off Vera Cruz in 1914.

Above:
S.S. *Lusitania*, sunk by a German U-boat in 1915.

Right:
Enlistment poster commemorating the loss of the *Lusitania*.

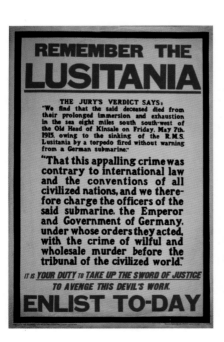

REMEMBER THE
LUSITANIA

THE JURY'S VERDICT SAYS:
"We find that the said deceased died from their prolonged immersion and exhaustion in the sea eight miles south south-west of the Old Head of Kinsale on Friday. May 7th. 1915. owing to the sinking of the R.M.S. Lusitania by a torpedo fired without warning from a German submarine."

"That this appalling crime was contrary to international law and the conventions of all civilized nations, and we therefore charge the officers of the said submarine. the Emperor and Government of Germany. under whose orders they acted, with the crime of wilful and wholesale murder before the tribunal of the civilized world."

IT IS *YOUR DUTY* TO *TAKE UP THE SWORD OF JUSTICE TO AVENGE THIS DEVIL'S WORK.*

ENLIST TO-DAY

The Burgess-Dunne Flying Boat was acquired by the Second Battalion of the New York Naval Militia in May 1915.

To create a reserve manpower component for its growing aviation arm, the Navy established an aircraft loan program for the various naval militias. Included with each aircraft the naval militia unit received:

- *One spare motor*
- *One spare magneto*
- *One spare propeller*
- *One hangar*

- *One hangar tool outfit (Steam engineering)*
- *One hangar tool outfit (Construction and Repair)*

- *One aeroplane launch truck*
- *Two helmets*
- *Two safety jackets*
- *Two pairs of goggles*

Operating expenses were provided to purchase fuel, oil, and other needed supplies.

Two weeks following the loss of *Lusitania* to U-20, the Illinois Naval Militia claimed the honor of being first to launch a hydro-aeroplane—a fitting sequence of events, given the Naval Reserve's future contribution to the Navy's anti-submarine warfare assets.

By July 1, 1916, the naval militias had grown to a total 9,806 officers and enlisted men. In May 1916 the Division of Naval Militia Affairs was transferred to the office of the recently established Chief of Naval Operations.

Ensign Samuel S. Pierce, Second Battalion, Naval Militia, New York, stands aside the Burgess-Dunne Flying Boat. Pierce was one of two officers who organized the aviation branch of the New York Naval Militia.

CREATION OF THE NAVAL RESERVE FORCE

Unfortunately, the Navy-veteran manpower pool that the Navy hoped to create following the March 3, 1915, legislation did not quickly materialize. Eight months after the passage of the legislation, only 176 men had joined. Therefore in early 1916, Secretary Daniels wrote the chairman of the House Naval Affairs Committee that proposed amendments would be forthcoming. Captain Blue again appeared before the committee to propose the increase of monetary incentives as well as the potential pension. He also noted that the 1915 act only applied to enlisted Sailors—no officers. Blue sought to amend that. Finally, Blue sought to expand the civilian pool beyond Navy veterans from which the Naval Reserve could draw and initially proposed five classes of naval reservists. After discussions and revisions the Naval Reserve morphed into six classes:

1 Fleet Naval Reserve consisting of Navy veterans.

2 Naval Reserve of seafaring officers and men of the Merchant Marine who trained on Navy ships and could be called to serve on warships.

3 Naval Auxiliary Reserve of seafaring men who could serve on auxiliary ships.

4 Naval Coast Defense Reserve who could perform limited duties such as coastal defense and would undergo training to do so.

5 The Naval Reserve Flying Corps of veterans of the Naval Flying Corps or men skilled in civilian aviation.

6 The Volunteer Naval Reserve of men who could offer services in wartime such as powerboat owners.

This structure, collectively called the Naval Reserve Force, became the law of the land on August 29, 1916, with the passage of the Naval Preparedness Act of 1916. A comprehensive piece of legislation, the act called for a three-year construction program to build ten battleships, six battle cruisers, ten scout cruisers, fifty destroyers, sixty-seven submarines, and sixteen auxiliary ships. This legislation also established the U.S. Marine Corps Reserve.

Enrollment card for Seaman William B. D. Gray who enrolled on April 12 in Class 4 of the U.S. Naval Reserve Force.

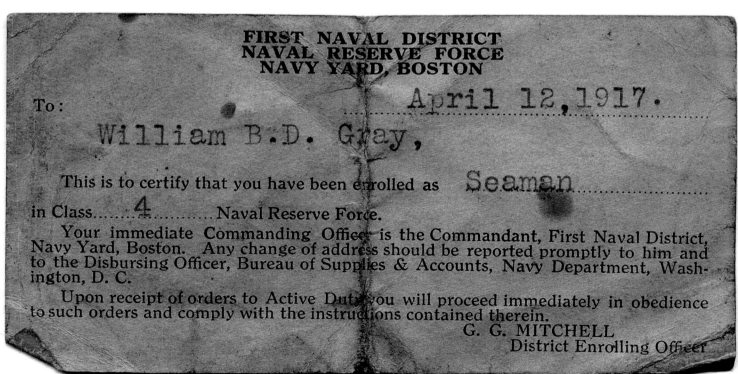

FIRST NAVAL DISTRICT
NAVAL RESERVE FORCE
NAVY YARD, BOSTON

April 12, 1917.

To:

William B.D. Gray,

This is to certify that you have been enrolled as Seaman

in Class 4 Naval Reserve Force.

Your immediate Commanding Officer is the Commandant, First Naval District, Navy Yard, Boston. Any change of address should be reported promptly to him and to the Disbursing Officer, Bureau of Supplies & Accounts, Navy Department, Washington, D. C.

Upon receipt of orders to Active Duty you will proceed immediately in obedience to such orders and comply with the instructions contained therein.

G. G. MITCHELL
District Enrolling Officer

With the creation of the Naval Reserve Force, an infrastructure now existed to identify and raise an adequate naval reserve manpower pool. As land warfare in Europe devoured the manpower reserves of the Allied and Central Powers, naval warfare proved to be just as life-consuming. Four months earlier during the Battle of Jutland, the British lost 6,094 sailors in the span of a few hours during their duel with the Imperial German High Seas Fleet.

To accommodate the use of the naval militias in what certainly promised to be an overseas war, a provision in the Naval Preparedness Act provided the authority to federalize the naval militias so they could be used domestically or abroad. To do this the Navy created the National Naval Volunteers as the mechanism to bring militias out from under state jurisdiction. By enrolling as a National Naval Volunteer, a Navy militiaman severed his ties with his state's militia unit. Of significance,

Sampson was one of Commander Joseph Taussig's destroyers that included National Naval Volunteers as crewmembers.

during wartime or a national emergency, there was nothing voluntary about the National Naval Volunteers, as the president could order the enrollment of a naval militiaman whether he volunteered or not.

NAVAL RESERVE UNIFORMS IN WORLD WAR I

By Master Chief James L. Leuci
U.S. Navy Reserve

Naval Reserve uniforms, while generally identical to those worn by regular Navy Sailors, did have some differences. In 1917, nearly two years after the establishment of the Naval Reserve, Navy Uniform Regulations were revised to include uniforms of Naval Reserve Force Sailors.

Unique brass buttons for reserve officers and chief petty officers distinguished them from regular Navy personnel. USNR buttons replaced regular Navy buttons on officer's coats, caps, and

shoulder marks. Chief petty officers also replaced the buttons on their coats and caps. The Naval Reserve Force officer cap device, while identical in style to the regular Navy officer cap device, was smaller—only one inch high. The reserve officer device consisted of a metal pin instead of the elaborately embroidered bullion patch sewn on the regular officer's cap band.

Enlisted reserve Sailors below chief petty officer wore blue cap ribbons bearing "U.S. Naval Reserve Force" instead of "U.S. Navy". When women entered the Navy in 1917, blue and white reserve cap ribbons became part of their seabag.

Change 20 to 1913 Navy Uniform Regulations, promulgated in the summer of 1918, modified reserve uniforms to further distinguish them from the regular Navy. In order to prevent any misidentification as

(A) **1918 Storekeeper First Class Petty Officer** with two War Service Chevrons. War Service Chevrons were worn by eligible reserve and regular officer and enlisted Sailors. **(B)** **1915-1918 Naval Reserve Button** worn by officers, chief petty officers and women. **(C)** **1918 U.S. Naval Reserve cap ribbon.** **(D)** **1916 Enlisted Blue cap** with USNRF ribbon. **(E)** **1918 USNRF Line Commander Shoulder Mark.** Change 20 to Navy Uniform Regulations modified reserve officer shoulder and sleeve mark to distinguish them from Regular Navy Line Officers.

A.

THE RECRUITMENT OF WOMEN

The coming of the Naval Reserve Force and the National Naval Volunteers created the requirement for a large bureaucratic administrative infrastructure to generate circulars, correspondence, orders, instructions, purchase requests, and so on. Suddenly, the Navy found those who could master the typewriter keyboard were just as critical as those who could tie a knot. On March 19, 1917, the commandants of the various naval districts around the nation received an interesting circular from the Bureau of Navigation stating that nothing in the Naval Preparedness Act prohibited the recruitment of women into the Naval Coast Defense Reserve—one of the components of the newly established Naval Reserve Force. The circular concluded:

> *The Bureau authorizes the enrollment of women in the Naval Coast Defense Reserve in the ratings of yeoman, electrician (radio), or in such other ratings as the commandant may consider essential to the district organizations.*

In an era where women still were disenfranchised, the response to the call for volunteers would be astonishing.

1917 Navy recruiting poster World War I by Howard Chandler Christy.

regular line officers, reserve line officer rank insignia changed. The line officer five-point star located on shoulder marks and sleeves became inscribed in a circle. The same design had already been in use by state naval militias and the National Naval Volunteers.

E.

The change in uniform regulations also provided that the "cap device for chief petty officers shall bear the letters 'U.S.N.R.' instead of 'U.S.N.' " The "U.S. Naval Reserve Force" enlisted cap ribbon was changed to "U.S. Naval Reserve".

However, most of the change 20 reserve uniform modifications only remained on the books a short time and generally were not implemented. On August 27, 1918, Secretary of the Navy Josephus Daniels issued General Order 418 stating that the uniforms for "regulars and reservists...shall

F.

hereafter be identical." However, reserve Sailors in inactive status would continue to wear U.S. Naval Reserve cap ribbons.

Navy reserve and regular uniforms did have some common distinguishing marks. General Order 422, dated September 25, 1918, authorized war service chevrons and wound chevrons for all naval enlisted and officer personnel. Wound chevrons were identical to war service chevrons, both resembling an inverted "V". War service chevrons worn on the lower left sleeve indicated overseas service. Wound chevrons, worn on the lower right sleeve, showed a Sailor had been wounded in combat with the enemy.

General Order 482, dated June 30, 1919, abolished war service chevrons, replacing them with the Victory Medal (renamed the World War I Victory Medal in 1947). The wound chevrons were also eventually dropped. In 1942, the Navy adopted the Purple Heart to recognize Sailors wounded in action.

G.

(F) 1918 Chief Petty Officer (CPO) cap device. Change 20 to 1913 Navy Uniform Regulations authorized a USNR chief petty officer cap device. The change was canceled before any USNR devices were produced. **(G) 1919 Victory Medal** (shown with Naval Battery clasp) authorized for personnel who served on active duty from April 6, 1917, through November 11, 1918, replacing War Service Chevrons.

Top: Recruiting poster for women in New York City, World War I.

Bottom: Naval Militia New York recruiting poster, World War I.

The Navy would need these women as events unfolded in early 1917 that drew the nation into the Great War. Following the international outcry about the *Lusitania* sinking, Germany agreed to forewarn potential torpedo attack victims by surfacing and communicating intent. With this restriction on its U-boat commanders, the Imperial German Navy high command gave away a tactical advantage which the British exploited through the deployment of Q-ships, seemingly innocent-looking commercial vessels that were in fact heavily armed. Seeking to tighten its stranglehold on vital materials bound for the British Isles, Germany announced on February 1, 1917, that its submarine commanders would resume unrestricted submarine warfare.

AMERICA DECLARES WAR!

The United States immediately broke off diplomatic relations. Americans were further incensed to learn of a message from the German Foreign Secretary Arthur Zimmermann to the German ambassador to Mexico proposing an alliance that would grant Mexico territories lost during the Mexican-American War. The British, who had intercepted and decoded the message, briefed the American ambassador on February 23. When the news of the telegram became public, accusations of an elaborate hoax crafted by British intelligence were widespread. However, on March 3, 1917, Zimmermann confirmed the telegram to an American reporter. Perhaps in being honest he was dismissive of a potential American contribution to the Allied effort on the Western Front. In Russia, Czar Nicholas II's abdication further demoralized a floundering Russian Army. If Russia could be knocked out of the war, tens of thousands of German troops could be decisively redeployed into France.

As of April 1, 1917, the Naval Reserve Force had enrolled approximately 10,000 officers and enlisted men having prior service.

Five days later, the United States declared war against Germany. A few days later in London, the First Sea Lord Admiral Jellicoe briefed Rear Admiral William S. Sims that the German U-boat campaign had been far more devastating than the public had been led to believe. Over a million tons of allied shipping had been lost in February and March, and German U-boats were on pace to match that number in April. The prognosis was grim. With a depleting reserve of three weeks of grain, the admiralty predicted that Britain would need to sue for peace by November or subject its population to starvation.

The Navy's greatest challenge during World War I would be to counter the German submarine menace to prevent the starvation of the British Isles and then to assure the safe transport of the American Army to France. To counter the German submarine threat, the United States quickly deployed a division of six destroyers with Commander Joseph Taussig in *Wadsworth* in command. Arriving in Queenstown, Ireland, on May 4, Taussig stunned British Vice Admiral Sir Lewis Bayly, who asked how long it would be until the Americans could be of service. Taussig could quickly respond: "I shall be ready when fueled," in part because his ships had fully manned crews augmented by National Naval Volunteers.

Before and After! Five Recruits are escorted into the receiving building at Naval Training Station Great Lakes and emerge as new Bluejackets.

MOBILIZATION AND TRAINING

With the declaration of war, men of the Naval Reserve Force were recalled to active duty. In addition, the president federalized the naval militias into the National Naval Volunteers—some 10,160 officers and enlisted men. Prepared for mobilization, units such as the Illinois Naval Militia of 579 men boarded trains and left Chicago within 48 hours of war being declared. Arriving at the Philadelphia Navy Yard, many were at sea on coastal patrol within the week and others would be assigned to Taussig's Europe-bound destroyers.

Unfortunately, following the arrival of Taussig's token force, months passed before the British received real help from their cross-Atlantic ally. Part of the problem was that the Navy enlistments before the war had not kept up with the manning requirements of a growing fleet. The combination of some 20,000 Naval Reserve Force and National Naval Volunteers would hardly fill the void, let alone crew new ships that would be acquired for the service. To man the wartime Navy, the service would have to recruit and train tens of thousands of civilians who either volunteered or were drafted after America declared war. To train all of these landsmen, experienced naval militiamen would play an important role.

Such was the case with Frank Bailey. Instead of augmenting a battleship after he was mobilized, National Naval Volunteer Lieutenant (j.g.) Bailey found himself remaining in Buffalo to recruit and train a new division. Finally, on October 22, 1917, Bailey sent approximately 100 men he had enlisted to an armory in Brooklyn, and he reported to a training camp near Rochester to serve as executive officer. With cold weather coming, Bailey and the estimated 500 recruits at the camp headed to Pelham Bay Naval Training Station, which was opening in the

Bronx, arriving there on November 2. Two weeks later Bailey finally received orders to the battleship *Nebraska*.

Under the framework of the National Naval Volunteers and Naval Reserve Force, the Navy recruited individuals who had or demonstrated the potential to attain needed skills. In some cases, civilians with highly technical skills were offered direct commissions. Chaplains, surgeons, civil engineers, naval architects, and other experts suddenly found themselves wearing service dress blues. For example, a group of 170 electrical engineers were commissioned and sent to a one-month orientation school at the Naval Academy. John Philip Sousa received a Navy commission. Women would not receive commissions, however, some 12,000 women would fill clerical billets under the title "yeoman (F)," though many

Sailors muster in Queenstown, Ireland.

I WAS A YEOMAN (F)

In 1967, the Naval Historical Foundation published a short monograph by Mrs. Henry F. Butler (Estelle Kemper) of her enlistment in the Navy during World War I. After graduating from college in Virginia the spring of 1918, Kemper decided to go to Washington from Richmond, against the wishes of her parents, with the intent of securing a civilian position with the Army.

Father warned me that Washington, in wartime, was a dangerous place for a girl, and that if I went to the capital city, I should 'expect to be insulted on every street-corner.'

Kemper promised her parents she would stay with friends across the Potomac and that her train would be met by an ensign she had met at her cousin's home.

On arrival in the wicked city I was met by the Ensign, as planned, but since he too was young and filled with patriotic fervor, he had dreamed up a wonderful plan for me. He suggested that if I really wanted to serve my country, I should join the Navy.

Kemper described the enlistment process as simple and speedy, consisting of an interview by a chief clerk, an exam at the Naval Hospital, "an oath of allegiance and, presto, one was a 'Yeoman (F)'." Following her first day of duty she called her father.

I told him proudly that I had joined the Navy. He gulped and said quickly: "I'll call your mother." When I repeated my announcement to her, she was stunned into silence for a moment, then asked weakly: "Oh, sister, can you ever get out?"

Kemper joined hundreds of other yeoman (F) Sailors in the new Main Navy Building, serving in the Supply Section of the Division of Aeronautics of the Bureau of Steam Engineering. The division supervised building gasoline engines, propellers, and incidental equipment for aircraft. Kemper tracked spare parts from factories to naval air stations and bases at home and abroad. For quarters Kemper joined with a group of seven Vassar graduates to rent a house. They worked six days a week, sometimes on Sunday, to pursue their patriotic duty. She recalled making less than $150 a month and her rent and food costs left little for entertainment. Unfortunately, she discovered the young naval officers they dated were as broke as they were. Overall, though, she took great pride in having joined the Navy, except for the uniforms.

She described the skirts as straight, tight and of the most awkward length possible. The jackets were shapeless. Kemper felt the uniform was as flattering to the female form as her father's business suits. She observed the flat hats were just the wrong size and shape for any girl, "except when taking a comic part on the stage."

My seven Vassar friends and I tried on our new uniforms for the first time, and were struck dumb by what we saw in the mirror, and when we looked at each other. Normally we were not a bad-looking lot. In those uniforms we could have been outdone in looks by the Salvation Army!

Following the end of the war Kemper attended to the collection and disposition of Naval Aviation matériel. In addition, she provided logistical support for the flight of three Navy seaplanes that attempted to cross the Atlantic in 1919. Shortly afterwards, she received her honorable discharge. Kemper took pride in receiving the World War I Victory Medal from Navy Secretary Josephus Daniels "with the conventional kiss on each cheek. A little French, to be sure, but a very satisfactory honor!"

preferred to be called "yeowomen." By the end of the war some 2,000 of this number would be working daily on the massive new 940,000-square-foot Main Navy Building that was constructed in five months at the location of the present Vietnam Veterans Memorial. To assist with logistical issues, 200 of these women would work in the Bureau of Supply and Accounts.

Many of the male enlisted and officer recruits would pass through the constantly growing Pelham Bay complex on the western end of Long Island Sound that would be dubbed "the Reserve Academy." Where at one time the Navy saw the merchant marine as a source of manpower, the state of the merchant marine was such that the Navy had to train officers and crews for the needed merchantmen that were being acquired or built for the war effort. By the end of the war the Naval Overseas Transportation Service would operate some 450 cargo ships with Naval Reserve officers and crews. Pelham Bay, commanded by Captain William B. Franklin, trained deck officer candidates for topside duties and offered advanced courses for enlisted quartermasters, radiomen, cooks, winch operators, and hydrophone operators. With an initial annual capacity of 6,000 trainees, the center expanded to handle 25,000 per year.

THE SECRETARY OF THE NAVY.

WASHINGTON.

October 12, 1917.

My dear Mr. Gallivan:

I am very glad to hear of the excellent work which Chief Yeoman Daisy M. Erd has been doing. It justifies my belief in the capacity of women to do important work and to relieve the men who must go to sea. When I authorized the enlistment of women as yeomen in the time of emergency there was a good deal of doubt whether I had the authority to do so. I have no authority to do so except in the Naval Reserve, and there was some question raised about that. I held that I had the power and nobody has since questioned it. But I have no authority to make a woman an ensign and I have given orders that no men shall be made ensigns who do not pass the examinations necessary to qualify them for important duty at sea.

Sincerely yours,

Josephus Daniels

Hon. James A. Gallivan, M.C.,
No. 354 West Broadway,
South Boston, Mass.

Above: Loretta P. Walsh was the first woman enrolled in the U.S. Naval Reserve Force, Class 4, during World War 1. Walsh enlisted as a chief yeoman.

Left: A letter from Secretary of the Navy Josephus Daniels in response to an inquiry by Congressman James Gallivan of Massachusetts, who sought a commission for Chief Yeoman Daisy M.P. Erd (pictured below).

New Jersey's Stevens Institute of Technology served as a counterpart to Pelham Bay in the training of engineering officers. The Naval Academy also hosted a fifteen-week training course to prepare officers to serve on merchant marine vessels.

The emerging technology of radio communications would prove critical to naval operations, especially anti-submarine warfare. In June 1917, arrangements were made to establish a Naval Reserve Radio School at Harvard University capable of training upwards of 500 men and women simultaneously. Many of the students had civilian backgrounds as amateur or commercial radio operators. Back in New York, Columbia University hosted a gas-engine training program.

BUILDING THE NAVAL RESERVE FLYING CORPS

In the Upper Midwest, the recently opened Dunwoody Institute in Minneapolis provided advanced technical training to Sailors who had received basic training at Great Lakes Recruit Training Center. Impressed with the quality of training, the chief of the Bureau of Navigation, Rear Admiral Leigh C. Palmer, approved an expansion of Dunwoody Institute training programs. Along with the Massachusetts Institute of Technology and the University of Washington, Dunwoody would serve as a ground school for the Navy's infant Flying Corps.

Above: Comic from the Pelham Bay Camp Newspaper. Among the Pelham Bay graduates was Humphrey Bogart, who served as a coxswain in the troopship *Leviathan*.

Bottom: Circa 1918 lighter-than-air Aviators at blimp school at NAS Pensacola, Florida.

Opposite top: Harvard Radio School students receive small-boat training.

Opposite bottom: 1918 Naval Training Camp Gulfport, Mississippi. Naval Reserve and Regular Navy Sailors of the supply department pose for a group photograph.

In June 1917 guidelines were established to qualify officers and petty officers in the Naval Reserve Flying Corps. Program applicants would enlist into this component of the Naval Reserve Force and were sent to schools and training camps. By the end of the war, some 2,700 naval aviators would be produced through this program with most being assigned to coastal naval air stations, though some were trained to operate ship-based kite balloons that would be serve as portable observation platforms.

THE AMALGAMATION

The number of men and women entering the Navy through the Naval Reserve Force framework accelerated. On November 30, 1917, the number enrolled totaled 49,246. A year later it was 290,000.

Organizing, training and placing tens of thousands of newly minted officers and men and women did not occur without hiccups. However, the needs of the service were met. Except for their commanding officers, a fleet of former German merchant ships that had been seized at the outbreak of hostilities, including ocean liners, were crewed by naval reservists. The German liners alone would transport over a half million American doughboys to France. Some 300 reserve officers performed censor duties at telegraph offices. Twenty Naval Reserve officers performed naval attaché duties in London and another six performed similar roles in Paris.

One hiccup that needed resolution was rank and precedence of officers who were recalled as members of the Naval Reserve Force and those naval militiamen who were federalized as National Naval Volunteers. That these two reserve manpower pools were managed from separate offices also created administration duplications and coordination issues. Unfortunately for the National Naval Volunteers, regulations conveyed benefits and promotion precedence to the Naval Reserve Force over National Naval Volunteers, despite the latter having served as the Navy's sole reserve manpower pool for over a quarter century. Senior naval officials were quick to recognize this treatment as second-class reservists as unfair. Thus leaders of the Naval Militia Association, looking out for the interests of their men as well as

THE FIRST YALE UNIT

By Joseph F. Callo
Rear Admiral U.S. Navy Reserve (Retired)

F. Trubee Davison.

A visionary who foresaw how aviation would play an important role for the United States in World War I, F. Trubee Davison decided to form a flying unit for the U.S. Navy when he returned for his sophomore year at Yale University in September 1915. The group he organized—ultimately known as the First Yale Unit—made naval aviation history.

Nine Yale undergraduates joined his group: Alan W. Ames, Henry P. Davison (Trubee Davison's brother), John V. Farwell, Artemus L. Gates, Erl C.B. Gould, Robert A. Lovett, Albert D. Sturtevant, John M. Vorys, and Charles D. Wiman. In addition, Davison enrolled two non-Yale friends, Wellesley Laud Brown and Albert J. Ditman.

Davison first succeeded to convert his father from a naysayer into an enthusiastic supporter—an important step, since the senior Davison, a Wall Street financier with J.P. Morgan & Co., helped to raise $300,000 for the unit's equipment and training. During the summer 1916 school break, the unit trained at Port Washington, New York, with one old flying boat named "Mary Ann" and a civilian flight instructor named Dave McCulloch. Department store magnate John Wanamaker helped to underwrite the costs.

During the fall semester, the group participated as volunteers in a Navy training exercise in Gravesend Bay off Brooklyn. During the exercise, the young flyers convinced the Navy that a group of motivated volunteer pilots, driven by courage and patriotism, could perform serious naval operational functions. As a result, the Navy designated Davison's group as "Volunteer Aerial Coast Patrol Unit Number 1." They still were not official, but they were getting close.

Then, based on the Naval Reserve Appropriations Act of August 29, 1916 (now considered the birth date of the Naval Air Reserve) the entire unit—which had grown to twenty-six—was sworn into the Naval Reserve Force. Within weeks, the United States entered World War I.

Of the original group of twelve, Wellesly Brown, Trubee Davison and Charles Wiman did not earn their wings. In Davison's case his flying career ended with a serious training accident in July 1917. Following the War, however, he was awarded the Navy Cross for his leadership in establishing the First Yale Unit, and in 1966 he was designated an Honorary Naval Aviator.

The unit was quickly assimilated into the U.S. war effort in Europe, and the first two members of the Naval Reserve Flying Corps to be assigned overseas were from the original Yale contingent. Unit member David S. Ingalls became the first Navy ace, flying a Sopwith Camel with the Royal Air Force. Following the war Ingalls served as assistant secretary of the Navy. A fellow unit member, Artemus Gates, was awarded the Navy Distinguished Service Medal, Great Britain's Distinguished Flying Cross, and the French Croix de Guerre. In the 1940s Gates served as assistant secretary of the Navy (Air). Another member of the original group, Albert Sturtevant, was the first naval aviator to be killed in the service of his country.

Admiral William S. Sims, who commanded U.S. naval forces in Europe during World War I, summarized the First Yale Unit's reputation: "Whenever the French and English asked us to send a couple of our crack men to reinforce a squadron, I would say, 'Let's get some of the Yale gang.' We never made a mistake when we did this."

Lieutenant David S. Ingalls, USNRF Flying Corps was the Navy's first and only Ace during the first World War.

Painting by Bruce Ungerland depicting an aerial victory of Naval Reserve Flying Corps Ace Lieutenant David S. Ingalls over Western Europe.

the Navy, worked with the Navy to develop legislation that would merge the National Naval Volunteers into the Naval Reserve Force, recognizing that they were probably legislating themselves out of existence.

The bill amalgamating the two reserve organizations became law on July 1, 1918. The majority of the Naval Volunteers transferred were qualified to serve at sea on combatant vessels. For those who operated aeroplanes, they were formally shifted to the Naval Reserve Flying Corps. Before the armistice, some 785 officers and nearly 17,000 enlisted shifted from National Naval Volunteers to naval reservists. In addition, the amalgamation brought the previously established Medical Reserve Corps and Dental Reserve Corps under the Naval Reserve Force umbrella.

WINNING THE WAR

Dudley W. Knox, who served with Rear Admiral Sims in London in the planning and historical sections, documented the contributions of naval reservists and naval volunteers during the war. In his *A History of the United States Navy*, Knox credited the implementation of the convoy system, protected by escorts, for loosening the noose around the British Isles. Whereas the allies lost 881,000 tons of shipping in April 1917, with convoys the losses plummeted to 289,000 in November. Those cargo ships bringing food and war supplies to Britain and France would now also be available to bring the hundreds of thousands of American troops who ultimately would turn back the German Spring Offensive in 1918 and go on the war-ending counteroffensive.

Convoys alone did not turn the tide against the U-boat menace. A combination of platforms and tactics, all involving naval reservists, gave the allies the edge. Naval reservists operated mine layers, naval aeroplanes, and sub-chasers, and provided gun crews for merchant ships. Of some 220 merchant ships with naval armed guards that came under attack by surfaced U-boats, 193 were able to drive off the attacker.

An irony of the war at sea was that most of the Naval Academy graduates who trained for big-gun combat basically sat on the sidelines. Many of those not assigned to the Navy's combatants were busy training the naval reservists who actually wound up doing the fighting. Admiral Sims would later lament that it was a minor tragedy of the war "that many of our Annapolis men" who desired to engage the enemy, "had to stay on this side, in order to instruct these young men from civil life."

Naval reservists made up almost all the over 16,000 men operating 500 aircraft in the European theater. Besides scouting and reporting the presence of U-boats, some of the American aircraft were able to launch attacks. Later in the war, the Navy's "Northern Bombing Group" operated directly against the Germans in support of British Army operations. Besides dropping nearly 100 tons of high explosives on enemy targets, the American naval aviators, many graduates of a program that was started at Yale University, took on German pilots. Flying a Sopwith Camel, Lieutenant David S. Ingalls, a Naval Reserve officer who came through the Yale program, became the Navy's first and only ace of the First World War. While Ingalls would earn fame as naval aviation's first ace, Charles H. Hammann would be the first to earn a Medal of Honor due to his successful recovery of Ensign George Ludlow in the Adriatic after Ludlow had been shot down by Austro-Hungarian aircraft.

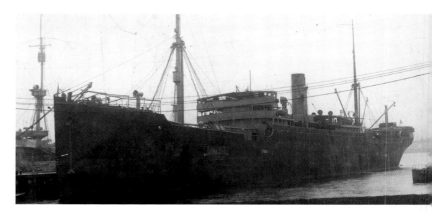

The cargo steamship *Ticonderoga* lost 217 sailors to a German U-boat attack in 1918. Her Naval Reserve Force commanding officer would receive a Medal of Honor for his actions.

Knox cited the contributions of hundreds of undergraduates from universities such as Yale, Harvard, and Princeton who comprised the crews of 120 sub-chasers that were sent to Europe to serve along the French and British coastlines as well as in the Mediterranean. In the Mediterranean the Naval Reserve crews operated against Austro-Hungarian submarines. Several of the sub-chasers apparently had success in at least damaging enemy submarines.

In addition to building sub-chasers, the Navy acquired a number of ocean-going yachts and refitted them for combat. While some were sent overseas, several yachts and other small craft operated off the Eastern seaboard to seek out German U-boats that eventually made trans-Atlantic forays in 1918.

WORLD WAR I NAVAL RESERVE FORCE MEDAL OF HONOR RECIPIENTS.

Compiled by Captain John Lynn Shanton
U.S. Navy Reserve (Retired)

Tedford H. Cann earned his recognition for actions taken in the patrol vessel *May*. On November 5, 1917, he courageously worked in a flooded compartment, locating and closing a leak that endangered his ship. In April 1918, Cann was commissioned as an ensign in the Naval Reserve Force, continuing to serve in *May* into July. He spent the rest of the war assigned to the *Noma*.

Charles Hazeltine Hammann joined the Naval Reserve Force in October 1917. On August 21 1918, as a pilot of a Macchi M.5 seaplane off the Austro-Hungarian coast, Ensign Hammann landed next to a downed fellow pilot (Ensign George H. Ludlow), brought him aboard, and brought him to safety amid constant danger of attack by Austrian planes. Hammann was killed while on active duty at Langley Field, Virginia, June 14, 1919.

John MacKenzie became the first naval reservist to be awarded the Medal of Honor while serving in a converted yacht commissioned as the *Remlik*. On December 17, 1917, *Remlik* encountered a German U-boat during an Atlantic storm and as the ship maneuvered, a depth charge broke loose, lost its safety pin, and began rolling around the deck. Chief Boatswain's Mate MacKenzie threw himself on the depth charge and managed to safely secure it.

James Jonas Madison was appointed lieutenant in the Naval Reserve Force on May 8, 1917. He was commanding the cargo steamship *Ticonderoga*, when on September 30, 1918, the ship was attacked and sunk by the German submarine U-152. Commander Madison in spite of severe wounds that later necessitated the amputation of a leg, continued to direct and maneuver the ship until he ordered her to be abandoned. Due to his injuries, he retired in August 1920 and remained hospitalized until he succumbed at the Naval Hospital in Brooklyn, New York, on December 25, 1922.

Orlando Henderson Petty graduated from Jefferson Medical College in Philadelphia in 1904 and joined the Medical Reserve Corps in December 1916. After the United States' entry into World War I, he was sent to France where he worked as an assistant surgeon. By June 11, 1918, Petty was attached to the 5th Marine Regiment as the unit took part in the Battle of Belleau Wood. On that day, his dressing station in Lucy-le-Bocage came under heavy fire from German artillery, some of which were firing poison gas shells. He continued to evacuate and treat the wounded, even after he was knocked to the ground and his gas mask rendered useless by an exploding shell. After his military service, Petty returned to Philadelphia and resumed teaching medicine.

Daniel Augustus Joseph Sullivan, born in Charleston, South Carolina, attended Clemson College and graduated in 1902. He joined the Naval Reserve Force on April 12, 1917, and received a commission. On May 21, 1918, while serving as an officer of the patrol vessel *Christabel*, he secured several live depth charges that had come loose during combat with a German U-boat. For this act, he was awarded the Medal of Honor. Later in 1918, Ensign Sullivan was assigned to the destroyers *Drayton* and *Ludlow*. Promoted to lieutenant in September 1918, he served with the U.S. Navy Headquarters in London, England, following the November 1918 armistice.

NAVAL RESERVES ON THE WESTERN FRONT

By Master Chief James L. Leuci
U.S. Navy Reserve

On November 11, 1918, U.S. Naval Railway Battery No. 4, commanded by a Naval Reserve Force officer and manned by Naval Reserve Sailors, fired the last round of American-made artillery on the Western Front—two minutes before the armistice took effect. Ironically, on September 6, 1918, U.S. Naval Railway Battery No. 2 fired the first American shell, from an American gun, manned by naval reserve gunners on the Western Front.

When the United States entered the war in April 1917, the German Army had been using long-range heavy artillery that had greater range than allied artillery. The U.S. Navy solution was to mount fourteen-inch naval guns on railway cars. The guns and railway cars were shipped, unassembled, to St. Nazaire, France.

Rear Admiral (then-Captain) Charles P. Plunkett became commander of the naval railway batteries. Five-hundred enlisted men and thirty officers, 90 percent of them reservists, volunteered to man the batteries. Many came from the Michigan State Naval Militia, which included Lieutenant Joseph Ralston Hayden, commanding officer of Battery 4, and Lieutenant J.L. Rodgers, commanding officer of Battery 5.

1918: RADM Charles P. Plunkett, USN Commander of Naval Railway Battalions in Western Europe.

In early summer of 1918, the naval railway battery crews began arriving in St. Nazaire to assemble the five battery trains and a staff train. Each battery train consisted of fifteen cars, including the locomotive. The staff train included eight cars. In August 1918, the naval batteries began deploying to the Western Front.

Prior to the arrival of the naval batteries, U.S. Army artillery units were supplied with French-made guns and ammunition. Naval Battery 2 fired the first American-made artillery shell from an American-made gun on September 6. The guns were in high demand during the final months of the war, firing 782 rounds at strategic targets such as railway centers and troop concentration areas. On November 11, 1918, Battery 4 fired the last American shell two minutes before the Armistice went into effect.

After the signing of the armistice, Rear Admiral Plunkett spoke to the assembled battery crews to express his admiration for the performance of the naval reservists, stating: "...there never will come again in my mind any question in regard to the American manhood meeting any situation. When we started out on this thing, the Navy Department told us that we could not have any Regular Navy people. They said: if you are going to make this thing through, you are to make it with people that you make yourself and that you can find somewhere, and I must admit that I had some misgiving at one time; but after we finished the 'Battle of St. Nazaire' I was satisfied that this outfit would go to Berlin and there was nothing that could stop them."

1918 Naval Railway Battery Uniform Sailors wore U.S.M.C. field uniforms. A chief petty officer cap device was worn by all enlisted men to show they were Sailors. 90 percent of the Railway Battery Sailors were from the Naval Reserve Force.

To put an end to the German submarine threat, naval commanders decided to lay a great mine barrage across the North Sea. American-made mine components were shipped to Scotland by twenty-four cargo steamers manned by naval reservists and transported to an assembly plant. Once assembled, the mines were taken aboard one of ten large mine-layers and sent out to sow the fields. Of the 70,323 mines laid by Britain, Norway, and the United States, 56,611 were American. Through the fall of 1918, the mines inflicted damage and destruction on a growing number of U-boats. Perhaps more damaging was the blow to morale.

By then the tide had turned on land. With the Bolshevik Revolution in November 1917 leading to the cessation of hostilities in the East, the Germans massed divisions for a massive offensive in the summer of 1918. The French and British, now being fed American reinforcements, were able to blunt the German offensive. At Belleau Wood, the Germans were stymied by the tenacity of the U.S. Marines who were supported by the heroic efforts of Navy medical personnel.

The American entry into the war proved decisive. By October 1918, the Germans came to a realization that they were in a war of attrition that they could not sustain. They chose to end the war. On the eleventh hour of the eleventh day of the eleventh month, an armistice was signed.

After the war, Secretary of the Navy Josephus Daniels would write of the naval reserves: "Never again will men dare ridicule the Volunteer, the Reservist, the man who in a national crisis lays aside civilian duty to become a soldier or sailor—They fought well. They died well. They have left in deeds and words a record that will be an inspiration to unborn generations."

Total in Navy each month. Enlisted personnel, 1917-1918.

	Allowed by law. [1]	Regulars in service.	Reserves.	Total.
Apr. 1, 1917	6,982	62,667	8,079	70,746
May 1, 1917	96,982	87,076	24,450	111,526
June 1, 1917	162,466	109,010	38,064	147,074
July 1, 1917	162,466	128,666	46,319	174,985
Aug. 1, 1917	162,466	137,374	64,824	192,198
Sept. 1, 1917	162,466	142,005	59,011	201,016
Oct. 1, 1917	162,466	144,030	61,406	205,436
Nov. 1, 1917	162,466	147,327	64,994	212,321
Dec. 1, 1917	162,466	153,104	71,538	224,642
Jan. 1, 1918	162,466	177,348	90,267	267,615
Feb. 1, 1918		188,180	88,715	276,895
Mar. 1, 1918		191,035	92,586	283,621
Apr. 1, 1918		194,185	101,520	296,705
May 1, 1918		198,390	120,959	319,349
June 1, 1918		202,419	163,201	365,620
July 1, 1918		206,950	213,414	420,364
Aug. 1, 1918		211,599	253,971	465,570
Sep. 1, 1918		218,223	263,679	481,902
Oct. 1, 1918		218,457	264,342	482,799
Nov. 1, 1918		217,276	271,571	488,847
Dec. 1, 1918		215,672	269,006	484,678
Jan. 1, 1919		210,365	245,789	456,154

[1] This allowed strength includes the hospital corps (3 1/2 per cent of allowed strength of the Navy and Marine Corps).

3

FROM THE NAVAL RESERVE FORCE
TO THE NAVAL RESERVE

(1919-1940)

Naval Training Station San Francisco drill hall/sleeping quarters with protective sheeting

Sign Posted at the Naval Aircraft Factory, Philadelphia

Spanish Influenza has endangered the prosecution of the WAR in Europe. There are 1500 cases in the Navy Yard 30 deaths have already resulted SPITTING SPREADS SPANISH INFLUENZA DONT SPIT

Navy nurse Josie Brown reflected on the horrible ordeal that she and her colleagues had to confront in 1918:

> *The morgues were packed almost to the ceiling with bodies stacked one on top of another. The morticians worked day and night. You could never turn around without seeing a big red truck loaded with caskets for the train station so bodies could be sent home.*

THE GREAT PANDEMIC

The scene Brown described was not behind the front lines in France but at the new Navy Training Station in Illinois along the shores of Lake Michigan. Thousands of regular Navy and Naval Reserve Force recruits arrived there eager to become bluejackets in a growing U.S. Navy. Many went home in coffins. Brown recalled:

> *We would give them a little hot whiskey toddy; that's about all we had time to do. They would have terrific nosebleeds with it. Sometimes the blood would just shoot across the room.*

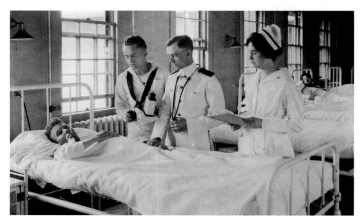

Caring for a patient at U.S. Naval Hospital Chelsea, Mass.

An influenza pandemic had spread around the world. By the time the virus had run its course, an estimated 30 million to 50 million lives would be lost—more than had been lost in World War I. The Navy would not be immune. In 1918 alone, Navy medical personnel, many of them reservists, treated some 121,225 Sailors and Marines who were admitted to Navy medical facilities with influenza. Of these, 4,158 died of the virus. Those treating the illness were not immune. Among the dead were thirty-two Navy nurses.

More Sailors were lost during World War I due to the influenza pandemic than to enemy action. For those National Naval Volunteers and naval reservists who had been assigned to ships at ship, the odds of survival were somewhat better. The virus began to go to sea in September 1918, first on the overcrowded transport ships and then on fleet units. The secretary of the Navy's 1919 report showed the infection rate as follows on the various ship types:

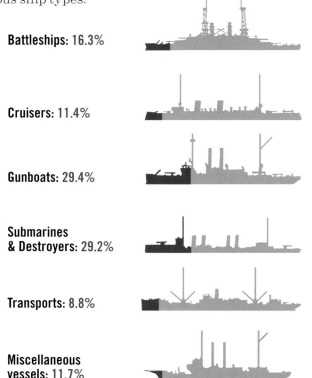

Battleships: 16.3%

Cruisers: 11.4%

Gunboats: 29.4%

Submarines & Destroyers: 29.2%

Transports: 8.8%

Miscellaneous vessels: 11.7%

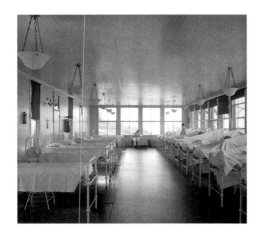

Hospital Ward "D" at Naval Training Station San Francisco.

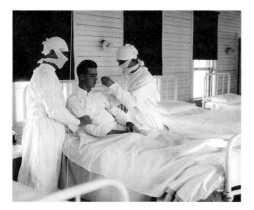

Despite precautions taken by Navy and Naval Reserve Force nurses to protect themselves from a deadly strain of influenza, 32 would lose their lives in the line of duty.

Nurses pose at Naval Training Camp, Gulfport, Miss.

Opposite page: The release of naval reservists in late 1919 left the Navy shorthanded in 1920 as evidenced in this appeal to naval reservists and ex-enlisted.

The steam yacht *Yacona* was one of the unfortunate exceptions. The steel screw vessel, which had been acquired from noted financier Henry Clay Pierce in September 1917, was crewed mainly by naval reservists. Between November 17 and 29, 1918, 80 of her crew of 95—84 percent—came down with influenza.

The Navy secretary's report noted that *Yacona*, which had been operating from New England, suffered its outbreak after the two waves of the virus had run their course ashore. The first wave spread in early 1918. For example, the report showed that earlier in the year in February the Naval Radio School at Harvard suffered between 350 and 400 cases. Included in this number were 11 cases of pneumococcus-streptococcus. Two months later the Naval Training Camp at San Diego reported similar numbers, with 410 cases and pneumonia affecting a dozen Sailors.

In July and August a more deadly outbreak of the virus occurred in Europe. The impact could be felt at U.S. Naval Air Stations in Ireland and France, with seven air stations reporting 690 cases. As noted by historian Dudley Knox, a large percentage of the naval aviation component was of the Naval Reserve Force.

This deadlier wave hit the United States hard in September. Naval reservists enrolled in courses at the Naval Training Camp at Pelham Bay Park in New York began reporting symptoms of the flu on September 24. Fortunately, the layout of the camp and the high hygiene standards enforced at that facility blunted the spread of the virus and there were only three reported deaths. At Pelham Bay, the hospital actually reported more cases of injuries due to trainees falling out of hammocks. Elsewhere the story was grimly different. Four days later a severe outbreak began at the Naval Training Camp at Gulfport, Mississippi. By November, this portion of the pandemic had claimed a majority of the estimated 675,000 Americans who would succumb to influenza during a span covering 1918 into 1919.

THE POST-WAR NAVAL RESERVE FORCE

The Great Pandemic of 1918-1919 is a part of the Navy Reserve legacy for reasons beyond those who suffered the ill effects of the flu, those families who lost a loved one in the service, and the heroism displayed by Naval Reserve Force medical personnel, many of whom lost their lives as a result of caring for the sick. Another part of the legacy was in addressing the twin challenges of fighting a major war in Europe and confronting the outbreak of a global influenza pandemic. Navy leaders could not focus on a post-war structure for its Naval Reserve Force. Thus when the Germans agreed to an armistice on November 11, the needed extensive planning for the re-organization of a peacetime Naval Reserve Force had yet to be contemplated. The creation of a Naval Reserve Force Division within the Bureau of Navigation to manage this planning finally occurred in September 1919, some ten months after the cessation of hostilities.

Demobilization greatly complicated the problem. By November 1, 1919, 29,026 of the 30,385 Naval Reserve Force commissioned and warrant officers had been released from active duty. Likewise on the enlisted side,

A CRUISE TO EUROPE AND THE NEAR EAST

for

NAVAL RESERVES AND EX-SERVICE MEN

6 AuG 1920

The new destroyers BROOKS, KANE, GILMER, HUMPHREY, FOX and OVER-TON are fitting out at Philadelphia for a cruise to Europe and the Near East.

These vessels are the fastest in the world. They have attained 44 miles an hour at sea.

The United States now has the finest and largest force of destroyers in the world.

Our small force of 35 before the War has been increased to over 300.

This condition results in a shortage of men and gives quick promotion to the right kind of men.

One of our Navy men writes that his pay under the new pay bill amounts to $391.58. As an example of the possibilities of the new pay bill, an enlisted man on Aviation Duty may find it possible to make $469.87 per month.

Call and verify these figures.

Unlike civil life, the Navy gives a man the chance to save practically all he makes.

This opportunity is offered you to get the bonus, interesting travel, fine pay, a chance to save, and quick promotion.

Ex-Navy men may reenlist and Naval Reserves transfer to take this cruise.

N R B 7 26 20 3754 20M

THE NEED FOR PILOTS

The need for the Navy to boost its officer corps with Naval Reserve officers reflected the reality that the Naval Academy could not keep pace with providing newly commissioned officers for a larger fleet that now included an air arm. On April, 6, 1917, the total number of officers and men assigned to naval aviation was 201, with thirty-eight designated as naval aviators. By the end of the war the war the tally had climbed to 36,909, of which some 26,000 were reservists. During the rapid demobilization the newly formed naval aviation community was hit especially hard, with a majority of its personnel rejoining the civilian world. Allowing Naval Reserve Flying Corps officers to obtain regular commissions sustained naval aviation during a critical period when the Navy introduced an aircraft carrier to the fleet with the converted collier *Jupiter* rejoining the fleet on March 20, 1922, recommissioned as the *Langley*. With the terms of the 1921-22 Washington Naval Conference placing battleship tonnage limitations on the five major signatories, the United States decided to convert two battle cruisers then being built into the aircraft carriers *Lexington* and *Saratoga*. Pilots would be needed to fly planes off these carriers as well as the Navy's seaplanes and projected fleet of dirigibles.

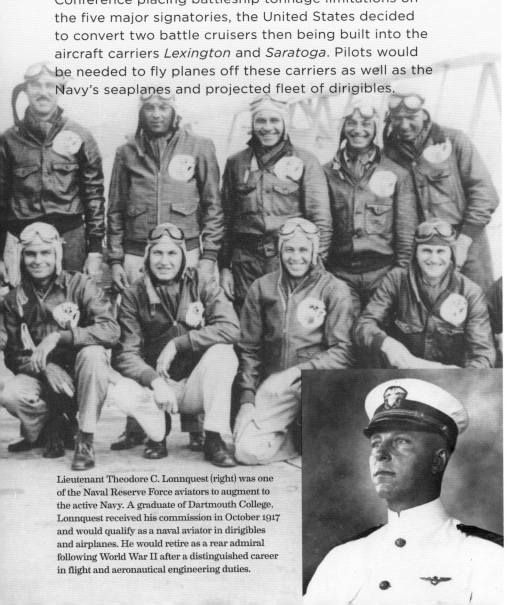

Lieutenant Theodore C. Lonnquest (right) was one of the Naval Reserve Force aviators to augment to the active Navy. A graduate of Dartmouth College, Lonnquest received his commission in October 1917 and would qualify as a naval aviator in dirigibles and airplanes. He would retire as a rear admiral following World War II after a distinguished career in flight and aeronautical engineering duties.

some 286,000 had been released. Many, upon discharge, did not inform the Navy Department of their new addresses. The U.S. Post Office returned over 60,000 retainer pay checks totaling $2.5 million to the bureau as undeliverable. Part of the problem was the 1918 act granted reservists a retainer, as it had been assumed that they would organize into drill units. The retainer, however, had not been made dependent on drill participation.

Led by Captain Henry J. Ziegemeier, the Naval Reserve Force Division persevered. A vision developed for a Naval Reserve Force of 120,000 reservists who would perform at least 36 drills a year in government-provided armories. Additional ships would also be provided to the Naval Reserve Force for training purposes. In 1920, Chief of the Bureau of Navigation Rear Admiral Thomas Washington signed the Regulations Governing the Organization and Administration of the Naval Reserve Force.

To use contemporary terminology, the Bureau of Navigation took extraordinary measures to "right size" the force. The Navy wanted a "sea-going" reserve. Testifying before Congress Rear Admiral Washington stated: "We are limiting this naval reserve force to actual seagoing men," noting there needed to be exceptions for paymasters, doctors and naval constructors. Of the 31,158 officers and 246,134 enlisted affiliated with the Naval Reserve Force at the time of the hearings, 51 percent of the officers had sea duty and 38 percent of the enlisted had spent time at sea. With this guiding philosophy, as a result of a records review of Naval Reserve Force officers for retention/dismissal, over half did not make the cut. On a positive note, Congress passed legislation on

June 4, 1920, that assisted the Naval Reserve Force to cut down its officer end-strength in another way: by allowing up to 1,200 officers to apply and receive regular Navy commissions, with up to 600 being naval aviators.

Unfortunately, the augmentation of the regular naval aviation community by Naval Reserve Flying Corps aviators had an unintended consequence when combined with budget cuts: It nearly put an end to the Naval Reserve Flying Corps.

Symbolic of the problems that beset the Naval Reserve Force was the loss of the *Granite State* due to fire in mid-1921.

ALNAV 67

With change in administrations, the Naval Reserve Force lost a strong friend in Secretary of the Navy Josephus Daniels, who wrote a long article in the *Saturday Evening Post* titled "The Naval Reserve—A Great National Asset" after he left office. The new administration of Warren G. Harding and a Republican-majority Congress entered office during an economic downturn and sought cuts. The military was not immune—hence Harding's eagerness to host the Washington Naval Conference during the winter months of 1921-22. Testifying before a House hearing in January 1921, Rear Admiral Washington requested $17.5 million for the Naval Reserve Force for fiscal 1922 to cover retainer pay and other expenses. Congress only appropriated $7 million. As a consequence, on September 21, 1921, the Navy Department promulgated ALNAV 67:

```
The Department regrets that
owing to lack of funds
through reduced Congressional
appropriations it finds it
necessary to disenroll or
transfer on their own request
to the Volunteer Naval Reserve
all members of the Naval
Reserve Force except classes
one and six. Those of classes
two, three, four, and five now
on active duty and those of the
Reserve Force who have taken
the examination for transfer
to the permanent Navy are not
affected by this order.
```

The ALNAV's impact was immediate and drastic. At the end of that month approximately 25,000 officers and 200,000 enlisted reservists, almost the entire Naval Reserve Force, were transferred to the Volunteer Naval Reserve. Not surprisingly, many who were disenrolled wrote their representatives in Washington, who pressed

the Navy for explanations for the dramatic reduction. Secretary of the Navy Edwin Denby and Assistant Secretary of the Navy Theodore Roosevelt, son of the recently deceased president, wrote to explain their fiscal responsibilities and suggested that a careful remodeling of the 1918 Reserve Act could help to improve the situation.

President Harding also received numerous letters from upset reservists. In writing a response to one complainant, the president argued that the Navy had no intention in doing away with the reserve but organizational changes were necessary. Harding urged patience and patriotism. To consider organizational changes, Rear Admiral Washington chaired a board convened from October 10 to November 23, 1921, to review the consequences of earlier legislation regarding the Naval Reserve Force.

REORGANIZATION

As a result of the findings of the board, Secretary Denby forwarded proposals to the speaker of the House for legislative consideration in 1922. No action was taken.

Congress did act, though, to allocate $3 million for fiscal 1923 to pay 1,500 officers and 5,000 enlisted men to

Good Shooting! Naval reservists proudly display a target kite.

EAGLE BOATS

By Captain John Lynn Stanton
U.S. Navy Reserve (Retired)

In June 1917, President Woodrow Wilson asked Henry Ford to serve on the United States Shipping Board. Told of the need for anti-submarine vessels to combat the U-boat menace, Ford replied, "What we want is one type of ship in large numbers." The Eagle was born. The blueprints were finished in a matter of weeks and the tooling was cast by Ford Motors' Highland Park plant in Detroit. Ford started construction and some 60 were built.

A new factory (the Ford River Rouge plant) was constructed to build the Eagle boats. Ford's original concept envisioned a massive building hall terminating at the water's edge, where Eagle boats were built on an assembly line, like his cars. This was not practical and a modified incremental process was used.

Ford insisted on the flat steel plates for the hull and geared steam turbine propulsion, but did not meddle with the actual design. The rest of the design was fairly conservative. A rowboat was carried amidships, and the boats had no sonar or radar.

An effect of using the flat hull plates was that there was no sheer to the bows or flare of the hull; the Eagle boats, while still safer than the old wooden sub-chasers, were bad hoggers (an upward stress on the keel) and unpleasant in a storm.

For the Naval Reserve, the Eagle Boats served as an effective training platform. Although too small and underpowered, these vessels provided seamanship skills that would be critical in the late 1930s.

Eagle 56, sister ship of the *Eagle 55* shown here berthed at Jersey City, N.J., would be sunk off the coast of Maine by a German U-Boat on April 23, 1945.

conduct a 15-day training period, as well as retainer pay for six months. Individuals who were in non-pay status could reapply to fill one of these slots.

One of those officers who would re-affiliate was Frank Bailey. Detaching from *Nebraska* before the war ended, Bailey saw additional service in the transports *Tenadores* and *Northern Pacific* before being discharged on April 14, 1919. Returning to Buffalo, he eventually would be given command of the 11th Division. For afloat training, he utilized *Eagle 21*, which the Navy had provided to Buffalo. For an armory, the Navy acquired a Great Lakes wood-hulled freighter, the *Sturgeon Bay*. At the time *Eagle 21* was one of twenty-five Eagle boats, seventeen submarine chasers, and six miscellaneous vessels that the Navy provided for drill sites.

As legislation to restructure the Naval Reserve Force remained in limbo, the rebuilding of the force continued to be slow. An example of rebuilding from scratch was Naval Reserve aviation.

Initially, the Navy authorized three units to be located at Boston, New York, and Chicago. The New York unit, based at Fort Hamilton, began when the Navy supplied the New York City Aerial Police with four training seaplanes. The flying cops also just happened, conveniently, to be naval reservists. At Squantum, Massachusetts, Naval Reserve aviators worked through Lieutenant Richard E. Byrd to acquire an aircraft from the Bureau of Aeronautics. With plane in hand, the reservists covered the costs of gasoline and other incidental items. Squantum would lay claim to being the first Naval Reserve Air Station.

Whereas before World War I there had been a strong, vibrant Association of Naval Militias, after the war the Naval Reserve Officers Association (NROA) emerged as a successor organization. At its annual meeting in Washington in January 1923, the NROA established a legislative committee. As such, the committee reviewed the proposals that were being developed through a conference that was led by Assistant Secretary of the Navy Roosevelt.

Meeting on October 22, 1923, the NROA approved the proposed legislation and instructed its legislative committee "to do its utmost to secure passage." At hearings held the following spring, a subcommittee of the Senate Naval Affairs Committee heard testimony from Roosevelt on the proposed legislation: S.1807.

Roosevelt discussed the problems with the current structure and argued that the new plan gave the Navy Department a "concrete definite plan on which to proceed." Roosevelt also aimed to quash perceptions that the Naval Reserve Force had been an entity apart from the Navy by arguing the Naval Reserve Force was integral to the organization.

The most controversial piece of the legislation involved changes affecting retirement for active-duty Sailors. In 1924, Sailors could request transfer to the Fleet Naval Reserve after 16 years and receive one-third of their base pay plus allowances, or after 20 years and be eligible to receive half their base pay plus allowances. The Navy wanted to eliminate the 16-year option, citing the loss of talented Sailors at their prime value. Looking downstream, the Navy also saw a large number of Sailors reaching the twenty-year mark in the coming decade and wanted to mitigate their impact on the budget by offering only one-third their pay and allowances. In addition, there was a proposed provision that enlisted men who had completed 20 years of service would need to undergo examinations every four years to determine eligibility to continue receiving payments.

The naval officers called to testify following Roosevelt were not in lock step. While the president of NROA, Captain Charles F. Macklin, and the Judge Advocate General Rear Adm. Julian Latimer fully supported the legislation, Captain Charles E. Courtney of the Navy Recruiting Service strongly opposed the cut in pay to those transferred to the Naval Fleet Reserve. He was supported by a representative of another recently formed organization—the Fleet Reserve Association (FRA). FRA spokesman Chief Yeoman Robert W. White also attacked the provisions requiring four-year examinations to former active-duty bluejackets. The subcommittee retained the one-half pay feature—and did not require examinations.

THE NAVAL RESERVE ACT OF 1925

The revised Naval Reserve Act passed the full Senate Naval Affairs Committee and was then passed in both the House and Senate. It became law on February 28, 1925.

With the act set to be implemented on July 1, 1925, much scrambling needed to be completed within the Navy. Captain Zeno E. Briggs, who relieved Captain Alfred B. Fry as the Naval Reserve section head at the Bureau of Navigation, chaired a board of ten officers with representatives from the Office of the CNO, Judge

Advocate General and other bureaus convened to draft new naval reserve regulations.

The 1925 Naval Reserve Act would serve the Navy and the nation well for the next 13 years as the United States saw the rise of potential adversaries, first in Japan and later in Germany. However, four days after Congress passed the act, it also approved an omnibus bill that would have an even longer-term impact on the U.S. Navy. Buried in section 22 of H.R. 2688 was enabling legislation to establish a Naval Reserve Officer Training Corps (NROTC) at selected colleges and universities around the country.

NROTC

One of the positive outcomes from the Great War was the Navy discovery that young college men, given some intensive training, could go on to become competent junior officers out in the fleet. Desiring to reopen that spigot during peacetime, Assistant Secretary of the Navy Roosevelt and Rear Admiral Latimer opted to include the proposal with the omnibus bill versus the pending naval reserve bill for fear that the naval reserve bill was not assured of passage.

In testifying before the Senate Naval Affairs Committee, Roosevelt faced some harsh comments on a proposal that would provide a student a subsidy of 30 or 45 cents per day as they attended college. Senator Claude Swanson suggested that the Navy could simply enlarge the Naval Academy. However, Senator George Pepper backed the proposal, arguing that "by introducing a modicum of

naval discipline and experience" the program could "put a little backbone into a good many jellyfish."

Upon passage of the omnibus bill, the Navy planned to introduce the program to six selected colleges and universities in the fall of 1926.

With the passage of the Naval Reserve Act of 1925, the promised efficiencies actually enabled the Naval Reserve to do more with less. For fiscal 1925, an appropriation of $3.9 million paid for:

- *Drill pay and 15 days training duty for 1,000 officers and 8,000 enlisted men in the Fleet Naval Reserve.*

- *Drill pay and 15 days training duty for 188 officers and 70 enlisted men in the Fleet Naval Reserve (Aviation).*

- *Provide 15 days training duty to 250 officers of the Volunteer Naval Reserve.*

- *Provide 15 days flying training to 47 officers of the Volunteer Naval Reserve.*

- *Provide 90 days training with 92 hours of flight time to 88 student aviators.*

- *Drill pay and 15 days training duty for 188 officers and 70 enlisted men in the Fleet Naval Reserve (Aviation).*

- *Provide 90 days afloat training to 43 midshipmen of the Volunteer Naval Reserve.*

THE NEW ORGANIZATION   U.S. NAVAL RESERVE

The previous Naval Reserve Force classes were to be scaled to three classes in the new U.S. Naval Reserve.

The Fleet Naval Reserve would create and mobilize trained Sailors to serve in the ships and air squadrons of the fleet. Organized into battalions and divisions, the drilling reservists would know what ship or squadron would be their gaining command during mobilization and would have a billet assigned.

The Merchant Marine Naval Reserve set to train merchant marine crews on selected U.S. merchant

marine vessels that could be made into auxiliary ships during wartime. Upon mobilization, these crews could switch into their Navy uniforms and facilitate the quick transfer of their former commercial vessel into naval service.

The Volunteer Naval Reserve was established to provide individuals for general service, usually ashore. Within the Volunteer Naval Reserve was one group that could be mobilized to augment the fleet, but others were assigned billets ashore that required special skills during wartime.

THE NAVAL RESERVE GAINS STRENGTH

By mid-1926, the Fleet Naval Reserve had 149 divisions that trained to augment 135 ships. These divisions drilled at eighty-seven locations around the country. There were ten reserve air squadrons organized to conduct bombing, fighting, and scouting missions. Over the following years leading into the 1930s, the Navy worked hard to get the Fleet Naval Reservists to sea and if the reservists didn't go to the ships they were designated to augment, they would go to a similar ship type. For Buffalo-based Frank Bailey, he would have the opportunity to deploy on nine different destroyers over the next ten years. When not steaming in the Atlantic, he cruised on Lake Erie on *Sub Chaser 103*.

Subchaser SC-292: one initiative to facilitate training was to assign ships to the Fleet Naval Reserve for use on weekends and annual cruises. However, insufficient appropriations in 1927 forced the Navy to withdraw nine destroyers from the Naval Reserve. Still, the Fleet Naval Reserve operated a fairly impressive flotilla of vessels. In 1929 that flotilla consisted of three destroyers, fifteen Eagle Boats, thirteen submarine chasers, and eleven other craft.

In addition to hands-on training with ships and aircraft, the Bureau of Navigation sent out thousands of courses for officers and enlisted to master as a basis for advancement. Selection board procedures were established and in 1927 a commodore, eight line officer captains, four medical officer captains, and two pay captains were selected. By 1930, the examination process had achieved enough standardization to allow a retired Navy commander to profit through his publication *of Notes for U.S. Naval Reserve Deck Officers—an Aid for Promotion Examinations*.

To facilitate improved fleet and Naval Reserve interoperability, the Bureau of Navigation hosted conferences in Washington with the first gathering occurring in January 1927.

The 6th Battalion, Chicago Naval Reserve, 1931.

THE NAVAL RESERVE OFFICERS TRAINING CORPS

By Captain Alexander Monroe
U.S. Navy Reserve (Retired)

The Naval Reserve Officers Training Corps (NROTC) Program was established in the fall of 1926 after passage of the Naval Reserve Act of February 28, 1925. Initially, the Navy established NROTC units at Harvard, Yale, and Northwestern universities; Georgia Institute of Technology; the University of Washington; and the University of California at Berkeley.

The NROTC program began modestly with an authorized strength of 1,200 who would ultimately be commissioned in the Naval or Marine Corps Reserve. Officers of "suitable rank" were detailed as instructors, academic credit was to be given toward graduation for approved courses and the officers assigned were to have faculty rank. Didactic instruction in core subjects such as navigation, gunnery and engineering was to be given in the academic year and supplemented by summer cruises with fleet units. Students earned a modest stipend in the school year and were paid on summer cruise. The initial 1927 summer cruise period, conducted aboard battleships such as *Wyoming* and *Pennsylvania* and the aircraft carrier *Lexington*, proved successful. NROTC was judged successful not simply because of the excellence of the officers produced but because those in charge opined that it "was important to be represented in important institutions in all sections of the country."

The first graduates commissioned in the late spring of 1930 then joined the organized Naval Reserve. With the need for more officers later in the decade, in 1939 the Navy established units at the University of California at Los Angeles and Tulane. Wartime exigencies were such that by the end of 1941, twenty-seven units were in operation.

NROTC graduates proved themselves in combat and one of the first postwar tasks faced by then-Chief of Naval Personnel Vice Adm. James L. Holloway Jr. was to revamp how the Navy procured officers from sources apart from the Naval Academy. In so doing, the father of the twentieth chief of naval operations became the father of NROTC as we know it today. With the advice of civilian education leaders such as James P. Baxter, president of Williams College, the program evolved where students would be receive tuition, books, and a modest stipend in return for a period of service, initially three years, with the opportunity to augment to the regular Navy. Though there was some initial skepticism expressed by those who viewed the program as less rigorous than Naval Academy education, NROTC would become the Navy's largest stable commissioning source.

NROTC met, adapted to and overcome the tests of an unpopular war and societal change. The Vietnam War presented difficult times for the program, and units were disestablished at many of the universities, such as Yale and Harvard. In certain situations, faculty rank had been removed and academic credit for NROTC courses denied, a breach of agreements between the Navy and the host institution. At the same time, the program served as an engine of social change in the Navy. In 1968, the Navy established a unit at Prairie View A&M University, a historically black institution, and it has produced senior officers such as Vice Admiral David Brewer, who retired following his tour as commander of Military Sealift Command. In 1972, women could enroll in the NROTC, four years ahead of the Naval Academy. In 1990 a Nurse Corps option was introduced. As of 2015, the program is carried on in sixty-one units and "cross town arrangements" that enable students enrolled in over 150 colleges to participate.

In summary then, the NROTC program, which began as a venture to produce officers strictly for the Naval Reserve for potential mobilization, has proven its worth both for that initial purpose and as a way of producing high-quality officers for the Navy and Marine Corps of today.

Midshipman Jasper Burns (left) of Boston University NROTC unit receives the Vice Admiral Robert F. Dunn Award for outstanding scholarship in the field of Sea Power from Lieutenant Daren McCulley. The award is named for Dunn, who served as the 4th Chief of Naval Reserve.

The Merchant Marine Naval Reserve Flag.

To encourage higher standards of readiness, the bureau established an inspection board that initially was composed of regular Navy officers. By 1927, the inspections took on a competitive nature as well-graded divisions earned prizes. To enhance communication, the bureau began publishing the *Naval Reserve Bulletin*, which covered a wide range of topical information germane to drilling reservists.

Whereas the Fleet Naval Reserve component of the Naval Reserve Act of 1925 came together nicely, the vision for a Merchant Marine Naval Reserve could barely be implemented due to lack of congressional appropriations. However, with hardly any funds to work with, the Bureau of Navigation performed an admirable ad hoc effort to visit merchant vessels to recruit for the program. By 1931 some 2,898 merchant marine officers had signed up, exceeding expectations. These men served on 881 vessels. As part of the recruiting incentive, any vessel having its master and over 50 percent of its officers participating in the program was entitled to fly the Merchant Marine Naval Reserve flag. In 1931, 141 vessels qualified to fly this flag.

The Volunteer Naval Reserve also attracted an impressive cadre of individuals that the Navy could draw on. Some individuals qualified to serve at sea and could apply for annual fifteen-day at-sea training. Limited funding meant not all applications could be accepted. Others processed technical skills of value ashore, such as naval architects, lawyers, chaplains and communication experts.

With radio being the hot technology of the era, young men were eager to join what evolved in 1927 into a Volunteer Communications Reserve. Using Navy-supplied and personally owned equipment, these units spread across the country. By 1931, there were 453 officers and radioman enlistments into the program. Units not only operated in all of the domestic naval districts but also in the Panama Canal Zone and Puerto Rico.

Volunteers were also recruited to bolster the Medical Corps Volunteer Reserve. By June 30, 1931, this corps had 249 officers in its ranks who could be available to augment hospital staffs during an emergency.

NAVAL RESERVE AVIATION TAKES FLIGHT

In retrospect, perhaps the greatest impact that the reorganization of the Naval Reserve had during an era when battleships remained the capital warships at sea was in the area of naval aviation. Having a genesis with units in Massachusetts, New York, and Illinois, a fourth air station was established near Seattle. In the mid-1920s, the Bureau of Aeronautics, working with college and universities, created a viable pipeline for college students interested in flying Navy by setting up ground courses in the winter months and pilot training at the four naval air reserve stations as well as at Hampton Roads and San Diego during the summer. Within the framework of the 1925 Naval Reserve Act, the student aviators were placed in the Volunteer Naval Reserve and given the classification V-5. For fiscal 1927, Congress authorized the purchase of additional aircraft for the Naval Reserve and one year of active duty with the fleet to fifty newly minted Naval Air Reserve ensigns who had earned their Wings of Gold through the "V-5 Program."

Lieutenant Edwin Francis Conway, USN, Commanding Officer of Naval Reserve Air Base Floyd Bennett Field, New York. Conway was killed in a plane crash on January 17, 1933. Note the reserve air squadron insignia on the fuselage.

In 1928, Naval Reserve air bases came to Detroit and San Francisco. In addition, the Navy took steps to further integrate Naval Reserve aviator training with officers who had attained regular Navy commissions by sending candidates to an eight-month course at Pensacola, Florida. Upon graduation, the reserve aviator would be commissioned and sent to the fleet for a year of additional training before returning to civilian life and assignment to a reserve air squadron. By 1931, the number of Naval Reserve air bases was at fourteen and climbing.

The Navy's policy for its reserve component, as articulated by its General Board in 1932, called for procuring a number of reservists during peacetime who could augment and sustain the Navy during the first 120 days of war.

Two Naval Reserve commissioned aviators. The Naval Reserve contributions to increasing the naval aviator pool would make an impact during World War II.

Initially, with the onset of the Depression, funding for the aviation component and other Naval Reserve activities held up. Up in Buffalo, Frank Bailey, now employed as an insurance broker, had been promoted to lieutenant commander in the Naval Reserve and his 11th Fleet Division had grown to 102 men, of which 55 were in pay billets. As a result, the Naval Reserve approved of a second division to be incorporated with the 11th as part of the new Ninth USNR Battalion, with Bailey in command, effective January 1, 1932. That year also provided good fortune in the form of a newly completed boat house training facility that Bailey had long lobbied for and finally had funded through a $75,000 appropriation from New York under its governor, Franklin D. Roosevelt.

THE GREAT DEPRESSION

Unfortunately for Bailey, 1932 would be the year he missed his annual deployment to a destroyer. Depression-era budget cuts finally trickled down. For fiscal 1933, Congress cut 9 percent from the Navy's budget request. This meant a cut of $32,438,577 overall, of which the Naval Reserve portion was $1,549,336. This dollar figure represented 34 percent of the Naval Reserve proposed budget. As a result training cruises were canceled. Commander L.R. Rutter of the Naval Reserve Officers Association testified before the Senate that the one year "elimination of training duty strikes at national safety."

With president-elect Roosevelt's anticipated move from the State House to the White House following the 1932 election, there was confidence that training cruises-type cuts would be a thing of the past. However, a month after his election, Roosevelt called for a one-third cut in the Navy's budget. The proposed fiscal 1934 budget attempted to take some more draconian twists. The Navy proposed to restore funding for summer training cruises but only allowed for twenty-four drills. During hearings in February 1933, the president of the NROA and other reservists testified before the House Naval Affairs Committee to restore funding for a full forty-eight drills. NROA letters to Congress generated congressional letters to the White House, to the director of the budget, and to the secretary of the Navy.

As the assistant secretary of the Navy who helped bring about the birth of the Naval Reserve, the new president of the United States would not take a passive role. Calling in his Navy secretary, Claude Swanson, and director of the budget, Lewis Douglas, Roosevelt

ASSISTANT SECRETARY OF THE NAVY FOR AERONAUTICS

A reason for naval reserve aviation's growth during this period could be attributed, in part, to the second person to fill the newly created position of assistant secretary of the Navy for aeronautics—David Ingalls. The Navy's only World War I ace had returned to finish his undergraduate degree at Yale, attained a law degree from Harvard, and returned to his native Cleveland to join a legal firm. However, he maintained his interest in aviation and when he was elected to the Ohio House of Representative's he commuted to Columbus by airplane, earning him the moniker "the flying legislator."

With the inauguration of President Herbert Hoover in March 1929, the new administration not only tapped the still young Ingalls for the assistant Navy secretary post, but also recruited another Yale Naval Reserve aviator, Trubee Davison, to serve as Ingalls counterpart in the War Department. With the president interested in aviation, the two Yale classmates found themselves spending many weekends at the president's fishing camp at the headwaters of Virginia's Rapidan River.

When not spending time with the president, Ingalls had either a Boeing F4B fighter or a Curtiss F8C Helldiver with a fuselage painted deep Navy blue at his disposal to visit naval aviation facilities, including the naval air reserve bases. On one flight, Ingalls flew Will Rogers to and from the aircraft carrier *Langley*, from where the humorist and commentator wrote:

> *Am out here on the broad ocean on the aircraft carrier* Langley...*Flew down here this morning in a fast navy 'hell diver' with the Assistant Secretary of the Navy Dave Ingalls piloting. Just think: a man in charge of aviation who can fly; its almost like a general fighting his own war. And say, you haven't had any landings in an airplane till you land on the deck of one of these things. I was sure glad we hit it.*

Ingalls worked cordially with Rear Admiral William Moffett, who headed the Navy's Bureau of Aeronautics. During Ingalls three-year tenure during the early years of the Great Depression, the Ingalls-Moffett team tripled the number of aircraft in the inventory, with Ingalls test flying all of the new models. He also supported the concept of an independent aircraft carrier task force. Shortly before leaving office in 1932 for an unsuccessful run for governor, he was recommissioned in the Naval Reserve with a rank of lieutenant commander.

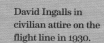

David Ingalls in civilian attire on the flight line in 1930.

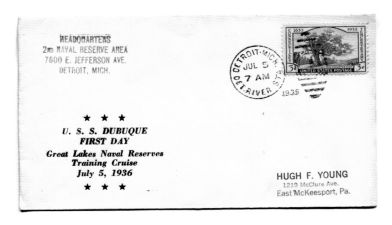
Envelope from the patrol craft *Dubuque,* which was homeported in Detroit between wars to provide training services to naval reservists.

directed sufficient additional funds restored to support pay for forty-eight drills. However, it came at the expense of the Voluntary and Merchant Marine Reserve programs. During 1934, no reservists would receive air training in Pensacola.

Naval Reserve representatives at the 1934 annual Naval Reserve Affairs meeting hosting by the Bureau of Navigation proposed a Naval Reserve Advisory Board to consist of representatives of the General Board, the Office of Chief of Naval Operations, the Bureau of Navigation, and at least six Naval Reserve officers on inactive duty. The concept received a lukewarm reception.

With members of Congress in 1935 having received much correspondence on Naval Reserve matters, House Naval Affairs Committee Chairman Carl Vinson asked the Navy's spokesman if a new Naval Reserve Act was needed.

THE COURSE TO LEGISLATIVE REFORM

To obtain the answer that the Navy spokesman would not provide, Vinson appointed Congressman John Delaney of New York to lead a subcommittee study of the structure of the Naval Reserve. Anticipating it would be called to testify, the NROA set up a committee to draft its own proposed legislation. Likewise, the Navy Department convened its own board to review the status quo and draft its own legislative package. The eight-man board, led by Captain Neil E. Nichols, met from May 8 to June 12, 1935. It produced a lengthy report advocating few changes to the 1925 legislation.

At the January 1936 annual convention of the NROA, the Nichols' report was shunned. Instead, the NROA decided to move forward with its own legislative agenda. For example, NROA called for the creation of a "superior authority, such as an assistant secretary, a reserve bureau (or both) or other equally efficacious and sovereign administrative unit."

Congressman Melvin J. Maas joined the Marines during World War I and would return to active duty in World War II.

Presented with NROA's proposals, the Delaney subcommittee put the Navy spokesmen on the defensive. Congressman Melvin J. Maas of Minnesota, a World War I veteran who held a commission in the Marine Corps Reserve (he would retire in 1952 as a major general), armed with documentation that funds intended for the Naval Reserve had been used to buy new aircraft for the fleet activities, questioned the chief of the Bureau of Aeronautics, Rear Admiral Ernest J. King, who responded that the Navy's action to divert funding seemed the right thing to do in the interests of national defense. The subcommittee also addressed the promotion and precedence of Naval Reserve officers. NROA representatives argued the system in place was unfair. Maas agreed and recommended a running mate system be put in place based on date of commission.

However, after all of the testimony, the subcommittee decided to hold back on recommendations for new legislation—for the time being. While this represented a tactical victory for the Navy Department, the hearings further exposed the chasm that existed between the department and those who wore the uniform on a part-time basis.

To fill the chasm in November 1936, the chief of the Bureau of Navigation, Rear Admiral Adolphus Andrews, convened a conference that recruited Naval Reserve officers from around the country to sit on committees to review aspects of the current reserve policies and organization. At a plenary session of the conference, CNO Admiral William Standley was blunt in is criticism of Naval Reserve lobbying efforts for increased appropriations:

> *So instead of helping the Reserve, these lobbyists in the end only hurt themselves and in hurting themselves, they hurt the Navy, because it is bound to create a feeling the Naval Reserve and the Navy are not working in unison to a common end.*

To address some concerns, especially those aired by Congressman Maas, the conference did revise the Navy legislation to establish a Reserve Policy Board for the purposes of advising the secretary of the Navy and establish a running-mate provision for the promotion of Naval Reserve officers.

The proposals did not entirely satisfy, Maas who envisioned a policy board that actually formulated Naval Reserve policies. He also wanted the director of the Naval Reserve Division within the Bureau of Navigation to be increased in rank to rear admiral.

With prodding from Maas, evolving legislation and initiatives satisfied interests within the Navy Department and the Naval Reserve community. For example, in 1937, a system of advisory policy boards were meeting in each naval district to forward recommendations from the drill deckplates to an annual policy board meeting in Washington. Legislative proposals that Maas planned to incorporate included changes to the promotion system and creation of a flag rank for the reserve. In mid-1937, Captain Felix Gygax relieved Captain William O. Spears as the head of the Naval Reserve Division.

NAVAL RESERVE ACT OF 1938

Because most of the contentious issues had been resolved, Gygax's tour as the division director would be less tumultuous. Congressman Maas drafted the legislation for the Naval Reserve Act of 1938 early that year. President Roosevelt reviewed the proposals and made a few minor changes. The legislation flowed through the House Naval Affairs Committee. One amendment added made the Naval Reserve Policy Board statutory. With passage through Congress, the new law became effective on July 1, 1938.

Among changes in the nomenclature the expansion from three to four classes of naval reservists. Those on active duty who retired after 20 or more years would be placed in Fleet Reserve status with no obligation to drill. Actively drilling reservists were classified as Organized Reserves. As before, the Merchant Marine Reserve and Volunteer Reserve remained. As part of the 1938 legislation, more extensive training was contemplated for these two classes.

One officer who would not be affected by the new reorganization was Frank Bailey, who retired on December 1, 1938, having reached the mandatory retirement age of 64. The Naval Reserve 9th Battalion and the 174th Infantry Regiment of the New York National Guard honored him with a "Review and Parade."

Frank Bailey honored, (courtesy NOSC Buffalo).

Retiring Navy Man Honored

Capt. Frank J. Bailey, right, retired commanding officer of the Ninth Battalion, New York Naval Militia, was honored last night at a review in the 174th Armory. At the left is Lieut. Edwin J. Lebherz, in command of the battalion review.

Fourth Naval District Reserve Radiomen training at Naval Station Philadelphia. Class V-3 of the Volunteer Naval Reserve consisted of hundreds of young amateur radio enthusiasts who became the nucleus for the rapid expansion of Naval Communications after 1939.

At the annual convention of the NROA in January 1939, Captain Gygax presented the administrative regulations that had to be written in the wake of the new law. The NROA attendees seemed content with the rule changes. However, the advocate for the Naval Reserve, Congressman Maas went on the offense. To prevent future friction between the regular Navy and the Naval Reserve, in March 1940 Maas drafted legislation to abolish the Naval Academy and turn to the NROTC program as the main source of naval officers. While Maas's proposal went nowhere, it apparently served as a shot across the bow that was heard. On July 15, 1940, the Naval Reserve Policy Division was established within the Office of Chief of Naval Operations.

THE GLOBAL SITUATION

The new reserve office did not survive for long. A month earlier, the German Army marched into Paris and an armistice was signed on June 22. Soon German submarines would be operating from French bases along the Atlantic to challenge shipping en route to the British Isles. Meanwhile, in the Far East, relations between the United States and Japan continued to deteriorate. Within a year the Naval Reserve would be mobilizing and with reserve and regular Navy Sailors shipping off together, the purpose of a Naval Reserve Policy Division became superfluous.

As the United States was drawn into the growing global conflict, the strength of its Naval Reserve began to reap benefits. Though the organization had budgetary and some morale issues during the years of the Great Depression, dollars spent on Naval Reserve programs during the inter-war years would provide an incalculable return on investment.

THE NAVAL RESERVE PREPARES FOR WAR

From 1932 to 1938 the organizational chart for the Naval Reserve remained consistent with 149 deck and engineering divisions drilling in 81 cities in the 48 states and one division located in Hawaii. For most of this period the aviation branch had 31 divisions located in 13 cities. For an enlisted reservist drilling in a deck division, the routine after arriving at the armory could include infantry drills performing the manual of arms, damage control drills, abandon ship drills, and gunnery drills with loading machines and training devices, followed by rate training which could include knotting, splicing, and signaling.

For divisions that drilled at seaports, the drill weekend could include a short underway period on a destroyer or smaller vessel assigned for such training duties. For the two-week underway period, the whole division would deploy for sea duty.

With the revised Naval Reserve regulations promulgated in the wake of the Naval Reserve Act of 1938, division compositions changed to contain a mix of ratings of those who served topside and others who worked in the engineering spaces. As the divisions shuffled their Sailors, they were provided more than ample funding to perform active duty. On September 8, 1939, following the German invasion of Poland, Roosevelt declared a state of national emergency. With this the Navy had authorization to bring naval reservists to active duty with their consent, to support neutrality and make preparations to improve the national defense. In 1940, many volunteered to receive orders to go on active duty for sea duty for upwards of a year to augment crews. Others were enrolled in technical schools or were assigned to ashore radio stations or other administrative duties.

With the advent of the war Europe, the spigot also opened wide for the Volunteer Naval Reserve. Operating during the Depression with virtually no federal funding, this component of the Naval Reserve expanded into a potent force that would provide great service to the nation. By the mid-1930s, a "Communication Reserve" included some 800 officers and 4,000 enlisted who maintained a network of 2,400 amateur radio stations. Besides becoming proficient on the radio waves, these men would support humanitarian relief efforts such as Red Cross efforts to steer relief to victims of floods.

For those in the Volunteer Reserve who were medical practitioners, the Bureau of Medicine and Surgery pushed for the creation of units assembled by "a Reserve officer to be known as Organizer, with desirable personal and professional characteristics." Ideally composed of "a surgeon, internist, urologist, roentgenologist, clinical pathologist, and opthalm-oto-laryn-gologist" at a minimum, with larger units including an assistant surgeon

Armored cruiser *Seattle,* circa 1916: with the national emergency declared in September 1939 cadets, along with other merchant marine officers, would receive orders for active duty in vessels of the Naval Transportation Service. Recognizing the need to further expand the training of officers in the merchant marine program, the Navy established a Merchant Marine Training Center in New York City. The eight-week course was conducted on the *Seattle,* by then a venerable vessel that had started her existence commissioned as the armored cruiser *Washington* in 1906. With her name changed in 1916 to free the state name for a future battleship, the cruiser performed convoy escort duty during World War I. For the next global war she served as a platform to train some of the officers who would serve in future convoys.

Irving M. McQuiston remained on active duty as a reservist until 1958, when he retired as a rear admiral.

With major American corporations having established offices overseas, many young college-educated Americans, many who were naval veterans from World War I, had an opportunity to live abroad to either work for these companies or pursue other endeavors. Not situated to participate in Fleet Reserve activities, many could still provide a service to the nation. In 1934, Rear Admiral William D. Leahy sent a reminder to district commandants that in corresponding with these individuals, plain envelopes were to be used and no ranks were to be indicated in the address. Leahy's emphasis was that the status and mission of these naval reserve intelligence officers must not be compromised. Clearly there was an appreciation for the quality of intelligence these individuals were sending from various locations abroad. As World War II approached, the number of officers recruited into the program dramatically expanded.

The limitations due to lack of funding of Merchant Marine Reserve Officer program have been touched on and the challenges continued throughout the depression years. One benefit of the Naval Reserve Act of 1938 was a provision to recruit merchant marine cadets from student bodies enrolled at the merchant marine academies in Massachusetts, California, Pennsylvania, and New York. Having a status similar to midshipmen at the Naval Academy, these cadets participated in coursework provided to the schools from the Bureau of Navigation that would prepare them for a commission in the Naval Reserve upon graduation.

THE NAVAL AIR CADET PROGRAM

In his dissertation on the development of the Naval Reserve, Harold Wieand argues that the reserve component that made the most gains during the interwar period was aviation—in part because it had further to go. Wieand credits Rear Admiral William Moffett, who persuaded Lieutenant Irving M. McQuiston to come on active duty to handle naval reserve aviation affairs. McQuiston, earning his Naval Reserve Force commission and designated as naval aviator No. 905 during World War I, had been discharged from active duty in 1921. Rejoining the Naval Reserve Force in 1923, the young officer impressed Moffett, who successfully arranged for McQuiston to return to active duty in 1930.

To provide resources for McQuiston to perform his critical administrative work, Wieand also lauded the role of naval reserve aviation's patron in Congress,

with "experience in orthopedics and an assistant internist having experience in psychiatry," these units could be used to augment staffs at naval hospitals or deploy independently to from the backbone of a medical department on a hospital ship or temporary base hospital ashore.

Granted the ability to grant new commissions at a rank above lieutenant commander, the Bureau of Medicine and Surgery in the mid-1930's recruited many of the nation's top medical and dental specialists to lead or serve in units that were tied to many of the nation's leading hospitals, such as the Mayo Clinic in Rochester, Minnesota. With no compensation in the form of drill pay, it seems that patriotism and a social status conferred with the granting of a commission provided the incentive to join. By June 1937, the Naval Reserve Medical Corps numbered 1,374 officers and the Dental Reserve Corps included 231 dental specialists.

the aforementioned Congressman Maas. Despite cutbacks, the number of Naval Reserve air stations slowly increased with qualitative improvements such as enhancements to allow night flying. The Great Lakes Naval Reserve Air Station was decommissioned in favor of a new base at Glenview. The Naval Reserve air stations supported the training of thirty-one fleet naval aviation divisions. Typically, the division drilled on a Saturday afternoons to coordinate squadron flying and multi-aircraft maneuvers. Each pilot had a forty-five flight hours per annum syllabus to improve skills in scouting, dive-bombing, night-flying and other facets of flight. To log in the flight hours, most pilots found time during the week to come out to the Naval Reserve air station.

With new aircraft carriers such as *Yorktown* and *Enterprise* being built, a requirement to train pilots to fill out new air wings would eventually become a

pressing need that the Naval Academy could not hope to meet. Lieutenant McQuiston developed legislation that caught the attention of the chief of the Bureau of Aeronautics, Rear Admiral King. Upon hearing the concept, President Roosevelt approved and named it the "Aviation Cadet Program."

Enacted by Congress on April 15, 1935, the program took off with an initial $3,228,252 appropriation that would be used to enlarge the infrastructure to support the program. Infrastructure included not only improved facilities and new cockpits, but the recall of 103 Naval Reserve aviators to help perform training duties at Pensacola and other locations.

The brilliance behind the Naval Aviation Cadet Program was its relative low investment to produce a pilot in short-order and then gain a strong return on that investment. To earn Wings of Gold through

Boeing F4B-1 aircraft of Fighter Squadron VF-5 in flight over Lexington (CV 2) circa 1930. Naval Reserve aviators trained with carrier air squadrons.

Naval Reserve in the movies? Navy Helldivers, like these based out of Floyd Bennett Field, were seen in the movies shooting King Kong off the Empire State Building.

the cadet program, a young man would enlist in the Navy as a seaman second class to receive preliminary training. Those who passed were appointed aviation cadets with orders for flight training at Pensacola. Upon graduation and earning his wings, the young man would be obligated to serve in the fleet for three years. Upon completion of his active-duty service, this fellow would receive a $1,500 bonus and then a commission as an ensign in the Naval Reserve. What further sold the program to the regular Navy was all of the training costs were to be taken from the Naval Reserve appropriation.

In 1936, of the 778 men who were enlisted to participate in the truncated flight-training experiment, 363 would complete flight training in Pensacola. The program continued to expand. By 1938, 526 new air cadets were at sea getting carrier-based training.

With the Naval Aviation Reserve Act of 1938 taking effect on July 1, 1938, the Navy now was authorized to award its naval air cadet graduates at Pensacola commissions as ensigns in the Naval Reserve and after three years of service, they would be eligible for promotion to lieutenant (junior grade). The active-duty requirement was extended to four years. The act also called for a statuary board to convene to review personnel matters involving all naval aviation programs within the Navy and Marine Corps.

The resultant board, chaired by Rear Admiral Frederick J. Horne, made procurement recommendations that quickly became outdated due to evolving world events. However, some recommendations were incorporated in the subsequent Naval Aviation Personnel Act of 1940 that gave the president carte blanche to appoint regular Navy commissions to as many Naval and Marine Corps Reserve aviators as he saw fit. With a cap on naval aviator end strength removed, the numbers of young men hoping to earn Wings of Gold quickly multiplied. During fiscal 1941, 3,835 young men entered aviation cadet training. Of these 1,022 would be designated naval aviators and be commissioned ensigns.

One change that increased the flow through the Naval Aviation Cadet pipeline was to shorten the pipe. Previously it took a cadet fourteen months to learn how to fly all of the aircraft in the Navy's inventory. By steering a cadet to specialize in carrier-based aircraft, land-based patrol planes, or battleship/cruiser-launched floatplanes, the cadet could earn his wings in half the time.

The interwar years for America's Naval Reserve were hardly smooth sailing. Budgetary challenges in the 1920s and during the mid-1930s interrupted training activities and caused friction between the drill decks and the bureaucracy in Washington. However, needed changes came about due to the Naval Reserve Acts of 1925 and 1938, which did provide the Navy and the nation an invaluable manpower resource pool when the national emergency came. Other congressional initiatives that led to the creation of the NROTC and Naval Aviation Cadet programs had longer-term impacts.

To simply say that the Naval Reserve contributed to America's victory in the forthcoming war with the Axis powers would be an understatement. In 1999, recognizing the pivotal role the Battle of Midway played in turning the tide of the war against Japan, Chief of Naval Operations Admiral Jay Johnson directed that the naval forces worldwide annually commemorate this June 3-6, 1942, battle along with the October 13, 1775, date that historians determined had been the birth of the Continental Navy.

At the Battle of Midway, 90 percent of the combat aviators had earned their wings through Naval Reserve aviation programs.

Naval Reserve Aviation
Cadets in Training.

4 TO DEFEND THE FREE WORLD
NAVAL RESERVISTS FIGHT A GLOBAL WAR

(1941-1945)

On the morning of December 7, 1941, the Navy cargo ship *Antares* approached the entrance of Pearl Harbor with a barge in tow when a lookout spotted a trailing object in the water. The *Antares* signaled the destroyer *Ward*, which was patrolling the approaches of the harbor that morning.

At 0637, the officer of the deck on the *Ward* called the captain, Lieutenant Commander William W. Outerbridge, to the bridge. Outerbridge, seeing a small conning tower with a periscope, ordered general quarters. At 0640, he ordered turns on the shafts for 25 knots and turned the World War I vintage flush deck destroyer toward what would be determined to be a Japanese mini-sub. Two minutes later his gun crew from the No. 1 forward 4-inch/50-caliber gun mount fired a shot that passed over the small conning tower. Then the crew from the No. 3 starboard side 4-inch/50-caliber took their turn. **Boatswain's Mate Second Class R.H. Knapp** was the *gun captain*. The rest of the crew consisted of:

⚓ **Seaman First Class C.W. Fenton** *Pointer*

⚓ **Seaman First Class R.B. Nolde** *Trainer*

⚓ **Seaman First Class A.A. De Demagall** *No. 1 Loader*

⚓ **Seaman First Class D.W. Gruening** *No. 2 Loader*

⚓ **Seaman First Class J.A. Paick** *No. 3 Loader*

⚓ **Seaman First Class H.P. Flanagan** *No. 4 Loader*

⚓ **Gunner's Mate Third Class E.J. Bakret** *Gunner's Mate*

⚓ **Coxswain K.C.J. Lasch** *Sightsetter*

In his official post-action report, Outerbridge wrote:

The shot from No. 3 gun fired at a range of 560 yards or less struck the submarine at the waterline which was the junction of the hull and conning tower. Damage was seen by several members of the crew. This was a square positive hit. There was no evidence of ricochet. The submarine was seen to heel over to starboard. The projectile was not seen to explode outside the hull of the submarine. There was no splash of any size that might result from an explosion or ricochet. Immediately after being hit the submarine appeared to slow and sink. She ran into our depth charge barrage and appeared to be directly over an exploding charge. The depth charges were set for 100 feet. The submarine sank in 1200 feet of water and could not be located with supersonic detector. There was a large amount of oil on the surface where the depth charges exploded. The attack was made at 0645 which was before Pearl Harbor was bombed by Japanese planes.

Naval reservists from the Fourth Naval District pose after being mobilized in May 1941.

MOBILIZATION FOR WAR

Whereas President Wilson's 1917 declaration of war against Germany led to a mobilization of the Naval Reserve and National Naval Volunteers, this was not the case when President Roosevelt declared December 7, 1941 "a date which will live in infamy." The No. 3 gun crew on *Ward* were all naval reservists who a year before had been drilling at the Naval Reserve Training Center in St. Paul, Minnesota. When the Japanese attacked Pearl Harbor, America's Naval Reserve was already on station to answer the call.

The mobilization had begun after the German invasion of Poland with Roosevelt's declaration of a state of emergency on September 8, 1939. The declaration authorized the voluntary recall of reservists to assist in the enforcement of neutrality and help bolster preparations to strengthen the nation's defenses. At the end of June 1940, following the fall of France, 816 officers and 1,136 enlisted men had voluntarily chosen to put the uniform on. At that time there were an additional 3,531 Fleet Reservists, men who had served a career on active duty who thought their days in uniform were behind them, back in uniform—and not all had volunteered to come back.

The voluntary recall approach challenged the various reserve divisions around the country that had trained together and had built successful unit cohesion, as would be demonstrated by those Minnesota reservists who fired the first deadly American shot of World War II. As reserve Sailors received orders to various ships and duty stations, divisions scrambled to backfill the vacant billets. However, the voluntary augmentation of the regular Navy halted late in 1940. As the Germans attempted to bomb Great Britain into submission in what would become known as the Battle of Britain, on October 5, 1940, Secretary of the Navy Frank Knox notified the Organized Reserve, including all drilling divisions and air squadrons, as well as members of the Fleet Reserve, that mobilization was pending.

The Second Division of the Organized Reserve, a unit that trained as a harbor defense unit that drilled at the Naval Reserve Training Center in Baltimore, received the call on October 14, 1940. Within two days they were heading to New York City to embark on a ship that departed on October 19 for deployment to the Panama Canal Zone. On November 21, four New York divisions received orders to augment the Atlantic Patrol Force destroyers *Breckenridge, Barney, Biddle,* and *Blakely.*

Left: As in World War I, the forthcoming Battle of the Atlantic would be over shipping lanes. In the early months of the war, German U-boats, like the one shown here, took a heavy toll on the Allied merchant marine.

Over the next seven-and-a-half months, Naval Reserve divisions and air squadrons departed for active duty. The three officers and 82 enlisted reservists who augmented the crew of the destroyer *Ward* were activated on January 25, 1941.

With the German Wehrmacht advancing into Denmark, Norway, and the Balkans, and making preparations to invade the Soviet Union, Britain and her commonwealth, including Canada, continued to fight on. With the Luftwaffe not able to secure the skies over Britain, Sea Lion, a proposed operation to invade the United Kingdom, was postponed by the German High Command. Instead, the German Fuehrer Adolph Hitler pressed his Kriegsmarine to pursue an aggressive U-boat campaign in an effort to starve Britain into submission. Now operating from French ports, German U-boat commanders, equipped with more enduring and lethal submarines, wreaked havoc against shipping heading to and from the British Isles.

Neutral America took some un-neutral actions to support its former World War I ally. In 1940 there was the orchestration of the Destroyers for Bases Agreement, in which Britain obtained 50 American World War I-era destroyers that had been laid up in reserve status. In March 1941, Congress passed the Lend-Lease Act to allow a greatly expanded shipment of war materials to Britain.

Not only were old destroyers being pulled out of mothballs for foreign use, they were being pulled out to bolster the U.S. Navy order of battle. In addition, the naval appropriation bill for fiscal 1941 and a follow-on authorization would create a two-ocean Navy by 1946 to include 35 battleships, 20 aircraft carriers, 88 cruisers, 378 destroyers, and 180 submarines. To crew the reactivated ships and numerous others that were on the building ways, the Navy needed to mobilize more reservists plus expand and create new manpower procurement programs.

For mobilization the Navy turned to the Volunteer Reserve and the Merchant Marine Reserve. On November 22, 1940, Navy Secretary Knox authorized bringing onto active duty all classes of the Naval Reserve except for the Merchant Marine Reserve. While the directive noted that a recall of an individual could be done without his consent, it did stress that the recall

Below: World War II recruitment posters for the Naval Reserve.

GET UNDER THIS FIGHTING TOP

NAVY AND NAVAL RESERVE RECRUITING STATION

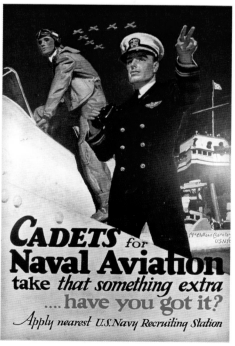

CADETS for Naval Aviation take *that something extra* .....have you got it?

Apply nearest U.S.Navy Recruiting Station

should be done in a way to reduce personal hardship. Thousands of young and not-so-young men who had skills, such as radio communications and clerical, freed Sailors qualified for sea duty to receive orders to afloat commands.

On April 28, 1941, all Fleet Reservists were recalled to active duty along with their decades of experience.

Roosevelt's May 27, 1941 declaration of an unlimited national emergency gave Knox the authority of June 10 to declare that Naval Reserve enlisted personnel on active duty and coming on active duty would be retained beyond enlistment expirations for the duration of the emergency. The next day Knox directed that Merchant Marine Reserve officers could soon be activated without their consent.

While the vast majority of naval reservists enthusiastically put on their uniforms to serve the nation, a small minority had reservations. Rear Admiral Chester W. Nimitz, as the chief of the Bureau of Navigation who oversaw the mobilization process, convened a deferment board to review requests for deferment and discharge. Over an eight-and-a-half-month period ending July 1, 1941, the board considered requests from 2,512 officers and 3,441 enlisted. The board was far more sympathetic to enlisted requests, granting discharges to nearly half of the applicants. For the officers—not so sympathetic—401 were granted discharges. Many others were given deferments to handle personal issues or finish an education, and these individuals would be called to duty at a later date.

Seen here berthed on the Hudson River, *Prairie State* served as a V-7 Midshipmen training ship during World War II. The former battleship *Illinois* of Great White Fleet fame was converted to be a floating armory in 1924 for the Naval Reserve in New York City and would be retained by the Naval Reserve as a training platform until 1955. The ship's name was changed in January 1941 to free the name for a potential new battleship.

For the procurement of Sailors, Senator Edward R. Burke of Nebraska and Representative James W. Wadsworth of New York introduced legislation during the summer of 1940 to conscript young men into the military. The passage of the Selective Training and Service Act on August 27, 1940, the first peacetime draft in U.S. history, initially subjected men ages 21 to 36 to conscription into the armed forces.

OFFICER PROCUREMENT

As for officer procurement, the Navy added schools to the NROTC program, first at Tulane University and the University of California at Los Angeles in 1939, and then at the Universities of Minnesota, Oklahoma, and Michigan the following year. In 1941, sixteen more units were created at major colleges around the country as Congress increased the enrollment from 2,400 to 7,200 students. The Navy also received permission to offer regular Navy commissions to NROTC midshipmen who were under 26 years old and had one year of active duty.

Additional pilot training facilities were established in Atlanta, New Orleans, and Dallas to increase the number of Naval Reserve pilots entering the service to 1,600 a month.

Established on June 25, 1940, the V-7 program provided a new path to commission in which a candidate with two years of collegiate academic experience could enlist as an apprentice seaman and be sent to sea for a month of unpaid duty. Those evaluated as having potential were designated as midshipmen and sent to one of three midshipmen schools established at Prairie State College, Northwestern University, and the U.S. Naval Academy.

News of the program spread quickly. Four days after the program was established, some 250 applicants boarded the Great White Fleet-era battleship *Illinois* berthed on the Hudson River at Manhattan's 137th Street to fill out the necessary paperwork and complete medical and dental exams. Many of these applicants and others—a total of 611—made an inaugural cruise in the training battleship *Wyoming*, which departed New York on July 16. A month later *Wyoming*, joined by *Arkansas* and *New York*, carried some 1,500 candidates.

Of the approximately 6,000 who applied, 5,367 survived the indoctrination cruise to go on to attend an intense three-month naval curriculum at one of the three midshipmen schools. After successful completion of the courses, the "90-day wonder" received his commission in the Naval Reserve.

FRESHMEN! SOPHOMORES!

McCLELLAND BARCLAY · U S N R

NOW you can stay in college and become a NAVAL OFFICER

SEE YOUR DEAN OR NEAREST NAVY RECRUITING STATION FOR FULL DETAILS

In charge of the Bureau of Navigation, which handled personnel matters before the war, Rear Admiral Chester W. Nimitz took the needed steps to mobilize and expand the Naval Reserve.

Opposite page: USNR manning statistics, 1945.

Navy Reserve Selective Service poster.

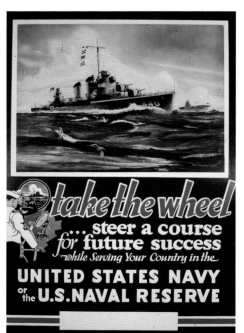

In May 1941, the Navy established a second V-7 program that targeted college graduates who had engineering degrees. The indoctrination cruise was eliminated due to ship scheduling priorities and a fourth month of training was added. By June 30, 1941, 4,868 men had applied for this program.

In the wake of the attack on Pearl Harbor, Rear Admiral Nimitz signed Naval Reserve Multiple Address Letter 117, which expressed satisfaction with the progress of the V-7 program and recommended continuation of the effort with modifications, to include reducing the enlistment age to 19, increasing the number of degrees that could be considered, and paying the candidates during their 30-day screening indoctrination.

He also signed a letter to all ships and stations on the subject of "Aviation Cadet Procurement." Recognizing the need for quality aviators for the war effort, Nimitz argued that reserve naval aviators "should be the best missionaries" to recruit more pilots.

Both letters, dated December 16, 1941, would be among the last pieces of correspondence that he signed as the chief of the Bureau of Navigation. Receiving orders the next day to relieve Admiral Husband Kimmel as commander in chief of the Pacific Fleet, Nimitz would head out to Pearl Harbor to take command of a fleet that included many of the men he had mobilized.

In his 1950 dissertation on "Organization and Administration of Naval Reserve Training," John Alexander Davis wrote: "The performance of the Naval Reserve during the war is a matter of record; only the narrative remains to be written." In lauding the Navy, Davis expressed wonderment on how such "a comparatively small organization could procure, train and absorb the large group of Reservists which they did; wield them into such an effective fighting force is one of the phenomenal incidents of naval history."

Perhaps in retrospect, when selecting a commander for the largest naval force that the world had ever seen, it helped that in his previous job he had responsibilities for procuring and training that force.

With Nimitz now commanding naval forces in the Pacific, he would continue to depend on the home front to provide trained officers and enlisted Sailors to support his operations. The V-7 program continued to expand, with Princeton and Columbia Universities offering space to support new midshipmen schools.

However, with five midshipmen schools now established to annually train recent college graduates, or juniors and seniors who had completed at least two mathematics courses, to become general line officers or perform specialized duties, the Navy faced a problem following an amendment of the Selective Training and Service Act to lower the draft age to 18.

THE SELECTIVE SERVICE ACT

The nation would draft over 10 million young men during the war years under terms that required them to serve on active duty for the duration of hostilities and then join the organized reserves for a six-month period. Whereas industries supporting the war effort would adapt to this loss of manpower by hiring older workers and women, the nation's colleges saw their student bodies being marched off to war with no replacements. One side effect of the draft age being lowered to 18 was to severely limit the number of college students who could apply for the Navy's V-7 program.

Early in the war, the Navy did not need to be part of the Selective Service process. Many young men were predisposed to join the Navy rather than risk being conscripted to wear Army green. This trend did not go unnoticed and on December 5, 1942, the government centralized military and industrial manpower procurement in the hands of the War Manpower Commission. With that, volunteer enlistments ended and starting on February 1, 1943, all conscripted males between 18 and 37 years old reported to one of 93 Selective Service Centers. Often the physical examination determined which service the inductee would join. For the Navy, color-blindness and venereal disease were causes for rejection—not so with the Army. After the inductee's education and skills were evaluated, a joint committee assigned him to either the Army/Army Air Forces group or the naval service group. If assigned to the naval group, the inductee was transported to the local Navy recruiting officer, where he could be placed into the Navy, Marines, or Coast Guard. If the inductee was selected for the Navy, he came in as an apprentice seaman USN-I. The inductee could either remain as USN-I and upon discharge could remain eligible to be drafted again for another decade, sign up for a six-year hitch in the regular Navy (assuming he was under 31 and could pass another physical), or opt to join the Naval Reserve—the choice made by the vast majority of inductees! With demobilization following World War II, a USNR Sailor would transfer to V-6 status remain in the reserves, not subject to future drafts.

THE V-12 PROGRAM

With the many of the nation's colleges facing bankruptcy and closure, President Roosevelt acted on the advice of British Prime Minister Winston Churchill, who warned him not to squander a university generation in one prolonged bloody campaign as the British had in World War I. In December 1942, the secretaries of War and the Navy issued a joint statement envisioning a role for colleges and universities in the war effort. The Army and Navy, however, took different

NAVY NOW 84% RESERVE

More than 84 out of every 100 people serving in the United States Navy are reserves, according to a recent analysis of the Navy's officer and enlisted personnel.

The figures, as of 30 June 1945, close of the Navy's fiscal year, are:

	Number	%
USN —Officers...	50,039	15.2
USNR—Officers...	278,363	84.8
Total officers....	328,402	
USN —Enlisted..	328,221	10.7
USNR—Enlisted..	2,584,608	84.5
USN-I—Inductees.	147,322	4.8
Total enlisted...	3,060,151	
Total personnel.	3,388,553	

Included in the reserves are 82,175 Waves—8,385 officers, 73,790 enlisted.

As of 30 Sept 1939 — 22 days after the declaration of the limited emergency — the Navy had 11,793 officers and 114,625 enlisted men on active duty.

approaches. The Army Specialized Training Program would use college facilities and faculty to provide advanced technical skills to selected enlisted personnel. In contrast, at a national conference held at Columbia University in May 1943, Vice Admiral Randall Jacobs, the chief of Naval Personnel, called for a joint venture between the Navy and the colleges and universities to provide two years of education, at government expense, to potential officer candidates. Upon graduation, the candidates would then attend one of the five midshipmen schools.

Designated as the V-12 program, the program was open to Navy and Naval Reserve enlisted Sailors on active duty between the ages of 17 and 23. Numerous schools applied to participate and a day before the program's inauguration on July 1, 1943, the Navy announced an initial list of 131 colleges and universities. Eventually, 212 schools would enroll in the program, with some hosting specialized units to provide selected candidates with educations in medicine, dentistry, and theology.

HOW THE NAVAL RESERVE SAVED COLLEGE FOOTBALL!

By Captain Wilbur Jones
U.S. Navy Reserve (Retired)

The Department of the Navy deservedly received credit for saving college football "from the junk pile of non-essentials" during the middle-dark days of World War II. How? By its injection in 1942-45 of thousands of officer candidates into colleges for education and conditioning prior to advanced training, including many All-Americans, National Football League stars, and other former players who then played briefly for those schools. Pundits called them "Lend-Lease" players. Navy officials claimed the program helped win the war.

To fight their Pacific War, the Navy, Marine Corps, and Coast Guard needed educated, tough, disciplined, motivated surface and submarine officers and naval aviators, their crews, and ground warfare lieutenants. The sea services instituted vigorous physical and mental conditioning programs at the colleges to train and develop teamwork, motor skills, endurance, leadership, and fortitude. Football fit this need perfectly. Even more so, Navy Commander Thomas J. Hamilton, the former Naval Academy coach who directed the pre-flight and physical training program, titled his training manual "Football! Navy! War!"*

Sometimes unconventionally administered, fluctuating and unpredictable, football and other sports generated competitive regimens that also provided a home-front morale boost.

Besides the department's program (the Army never established a similar one for its future lieutenants), nearly all the hundreds of armed forces bases formed teams that competed against each other and the colleges. High-quality clubs at the Navy's Bainbridge and Great Lakes training stations, the Marines' El Toro air station, and the Air Force's Randolph Field ranked high in national polls and endure as gridiron legends. In the greatest wartime game, Great Lakes defeated powerhouse Notre Dame, ranked No. 1 in the Associated Press poll, with its Navy V-12 players, on a last minute touchdown pass, 19-14.

Navy officer candidate programs included the pre-war NROTC, V-5 (five cadet pre-flight schools), V-1/V-7 (with NROTC integrated into V-12 in 1943), and the largest, V-12 (surface, infantry, and other line designators). To keep from closing from a lack of students, colleges ranging from the Ivy League to small private schools fiercely vied for V-12 designations.

An estimated 60,000 of the 125,000 enrollees completed V-12 and continued officer training. All were male and nearly unanimously white. Because their curricula required either eight or 24 months, they were not "90-day wonders." Most received reserve commissions. After the war, many returned to finish their degrees. V-12 produced more than 40 future Navy admirals and 18 Marine generals.

By 1943, the National Collegiate Athletic Association believed the V-programs supplied the backbone of American football. Outstanding V-12 candidate-civilian student college teams included Georgia Tech, Southern California, Ohio State, Duke, and Michigan. V-5 leaders were the Iowa and North Carolina pre-flight teams. After the war, many famous names emerged Navy V-programs and base teams as coaches— including Bear Bryant, Jim Tatum, Don Faurot, Paul Brown, and Bud Wilkinson—and players, including Elroy Hirsch, Marion Motley, Otto Graham, Bill Dudley, Charlie Justice, and Johnny Lujack.

Paul "Bear" Bryant.

*This is also the title of Captain Jones's widely reviewed book on wartime military and college football, subtitled "How Military 'Lend-Lease' Players Saved the College Game and Helped Win World War II."

BREAKING DOWN BARRIERS

A question posed by African American educators to the Bureau of Personnel regarded the eligibility of black Sailors to enroll in the V-12 program. Lieutenant Commander Alvin C. Eurich, USNR, who directed the curriculum and standards section of the program, felt stonewalled by his chain of command, so he sent a message directly to the White House to seek clarification. The response: "Of course Negroes will be tested! F.D.R."

A young Samuel L. Gravely, Jr. with Alma Bernice Clark, whom he married in 1946.

Assigned to the Naval Base at San Diego, a black fireman apprentice named Samuel L. Gravely Jr. pulled compartment cleaning duty. Having some college education prior to joining the service, Gravely volunteered for a Morale and Recreation job to run the base pool hall. It was there he caught the attention of a Lieutenant Stubbs, the Morale and Recreation officer, who urged Gravely to take a test for the V-12 program. Gravely responded: "Mr. Stubbs, I'm not sure if there is any reason for me to go down there and take this test. To the best of my knowledge, the Navy has no Negro officers, and I don't know of anything about them anticipating any." Stubbs simply said: "Get your ass down there and take the test."

Gravely was one of three Sailors who passed that day. Soon he was on his way to UCLA. Successfully completing his academic coursework, he moved on to the Midshipman School at Columbia University. However, just before he received his commission, Gravely learned he would be assigned to instructor duty to train other black Sailors at Camp Robert Smalls at Great Lakes Recruit Training Center.

Having imbibed a few beers while on liberty with his classmates, Gravely was heard yelling in the passageway, "Damn it, if all my friends are going to sea, I ought to go to sea too!" Apparently his plea was overheard, because after six weeks of instructor duty, Ensign Gravely found himself at sub-chaser school in Miami and then assigned to *PC-1264*, a patrol craft unique due to her all-black enlisted crew. Gravely became the first black officer in a five-officer wardroom.

With Gravely embarked, *PC-1264* performed convoy escort duties along the Atlantic coast and was en route to the Pacific when the war ended. With the decommissioning of *PC-1264*, he received orders to Fleet Training Group at Little Creek, Virginia, while he awaited his discharge so he could take advantage of the GI Bill to study history at Virginia Union University. He would earn his B.A. in 1948.

Above photos: *PC-1264* was commissioned in New York on April 25, 1944 with an all-black enlisted crew.

THE GOLDEN THIRTEEN, USNR

By Commander Paul Stillwell
U.S. Navy Reserve (Retired)

In late 1943, in the midst of World War II, the U.S. Navy had more than 60,000 black enlisted men on active duty and another 12,000 entering every month, but there were no black officers. Indeed, there had been none since the service's founding more than 150 years earlier. Though a few African American individuals were in training under the V-12 reserve officer program, commissioning was still a year away. From a political standpoint, it looked bad, and it was bad at a time when the nation was calling on its citizens to make heavy contributions to the war effort. Groups such as the National Association for the Advancement of Colored People and the Urban League were calling for action.

Adlai Stevenson, an assistant to Secretary of the Navy Frank Knox, proposed a quick solution that would answer the political demands: Train a group of highly qualified Negro enlisted men in a short course and then commission a dozen of them as officers in the Naval Reserve. The call went out to commands that had large numbers of black personnel to recommend candidates with demonstrated leadership skills. The FBI investigated the nominees to make sure their personal lives were above reproach. In January 1944, a group of sixteen mustered at the Great Lakes Naval Training Station near Chicago and began a concentrated training program. The nominees met early on and agreed to pool their knowledge rather than trying to compete with each other.

The training took place at the segregated Camp Robert Smalls—named for a black Civil War hero—that was part of the Great Lakes complex. The curriculum included a variety of professional subjects: navigation, seamanship, ship and aircraft recognition, gunnery, communications, engineering, and the qualities of officership. The instructors came to the men's barracks and taught classes. The pace was hectic, and the students felt the pressure. At night the officer candidates met and shared their individual expertise with their cohorts so that all came to know what each one knew. All sixteen passed the course, but not all became Naval Reserve officers. A supposition is that those running the program anticipated a 25 percent failure rate and thus started with a higher number. Of the group, twelve became ensigns and one became a warrant officer in March 1944. These individuals who made history were Ensigns Jesse Arbor, Phillip Barnes, Samuel Barnes, Dalton Baugh, George Cooper, Reginald Goodwin, James Hair, Graham Martin, Dennis Nelson, John Reagan, Frank Sublett, and William White, and Warrant Officer Charles Lear. The other three, though successful in learning the curriculum, remained enlisted men.

Once they became officers, the thirteen were assigned to duties below their demonstrated capabilities. Even though they received training that prepared them for shipboard duty, only Hair was eventually assigned to a warship with a black crew. The Navy did not want white personnel to have to serve under black officers. The others were assigned to small harbor craft, to public relations, or to command of segregated stevedore gangs on Pacific islands. After the war, only one of the thirteen, Nelson, augmented to the regular Navy and made a career of the service. The rest returned to civilian lives that included a great deal of professional accomplishment — a testimonial to the quality of the men selected for the program. Reagan remained in the reserve and was able to command an amphibious boat unit in the 1950s after he returned to active duty.

In the 1970s, after the Navy became proactive in increasing opportunities for African Americans, it retroactively made heroes of these pioneers, who got virtually no public recognition in 1944. Now they were invited to annual reunions and served as role models for a later generation. The group received a new identity at that point—the Golden Thirteen, based on their number and the gold stripes of their rank. They opened the door for the thousands of black officers who have since served in the Navy and Navy Reserve.

Gravely would be one of thirty-seven African Americans to earn commissions through the V-12 program. However, all of these officers earned their commissions after a select group of college-educated black Sailors had completed a two-month course at Camp Robert Smalls and were commissioned into the Naval Reserve in February 1944. Known as "The Golden Thirteen," these twelve ensigns and one warrant officer shared the distinction of being the Navy's first black officers.

Ensign Philip K. Lundeberg, USNR.

A more typical product of the V-12 experience was Philip K. Lundeberg, who attended Duke University. Having already enrolled there as a history major, Lundeberg enlisted in the Navy for the program shortly after it was announced and found himself billeted with other prospective officers in Duke's gothic West Campus dormitories. Lundeberg recalled taking navigation, trigonometry, electronics, engineering drawing, German, and naval orientation courses during his compressed three semesters at Duke. He recalled getting excellent physical training from the Duke Athletic Department. Because of his previous credits, Lundeberg actually earned a B.A. upon departing Duke in February 1944.

As with Gravely, Lundeberg attended the Columbia Midshipmen School. He recalled: "It amounted to four months trying to master, understand, at least part of what you could absorb at Annapolis in four years." Lundeberg remembers the graduation at the end of June 1944 at the Cathedral of St. John the Divine as one of a class of 1,386 new Naval Reserve ensigns. His was one of 26 classes that Columbia would graduate.

From New York, Lundeberg received orders to New Orleans to undergo anti-aircraft battery training and then on to Miami to the sub-chaser school for 10 weeks of anti-submarine warfare (ASW) training. From Miami, Lundeberg traveled to Key West to attend the Fleet Sound School to learn how to operate sonar equipment. After more than four months of training, Lundeberg returned to New York with orders to *Frederick C. Davis*, a destroyer escort named for a

Naval Reserve ensign killed on the battleship *Nevada* during the attack on Pearl Harbor. Lundeberg's new assignment was undergoing a refit at the Brooklyn Navy Yard following service in the Mediterranean Sea off Italy. Ironically, when he reported aboard, he discovered there was no need for an ASW officer and he was assigned as a deck division officer. Soon Lundeberg was back in the waters off Florida as the destroyer escort underwent refresher training and then returned to the North Atlantic to participate in Operation Teardrop, a massive ASW operation to flesh out any U-boats that naval intelligence believed could have launched an attack on an East Coast city.

Thanks to the NROTC, Naval Aviation Cadet, and V-12/V-7 programs; initiatives such as accepting individuals volunteering to come off the Honorary Retired List; offering direct commissions to civilians possessing specialized skills; new policies that allowed promotions to stellar enlisted personnel to hold temporary commissions as warrant officers and ensigns; and offering commission to women, the Navy had more than 286,000 reserve officers on active duty at the end of 1944.

One of the retirees who immediately volunteered to return was Frank Bailey. Initially supporting the war effort as a civilian naval engineer, Bailey persisted in returning to active duty and, found to be fit at age 68,

Rear Admiral David W. LeBreton presents the Navy Cross to Lieutenant Commander Robert W. Copeland, USNR, for his actions in command of the destroyer escort *Samuel B. Roberts* during the Battle of Leyte Gulf where *Samuel B. Roberts* engaged a superior Japanese surface force off Samar.

NOTABLE NAMES FROM THE BIG SCREEN AND LITTLE SCREEN

By Captain John Lynn Shanton
U.S. Navy Reserve (Retired)

Actor Douglas Fairbanks Jr. joined the Naval Reserve in 1941 and was assigned to Lord Louis Mountbatten's staff to observe and participate in British cross-channel commando operations. Returning to the States, he took lessons learned from the British operations and advocated for the creation of a unit that would attempt to deceive enemy forces by drawing attention away from an actual landing site. The organization he created, the U.S. Navy Beach Jumpers, would first be employed during the invasion of Sicily and used in subsequent Mediterranean operations. Other notable names who served in the Naval Reserve during World War II include actors Jackie Cooper, Robert Taylor, Gene Kelly, Henry Fonda and Jack Lemmon, late-night TV host Johnny Carson, and movie director John Ford.

donned his service dress blues on December 29, 1942. Assigned stateside, he served as a naval advisor to the War Production Board and spent much of his time stationed in Erie, monitoring Navy contracts with suppliers and manufacturers in northwestern Pennsylvania. He ended his time in service with the Navy's Material and Distribution offices in New York and Boston, assisting with the disposal or redistribution of excess material not required for the war effort. He was released on June 9, 1945, at age 70.

One example of a civilian having specialized skills was Harvard history professor Samuel Eliot Morison. After a meeting with President Roosevelt and Secretary Knox, Morison received a commission as lieutenant commander in the Naval Reserve on May 5, 1942, with an assignment to document and eventually write a narrative of naval operations during the global conflict.

Then there were civilians who had prior Navy service. David S. Ingalls had resigned his Naval Reserve commission and at the time of the attack on Pearl Harbor was a vice president for Pan American Airways, managing a contract to ferry military aircraft overseas. While he would be supporting the war effort in this civilian post, Ingalls felt he could make a greater contribution in uniform. Returning to active duty, Ingalls took on several staff jobs in the Pacific theater and by the end of the war was the commanding officer of Naval Air Station Honolulu.

Both Morison and Ingalls would leave active duty following V-J Day to stay in the Naval Reserve and provide additional service during the post-war period. Both would eventually be placed on the retirement list during the following decade at the rank of rear admiral.

Below: Lieutenant Robert Taylor, USNR (left), and Lieutenant (j.g.) Gene Kelly, USNR (right).

78

WAVES

On June 3, 1942, at the urging of Eleanor Roosevelt, Congress amended the Naval Reserve Act of 1938 to establish a Women's Auxiliary Reserve program. Not wanting to call the female Sailors WARS, some in the media dubbed them "goblettes." An English professor at Barnard College, Elizabeth Reynard, proposed the acronym WAVES, for Women Accepted for Volunteer Emergency Service. Under the WAVES program, V-9 officer and V-10 enlisted classifications for women to serve in staff positions were opened. Mildred H. McAfee, a brilliant scholar who took a leave of absence as president of Wellesley College, earned her direct commission in August 1942 as the Navy's first female officer at the rank of lieutenant commander to administer the program. Following training for the first 120 female officers at a Naval Reserve Training School established at Smith College in September 1942, McAfee oversaw the growth of the program to some 72,000 officers and enlisted by mid-1944.

Lieutenant Commander Mildred H. McAfee, USNR.

Lieutenant (JG) Grace Hopper, USNR.

Toward the end of the war, women filled approximately 18 percent of the billets ashore. Their billets, ranging from air traffic control to ship design, freed enough men to form a task force of two large carriers, a battleship, six cruisers, and fifteen destroyers.

One of the women breaking the stereotypes of what constituted women's work was Grace Murray Hopper. A mathematics instructor at Vassar College, she needed a waiver to get into the program as she was sixteen pounds shy of the weight limit. Commissioned as a lieutenant (junior grade) in June 1944, she found herself assigned to the Cruft Laboratory at Harvard programming the Navy's Automatic Sequence Controlled Calculator, a 51-foot long primitive computer having 3,300 electrical relays. During her time on active duty, Hopper had found her passion, which would continue on as she stayed affiliated with the Naval Reserve after she left active duty.

While women were initially prohibited from serving outside the continental United States or on board naval vessels or combat aircraft, by the end of the war many found themselves stationed in Hawaii, Alaska, and the Caribbean.

Impressed by the women's contributions to the war effort, Congressman Maas introduced legislation in early 1943 to extend the program after the war's conclusion. As with the male V-12/V-7 program, the V-9 program also provided a vehicle to break a racial barrier as three African American women received Naval Reserve commissions on November 13, 1944.

By mid-1945 the number of Naval Reserve officers approached 300,000 and the number of enlisted USNR, thanks in good part to the draft, hovered at 2.5 million. This constituted 84.6 percent of the active duty force as of July 31, 1945, when the Navy's manpower totals reached their peak.

With the ratio of reservist to regular Sailors steadily increasing as the war progressed, the situation mirrored that of Britain, where the Royal Navy Volunteer Reserve grew to constitute a majority of the Royal Navy's fighting force. In Britain the growing gap was visibly noticeable due to the jagged striping on the officer service dress blue sleeves. Due to the striping, reservists in Britain as well as in Canada were dubbed "The Wavy Navy." Royal Navy Reserve chronicler Stephen Howarth would note:

> *By 1942 there were as many RNVR officers as RN officers, and in June 1943, nearly four years into the conflict, a cartoon appeared in* **Punch** *that became a favourite with the Wavy Navy. Walking down a street, the girlfriend of a one stripe sub lieutenant RNVR notices a three-stripe commander RN— such an unusual sight by then that in answer to her unwritten question the sub lieutenant explains, "Straight stripes? Oh, those are the fellows who run the Navy in peace-time."*

IT'S A WOMAN'S WAR TOO!

By Master Chief James L. Leuci
U.S. Navy Reserve

Recruiting poster by John Falter, USNR.

Women Accepted for Volunteer Emergency Service (WAVES) became members of the newly established Women's Reserve (WR) on July 30, 1942. Women joined as apprentice seamen or officer candidates. An enlisted WAVES had to be between 20 and 36 years old and a high school or business school graduate. An officer candidate had to be at least 21 years but not over 50, and have a baccalaureate degree or completed at least two years of college. The first WAVES began reporting in the summer and fall of 1942. Within eighteen months, 56,000 women had entered the Navy, at a rate of nearly 1,000 a week.

Women volunteered to serve as officers (USNR Class V-9) or enlisted Sailors (USNR Class V-10). Officer candidates and enlisted recruits alike received four weeks of basic indoctrination as apprentice seamen. Upon completion of indoctrination training, officer candidates became midshipmen and enlisted women advanced to seaman second class.

Women were selected as officer candidates based on their civilian experience and the needs of the Navy. Women received commissions upon completion of training at the Naval Reserve Midshipmen's School at Smith College, Northampton, Massachusetts, or Mount Holyoke College, South Hadley, Massachusetts. Additional advanced training for WAVES officers included schools in naval communications, supplies and accounts, and aerology. Some reported directly to the staffs of training schools to oversee the supervision of enlisted WAVES. In June 1943, the first enlisted women selected for promotion to the officer ranks reported for training at Reserve Midshipmen's School at Northampton. A total of 7,000 WAVES officers were serving on active duty by the spring of 1944.

Enlisted women, unlike their World War I predecessors, did not receive direct appointments as petty officers and entered the Navy as apprentice seamen. Initially, enlisted WAVES attended basic indoctrination school (basic training) combined with service schools at various locations including Stillwater, Oklahoma; Bloomington, Indiana; Madison, Wisconsin; and Cedar Falls, Iowa. The Naval Training School established at Hunter College in the Bronx, New York, in February 1943, became the only school for enlisted WAVES basic training.

After basic training many WAVES went on to receive additional training as yeomen, radiomen, aerographers mates, aviation machinist's mates, hospital apprentices, pharmacist's mates, and other ratings. WAVES service schools were located in over twenty locations throughout the country. Some WAVES reported for general duty directly from basic training. Others found to be qualified without the need for additional training became yeoman third class petty officers.

The primary reason for bringing WAVES into the Navy was to replace men serving ashore in non-combatant billets, allowing them to transfer to sea-going billets. Women served as wartime volunteers and were not expected to remain on active duty after the war ended. Nearly 100,000 women served in the Naval Reserve during World War II, allowing men to serve at sea. However, when the war ended, women's service did not. They remained on active duty and in 1948 became a permanent part of the Navy.

1944: Members of the U.S. Navy Women's Reserve performed a variety of jobs in WWII. The two WAVES shown here are instructors on electrically operated .50-calibre machine gun turrets at the Naval Air Gunners School at Hollywood, Fla.

In the case of the U.S. Navy, the lack of uniform distinctions would make the integration of citizen and regular Navy Sailors more seamless.

SERVICE AND SACRIFICE

As the percentage of reserve Sailors in uniform climbed, so did the percentage of casualties. A survey of the 1,177 names listed on the USS *Arizona* Memorial Wall reveals only 47 were naval reservists. By the end of the war, of the 4,025 naval officers killed in combat, 2,983 had Naval Reserve commissions—nearly 75 percent. In contrast, combat death totals for enlisted Sailors were more balanced: 14,296 regular Navy and 18,136 Naval Reserve. The explanation for the higher death rate for reserve officers can be attributed to naval aviation, where 172 mostly Annapolis graduates were lost in combat in contrast to 1,341 aviators who were commissioned through Naval Reserve aviation programs. With enlisted men embarked in many combat and patrol aircraft, many were subject to hostile action. Of 1,659 airmen killed in air combat, 1,015 were USNR.

Lieutenant (j.g.) Alex Vraciu, USNR, following his shooting down six Japanese aircraft during the "Marianas Turkey Shoot" over the Philippine Sea on June 19, 1944.

Converted from a paddlewheel steamer to an aircraft carrier, *Wolverine* served as a practice landing platform operating in Lake Michigan.

While a total of 36,950 USN/USNR officer and enlisted personnel made the ultimate sacrifice fighting the enemy, it is sobering to review the non-combat death tallies, which indicate death notifications were delivered to the families of an additional 25,664 officers and enlisted during the war. More sobering are the aviation statistics. A total of 4,142 officers, 527 officer candidates, and 3,515 enlisted perished due to accidents. Of this combined tally of 8,184 non-combat action killed, 6,587 were USNR.

Nimitz, King, Leahy, Halsey, Spruance and hundreds of other Annapolis graduates enhanced the reputation of the Naval Academy through the leadership they provided as fleet and major combatant commanders. But as the war progressed, the quality of training and combat experience blurred the difference between Annapolis graduates and officers commissioned through the Naval Reserve. Toward the end of the war Admiral Halsey stated: "I do not know which of my officers are reserves." Illustrating why this was so, the percentage of department heads having USNR commissions on major combatants (fleet carriers, battleships, cruisers) ranged from 41 to 50 percent.

With Annapolis graduates having fleet and major combatant commands, more of the smaller combatants were entrusted to Naval Reserve officers as the war progressed. By July 1945, reserve officers commanded 302 destroyer escorts, 41 destroyers, and 33 submarines.

One destroyer escort with a Naval Reserve captain was the *Frederick C. Davis* with Lieutenant James Crosby, a Seattle native, in command. With allied forces having crossed Germany's eastern and western borders, the end of hostilities on land was a matter of weeks away. As a measure of desperation, German Admiral Eberhard Godt ordered seven U-boats of Gruppe "Seewolf" to the mid-Atlantic from bases in Norway in March 1945 to intercept Allied convoys. Aware of the deployment and believing this wolf pack had a more nefarious mission, Vice Admiral Jonas Ingram, the Atlantic Fleet commander, initiated Operation Teardrop—the largest Allied anti-submarine hunter-killer effort of the war.

The operation included land-based patrol aircraft operating from bases surrounding the North Atlantic basin to hunter-killer groups centered on escort carriers. However, with the Germans employing snorkels on their U-boats, they were difficult to sight in choppy seas. Thus, Ingram deployed destroyers and destroyer escorts to form two long lines abreast to create barriers. The first barrier successfully destroyed three of the German submarines.

On April 23, 1945, *Frederick C. Davis* was operating with the escort carrier *Bogue* as part of the second barrier line when its sonar detected U-546. A release of depth charges failed to damage the enemy boat. During the night Ensign Lundeberg had the mid-watch in the Combat Information Center. Figuring they would soon go back to general quarters, Lundeberg retired to the wardroom to sleep on the sofa. A classmate of his from the Columbia midshipmen school, Ensign Bob Minerd, who had relieved him in CIC, stepped into the wardroom to refill his cup of coffee and said, "Phil, there's nothing going on, why don't you go back aft and get some real sleep."

At about 0830, the CIC detected U-546 on sonar nearby. The U-boat's captain, Paul Just, had spotted *Bogue* on the horizon and was steering toward her when he swung his periscope abaft and spotted *Frederick C. Davis* coming about. With the American destroyer escort only 650 yards away, Just ordered a torpedo launch from his stern tube. The 306-foot-long vessel jack-knifed. Coxswain Levi Hancock, in the forward crew's mess, saw the bulkhead between the mess and the engine room collapse and caught a glimpse of all on watch below being killed instantly as he scampered up a ladder to the deck. The shock of the blast catapulted the officer of the deck, Lieutenant (Junior Grade) John McWhorter, down to the forward 3-inch/50-caliber gun tub. Sonar man Eugene Pakanowski witnessed a steel shroud from the mainmast slice Captain Crosby in half. The deck of the wardroom, where Lundeberg had been sleeping, was blown up nearly to the ceiling,

The speck on the distant ocean is the last remnant of the destroyer escort *Frederick C. Davis*.

Sleeping aft, Lundeberg was awoken by a metallic thud and quickly escaped his quarters, securing watertight hatches where he could. Getting topside, he quickly determined that *Frederick C. Davis* was going down and he made an effort to disarm the depth charges. Lundeberg recalled that, unlike at Midshipmen School where they plunged in the water from a 35-foot platform, he merely stepped into the cold waters of the Atlantic and managed to swim out to a life raft when a few of the depth charges that had been knocked over the side detonated. To several of the crew who had made it into the water, the blasts proved fatal. One rescue ship would eventually pull eighteen floating bodies and eight survivors from the ocean. A sister ship, *Flaherty*, quickly arrived and plucked three survivors, including Coxswain Hancock, aboard before breaking off to pursue U-546. *Flaherty*, named for Naval Reserve Ensign Francis Charles Flaherty, who was killed in *Oklahoma* on December 7, 1941, subsequently joined an intensive effort to surface U-546. Once surfaced, the German submarine was sunk by gunfire and *Flaherty* recovered Captain Just and four other German sailors.

For Lundeberg, the depth charging and hypothermia had caused shock to set in and he had no recollection of being recovered by the destroyer escort *Hayter*, which also recovered sixty-four of his shipmates. Lundeberg and two other junior Naval Reserve officers were the only survivors from the destroyer escort's wardroom. Over the next month, those three officers proceeded to write 115 condolence letters to the next-of-kin of Sailors lost that day.

As the remaining surviving officer, Lundeberg reviewed those letters 69 years later:

All of them were Naval Reserve.

In a letter he wrote to the parents of Seaman First Class Clifford Gregory O'Brien, USNR, Lundeberg's final paragraph echoed the sentiments shared in the other 114 letters as well as thousands of letters that were written to the next-of-kin of Sailors lost during the war.

```
To have the sinking of the DAVIS
occur on the very eve of victory in
the Atlantic makes your bereavement
a doubly tragic one. There is
nothing that I can say or do in any
way to ease your sorrow. If peace at
last has come, however, it is brave,
responsible, unselfish men like Cliff
that have made it possible. Your
loss is also very much ours, a loss
to the men who knew him as a friend
and whom he befriended, to the Navy
to which he was an outstanding
credit, and to his country for which
he died. Cliff was a gallant man who
went down with a gallant ship.
```

The five Sullivan brothers killed in November 1942 following the loss of the light cruiser *Juneau* to a Japanese submarine torpedo.

Above: Seabees celebrate news of Japan's surrender.

83

WORLD WAR II NAVAL RESERVE MEDAL OF HONOR RECIPIENTS

Compiled by Captain John Lynn Stanton
U.S. Navy Reserve (Retired)

Elmer Charles Bigelow was embarked in *Fletcher* when the destroyer came under fire on February 15, 1945, while operating in the vicinity of Corregidor Island. Struck by Japanese shore batteries, the destroyer lost its forward gun mount and a fire ignited in the forward magazine. Watertender First Class Bigelow reacted quickly, plunging into the burning magazine with two fire extinguishers and beat back the flames, saving the ship. His lungs seared by smoke, Bigelow succumbed that evening.

Robert Eugene Bush serving with the Marines on Okinawa on April 16, 1945 treating wounded Marines when a hand grenade fell within the group. Bush covered the grenade with his body and absorbed the blast, saving those around him. Miraculously surviving the blast, he would later go on to be president of the Congressional Medal of Honor Society.

Francis Charles Flaherty ignored orders to abandon ship from his battle station in a turret on the battleship *Oklahoma* as she rolled over in Pearl Harbor following hits by five torpedoes. Ensign Flaherty stayed on station with a flashlight to show members of his crew the escape route sacrificing his life for his shipmates.

Nathan Green Gordon, piloting a PBY on February 15, 1945, rescued the crews of Army B-25s that went down in Kavieng Harbor on New Ireland while his aircraft came under fire from Japanese shore batteries. By the time Lieutenant Gordon was airborne, he had recovered 16 Army aviators.

William Edward Hall flew combat air patrols in a Douglas SBD Dauntless dive bomber on May 8, 1942, the second day of the Battle of the Coral Sea. Spotting an approaching Japanese air attack force, Hall shot down four Japanese planes while battling superior Zero fighter aircraft. A day earlier Lieutenant (Junior Grade) Hall had participated in the attack that led to the sinking of the carrier *Shoho*.

William David Halyburton Jr. served as a pharmacist mate second class with the 2nd Battalion, 5th Marines, 1st Marine Division on Okinawa. On May 10, 1945, Halyburton exposed himself to enemy fire to aid a wounded Marine. Shielding the Marine with his body, Halyburton was fatally wounded.

Rufus Geddie Herring commanded the landing craft infantry (gunboat) *LCI(G)-449* at Iwo Jima on February 17, 1945, with a mission to provide cover to underwater demolition team frogmen who were clearing underwater and beach obstacles. Heavy enemy gunfire struck the LCI, killing several Sailors and wounding Lieutenant (Junior Grade) Herring. Despite his wounds, Herring maintained his position and continued to direct fire against enemy positions.

Johnnie David Hutchins was on the bridge of the tank landing ship *LST-473* off New Guinea on September 4, 1943, when the ship was hit by bombs during an air attack. Wounded, Seaman First Class Hutchins grabbed the helm to steer the ship clear of two incoming torpedoes. He died clinging to the helm.

Herbert Charpiot Jones led an ammunition handling detail on *California* on December 7, 1941, when the battleship was hit, fatally wounding Ensign Jones. Rather than having his men risk their lives to extract him, he ordered his Sailors from the space, assuring their survival.

Fred Faulkner Lester served as a hospital apprentice first class with the 1st Battalion, 22nd Marines, 6th Marine Division, during the battle for Okinawa. On June 8, 1945, Lester ran out to recover a wounded Marine. In doing so he was shot twice yet still brought the Marine back to safety and directed his treatment until succumbing to his own wounds.

Joseph Timothy O'Callahan was assigned as a chaplain in *Franklin* operating near Japan on March 19, 1945, when that aircraft carrier was hit by two bombs. In the ensuing inferno, Lieutenant Commander O'Callahan organized and led fire parties and directed the flooding of several magazines at a critical juncture.

John Joseph Parle, while serving in *LST-375* on the eve of the invasion of Sicily on July 10, 1943, discovered a smoking pot had ignited in one of the ship's boats and hurled the pot over the side before it could set off pyrotechnics in the boat. Ensign Parle died a week later from smoke inhalation.

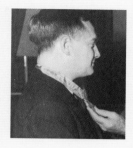

Arthur Murray Preston commanded Motor Torpedo Squadron 33 and on September 16, 1944, took two of his PT boats to perform a daring rescue of a Navy pilot who landed in a bay off the enemy-held island of Halmahera. Enduring two hours of enemy gunfire, *PT-363* and *PT-489* led by Lieutenant Preston returned with the rescued pilot.

George Edward Wahlen was assigned as a pharmacist mate second class to 2nd Battalion, 26th Marines, 5th Marine Division, ashore on Iwo Jima on March 3, 1945. During the assault of Hill 362B he was wounded for the third time in six days. Despite his wounds, he crawled 50 yards to assist another fallen Marine.

Jack Williams served as a pharmacist mate third class with the 3rd Battalion, 28th Marines, 5th Marine Division, ashore on Iwo Jima on March 3, 1945. During fighting that day, Williams treated 14 wounded Marines and moved forward under intense fire to rescue another fallen Marine and drag him into a depression, using his body as a shield while administering first aid. Shot three times, he moved on to treat another Marine before being shot by a sniper trying to return to friendly lines. He died later that day.

5 THE GREATEST GENERATION BECOMES
THE GREATEST NAVAL RESERVE

(1946-1949)

Secretary of the Navy James Forrestal, who had flown as a Naval Reserve Force pilot in World War I, warned the graduating class at the Naval Academy in June 1945 that "in order to obtain the officers needed to man the Navy which we must keep when this war is over we shall have to get large numbers from the ranks of Reserves who are serving and fighting in the Navy."

One of those officers would be Marmaduke Gresham Bayne.

"Duke" Bayne, a senior at the University of Tennessee when the Japanese attacked Pearl Harbor, returned to his native Norfolk, Virginia, upon graduation, and headed for the Navy recruiting office. Impressed with Bayne's skills in small craft handling that he had attained growing up in the Tidewater region, the recruiter offered him an accelerated path to a Naval Reserve commission. Bayne could skip the four-month V-7 midshipmen school by simply attending a six-week orientation course that would be opening at Dartmouth College. Upon graduating from the Dartmouth Naval Training School, Bayne received orders to take command of a YP—a converted fishing boat—to search for German submarines off the East Coast. After a year bobbing offshore, Bayne, desiring to see some real action, applied for and attended submarine school. Upon graduation, he joined *Becuna* for a successful war patrol in the Pacific. After the war he turned down an acceptance to attend graduate school at Harvard, as he loved submarines and decided to augment to the regular Navy to pursue a career serving his country.

Appearing before an Augmentation Board of three senior naval officers—graduates of the Naval Academy—Bayne was grilled on the seriousness of his intent. A final question to Bayne posed the hypothetical scenario of ten years down the line where he and two Naval Academy graduates might be recommended for a very fine assignment.

"Who do you think will be the third choice for that good assignment?"

Bayne responded:

> *If in ten years the people who made the decisions about those jobs were only Naval Academy graduates,*

> *I would have made a bad decision making the Navy a career, but I suspect that by then people like me who had fought a war and been augmented into the regular Navy would be having a say about such assignments.*

The panel was impressed with Bayne's faith in the system. He was accepted. "Duke" Bayne would retire from the Navy in 1977 as a vice admiral.

Shown here as a rear admiral in command of the Middle East Force, Duke Bayne would go on to become president of the National War College before retiring as a vice admiral.

DEMOBILIZATION

Bayne was just one of thousands of officer and enlisted Sailors who came into the Navy through reserve programs and would make the service a full-time career, bringing to the organization skill sets fostered through different educational backgrounds that would forever change the make-up and culture of the Navy. World War II had served as a catalyst for this change.

Despite the anticipated demobilization that would release millions of Sailors and scrap and mothball hundreds of ships, Forrestal understood that the Navy would need to retain at least 30,000 reserve officers to operate the peacetime Navy. With opportunities beckoning in the civilian sector, Forrestal was

Returning servicemen cram the decks of the attack transport *Hendry* steaming homeward from the Western Pacific.

concerned that an elitism that existed amongst Naval Academy graduates, hinted at during Duke Bayne's augmentation interview, would deter others from pursuing the Navy as a career. Those concerns probably factored into why only 24,000 officers responded to the offer to augment to the regular Navy to fill those 30,000 slots. Of the applications submitted, 18,000 were considered either outstanding or acceptable.

However, two other significant factors may have influenced reserve officers to stay reserve in the immediate post-war years:

    ↕ *For the Navy, it was the worst of times.*

    ↕ *For the Naval Reserve, it was the best of times.*

By September 2, 1945, the Navy had attained its zenith of strength. Over 1,200 combatant vessels included nearly 100 aircraft carriers, 23 battleships, 73 cruisers, 733 destroyers and destroyer escorts, and 234 submarines. Another 3,600 vessels, ranging from auxiliaries to mine warfare craft, also were included in the Navy's afloat inventory. As in all wars, there would be demobilization. Unfortunately for the Navy, a perfect storm of circumstances would render it nearly impotent in a span of less than half a decade.

The first circumstance that bode ill tidings was the

change of leadership at 1600 Pennsylvania Avenue. With the death of Franklin D. Roosevelt on April 12, 1945, the Navy lost a staunch supporter. His successor, Harry S. Truman, had served in World War I as an artillery officer from a Missouri National Guard unit. An associate from Truman's guard unit whom the new president brought into the administration observed, "... during the Roosevelt administration, the White House was a Navy wardroom; we're going to fix all that."

Then there were the atomic bombings of Hiroshima and Nagasaki that caused some analysts to declare such conventional forces as navies were obsolete. With the United States in sole possession of these powerful weapons, who would dare militarily confront America?

Another circumstance unique in history was that the outcome of the war left the United States Navy with no potential peer competitor that it could plan against. The navies of Germany, Japan, Italy, France, the Netherlands, and the Soviet Union had been savaged by the war. The Royal Navy, which had been a measuring stick for the U.S. Navy to justify planning and budgeting, remained; however, given the special relationship that had evolved between London and Washington over the course of two world wars, nobody could envision Great Britain as a potential foe in the post-war period.

BUDGET STRUGGLES

The chairman of the House Naval Affairs Committee, Congressman Carl Vinson, saw a perfect storm brewing and introduced a resolution in September 1945 to reaffirm the role of sea power in the nation's defense. Subsequently, the House of Representatives passed Concurrent Resolution 80 by a margin of 347-0.

Truman did not appreciate the resolution, which he felt usurped his executive authority. In addition, the Congressional seapower affirmation would not resonate with the general public, which demanded a rapid demobilization and saw no security threats to the nation in a world where the United States held sole possession of atomic weapons.

Truman, worried that the nation could slip into a recessionary economy, pushed for dramatic cuts and envisioned a military budget of $5 billion. Navy Secretary James Forrestal sought $6 billion for the Navy alone! The administration pushed for more efficiencies, which would be attained through the amalgamation of the Navy and War Departments into a Department of Defense that included a new service branch: the U.S. Air Force.

Demobilization proceeded faster than the Navy's leaders desired. Only six weeks after the Japanese surrender, an estimated one-third to one-half of the fleet was no longer combat ready as hundreds of thousands of discharged Sailors took off their jumpers in favor of civilian attire. To bring Soldiers and Sailors home from overseas, the Navy employed over 300 transport vessels, and used aircraft carriers, battleships and cruisers as personnel ferry boats in Operation Magic Carpet. In December 1945, the Navy was discharging Sailors at a rate of 15,000 a day.

For fiscal 1947, Truman initially submitted a budget of $7.1 billion for the Army and $4.5 billion for the Navy, and included in those funds were costs associated with the occupation of Germany and Japan. In August 1946, only a month into the fiscal 1947 budget, the president ordered the Navy to trim $650 million from the $4.5 billion it was expecting and to reduce its budget request for the following year to $3.5 billion. Adding to the Navy's budget woes were wartime contracts that had to be closed out and settled.

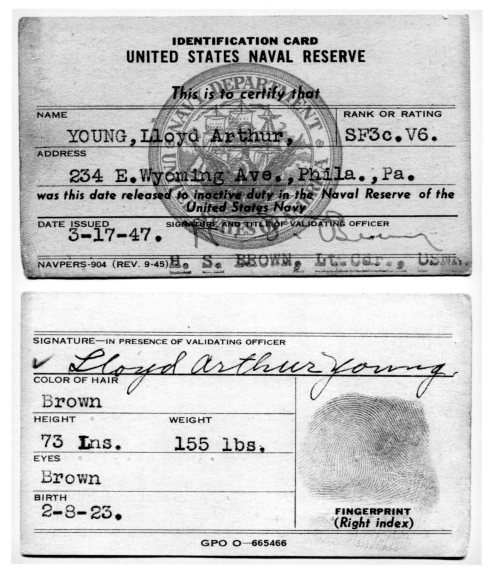

Hundreds of thousands of Sailors were issued these cards upon discharge from active duty at the conclusion of World War II.

With budget-conscience Republicans elected in November 1946 to majorities in both the House and Senate, there was little political will to buck the president and add funding to the Navy's budget. Indeed, the appropriation was cut to $3.3 billion.

Further complicating matters, the new Air Force benefited from a 1948 commission appointed by Truman to evaluate the nation's airpower strategy. Truman's Air Policy Commission argued that since no surface Navy threats existed, the Navy needed to focus on secondary missions such as overseas transport and that the Air Force needed a significant infusion of funding to build sufficient bomber and fighter forces. Using appropriated funding from Congress, the keel for the Navy's first supercarrier, the *United States*, was laid down on April 18, 1949. Five days later, Secretary of Defense Louis Johnson announced the cancellation of the supercarrier program. Furthermore, for the proposed fiscal 1950 budget, the Navy would need to reduce its carrier strength from eleven to eight flattops.

From Long Island in June 1949, retired Fleet Admiral Nimitz wrote to retired Fleet Admiral Ernest King, the

Chief of Naval Operations Admiral Louis E. Denfeld, USN, challenged the president's defense spending priorities before Congress and was asked to resign.

president of the Naval Historical Foundation: "I do not envy you your residence in Washington during these controversial times. I for one, am glad to be away from that trouble spot and I intend to stay away as long as I can."

Nimitz's successor as CNO, Admiral Louis E. Denfeld addressed a gathering of the Fleet Reserve Association in early September 1949 to explain that further budget cuts would force the Navy to reduce the number of active aircraft carriers to six. Testifying before Congress a month later, Denfeld bluntly expressed his concerns about the administration's defense spending priorities. Subsequently, the secretary of the Navy, Francis Matthews, relieved Denfeld from his duties as CNO on November 1, 1949.

Further cuts were forthcoming in fiscal 1951, beginning on July 1, 1950. Truman wanted a $13 billion cap on defense spending, of which the Navy would receive $3.9 billion—a cut of $50 million from the previous year's budget. To make the cut, Navy planners envisioned placing another two large carriers, three escort carriers, and five cruisers into inactive status.

PLANNING THE POST-WAR NAVAL RESERVE

Forrestal, having personally experienced the rapid demobilization of the Navy after World War I that nearly left the nation without a Naval Reserve capacity, worked during the war to have a viable Naval Reserve infrastructure in place.

With Italy's surrender and Allied armies and naval forces advancing toward the German and Japanese homelands, the Navy Department initiated preliminary planning in 1944 to map out a viable reserve organization. The guiding philosophy to assure effective training and high readiness would be for the reserve to be administered as an integral component of the regular Navy. The classifications of reservists, established in the Naval Reserve Act of 1938 remained: Organized Reserve, Volunteer Reserve, Merchant Marine Reserve, Fleet Reserve.

With the Bureau of Personnel succeeding the Bureau of Navigation in May 1942 as the Navy's people managing organization, general plans and policies for the administration of the Naval Reserve would be prepared and implemented by an Assistant Chief of Naval Personnel (Naval Reserve). To coordinate these policies within the various bureaus having reserve components, an officer would be assigned as the Assistant Chief of

Naval Operations (Naval Reserve). Monies, appropriated for Naval Reserve activities, would be managed through the different bureaus and commands that maintained reserve elements. At a regional level, Naval District commandants oversaw Naval Reserve activities within the various districts. Each district had an assigned billet of District Director of Naval Reserve. An exception to this framework would be Naval Reserve aviation where the Deputy Chief of Naval Operations for Air held overall responsibility to manage the program.

With a framework in place, but little funding to work with initially, Forrestal moved ahead with the formation of a peacetime reserve. On March 27, 1946, Naval District commandants received permission to start recruiting discharged Sailors. In May, 100 naval reservists who drilled at Fort Schuyler, New York, participated on a weekend training cruise on the destroyers *English* and *Haynesworth*. With funds made available in the fiscal 1947 budget, enrollment into a new Organized Reserve started on July 1, 1946.

As the regular Navy saw its fiscal 1947 budget slashed by another $650 million the following month, the Naval Reserve not only survived unscathed, but actually saw a small bump-up in appropriations. Eventually Congress budgeted $138.8 million to underwrite a drilling Naval Reserve of 24,000 officers and 200,000 enlisted. The Volunteer Reserve, however, retained the names of many who recently served, providing a pool of 300,000 officers and another 500,000 enlisted personnel. As was the case before the war, there was no requirement for these individuals to drill and limited funds were made available to allow some training opportunities.

For the active-duty leadership of the Navy, which was fighting a losing budget battle on Capitol Hill, the Naval Reserve provided a critical haven to shelter at least a part of the tremendous combat power that had been developed during the recent global war. In explaining to Congress why a strong shore infrastructure needed to be maintained, Admiral Denfeld argued that the nation would be unlikely have the luxury of 18 months, as was the case in World War II, to mobilize and prepare reservists for combat.

As previously noted, the fiscal 1948 Navy authorization was even more draconian at only $3.3 billion. Yet, Naval Reserve funding held firm. For the following year, Truman favored a 50 percent increase in reserve appropriations.

BUILDING RESERVE INFRASTRUCTURE

One reason for the increase in reserve appropriations was that the pre-war facility infrastructure, which mostly depended on the generosity of states that still retained naval militias, was not meeting the needs of a post-war Naval Reserve that needed more space and capacity to facilitate training with the latest technology. These requirements fueled an initial unprecedented building and modernization program of 287 facilities, as Congress happily supported construction projects for their home districts. For locations where there was waterfront, the Navy sent 145 ships to serve as training platforms, and in some cases, as temporary armories. Many of these ships had an active-duty complement of 30 percent of the wartime manning level. With reservists or NROTC midshipmen embarked, these vessels could get underway for short training evolutions.

The destroyer *English*.

The destroyer *Haynesworth*.

For the majority of the Naval Reserve officers and enlisted who anticipated going to sea upon recall, there was a radical change in the division organization. Whereas before the war Naval Reserve divisions focused on providing men to fill specific billets on specific ships, a lesson that came out of World War II was this arrangement hardly worked and reservists found themselves detailed to fill holes as needed throughout the fleet.

Hence, a new Surface Reserve Division would comprise 200 men, of which fifteen to nineteen were officers with the rest broken down into four to eight different rating groups. To facilitate quality training, new training centers shifted away from the drill-deck centered armories of the 1930s to facilities that resembled vocational technical schools.

Reserve radioman getting "Hands-On" training in Seattle.

The diesel boat *Cravelle* served as a reserve training platform after the war.

At some locations, the Navy reassigned eighteen of its World War II vintage submarines to support the training of naval reservists who had served in the silent service during World War II. In addition to maintaining these permanently moored boats, the 19,000 submarine reservists enrolled in the program were offered underway periods on active fleet submarines.

For the Naval Air Reserve the existence of an extensive World War II training infrastructure enabled a more seamless transition to peacetime flight training. With a headquarters established at Naval Air Station Glenview in Illinois under the command of Rear Admiral Edward Ewen, the Navy initially placed 1,600 aircraft dispersed to fifteen Naval Reserve Air Stations and seven joint USN-USNR facilities. To maintain proficiency, Naval Air Reserve pilots needed to log 100 hours of flight time during drill weekends or on active-duty. Initially, the Naval Air Reserve wanted to retain 7,500 officers and 19,000 enlisted. As the Soviet Union continued to morph into a growing international threat, funding for the Naval Air Reserve climbed. With a surplus of aircraft that had served on now-mothballed aircraft carriers and planes that were on the production lines at the end of the war, the number of aircraft in the reserve inventory climbed to 2,200, split among fifty-five carrier groups, twenty-five patrol squadrons, and twenty-five transport squadrons. The Naval Air Reserve also provided aircrews to support blimp operations.

Perhaps where the lessons of World War II had the greatest influence on the composition of the Naval Reserve was in non-afloat support activities. After the war, the Navy dramatically cut its construction battalion manning level to 4,000. By 1947, 200 Naval Reserve Seabee companies had been formed to provide access to an additional 615 officers and 5,000 experienced enlisted personnel.

Naval Intelligence maintained access to many of the analytical minds who served during World War II with the creation of 1,500 pay billets in the Organized Reserve and 2,500 billets in the Voluntary Reserve.

The Supply Corps Reserve was also created with 1,200 officers and 10,000 enlisted members. A subset of the Supply Corps reserve would be cargo handling units that were established in 1949.

WOMEN REMAIN

Unlike after World War I, the post-World War II Navy did not eliminate women from the ranks, though most of the women who served left the service as quickly as their male counterparts after the cessation of hostilities. Captain Jean Palmer became director of the WAVES, relieving Captain Mildred McAfee, who returned to academia. Palmer, after a short tenure, was relieved by Captain Joy Bright Hancock. Hancock had 9,800 WAVES under her purview. The WAVES Naval Reserve program officially ended on June 12, 1948, when President Truman signed the Women's Armed Services Integration Act, which allowed women to serve in the regular or reserve components of the armed forces. While the act gave women equal status to their male counterparts within the military hierarchy, it included restrictions that would, for several decades, deny the services the talents and skills these female Americans possessed. For the

Above: AM-1 Martin Maulers were introduced to the fleet in 1948 as aircraft that could deliver torpedoes and bombs. When the Navy found the AD-1 Douglas Skyraider to be more reliable, Maulers were turned over to the Naval Air Reserve.

Bottom left: Great Lakes WAVES Color Guard.

Bottom right: WAVES Captain Jean Palmer receives Legion of Merit on July 18, 1946 from Vice Admiral Louis E. Denfeld. Looking on is Commander Joy B. Hancock who succeeded Palmer, on July 26, 1946, becoming the third Director of the Women's Reserve.

Navy and Naval Reserve, the act limited the number of women enlisted to two percent of the enlisted end strength. The legislation also excluded women from serving in combat ships or aircraft and none could be promoted to the permanent rank of captain.

In addition to retaining some of its most capable individuals in the Naval Reserve, the Navy succeeded in creating opportunities for non-Navy veterans to join the service through officer commissioning programs that were dubbed "The Holloway Plan" for Chief of Naval Personnel Vice Admiral James L. Holloway, Jr. With the disestablishment of the V-12 and V-7 programs toward the end of the war, the Navy sought to expand the NROTC program, which had supplied 6,000 naval officers during the war. As the Navy phased out the V-12 program, a number of participants were moved into NROTC units. To create additional midshipmen slots, Congress authorized the Navy to select twenty-five additional colleges and universities to host NROTC units beginning in November 1945 to accommodate an enrollment of 14,000. A one-year ceiling of 24,000 was authorized to allow V-12 transferees to finish and receive their commissions.

RETURN OF THE DRAFT

With the NROTC program becoming the Navy's largest consistent source of officers, a complete Communist seizure of Czechoslovakia on February 24, 1948 encouraged Congress to act on Truman's request to reinstate the Selective Service program that had ended after World War II. The legislation signed by the president on June 19, 1948, re-established the draft, which would provide the Navy a pool of young men to fill out the junior ranks. The law had an unintentional benefit for the Naval Reserve in that young men who enlisted into the reserve would be exempt from being drafted into active duty.

On November 30, 1949, at a time when the combat capability of the regular Navy had nearly bottomed out, the Naval Reserve listed 1,068,780 men and women in its ranks. Of this number, 21,790 officers and 145,705 were in drill pay status in the Organized Reserve. An additional 29,612 officers and 13,564 enlisted drilled in an impressive array of thirty-one Volunteer Reserve programs in such specialties as dentistry, electronic warfare, industrial relations, intelligence, law, medicine, ordnance, petroleum, public relations, religion, and security.

These men and women now either drilled at 316 training centers, 21 Naval Reserve air stations, or on some 104 ships that the Navy had provided.

The majority of the Naval Reserve, though, consisted of just over 800,000 officers and enlisted in the inactive pool who could be recalled to service in a national crisis. Then there was a minority of Naval Reserve officers and enlisted who were brought back to active duty to fill short-term Navy manning requirements.

Phil Lundeberg and Sam Gravely were two of those officers. Both left active duty after the end of the war to complete college degrees in history. Lundeberg, with his B.A. from Duke in hand, decided to pursue a doctorate at Harvard. Gravely pursued a B.A. from Virginia Union University, earning it in 1948. Both Lundeberg and Gravely remained in inactive reserve status in the immediate post-war years. Lundeberg, studying under Samuel Eliot Morison, found himself writing on the War in the Atlantic. To assist with his research, Morison arranged for Lundeberg to be recalled to active duty to work in the Office of Naval History in Washington. Gravely also came to the nation's capital, having accepted an offer to return to active duty to perform recruiting duty. As Lundeberg reviewed historical documents and Gravely hit the pavement to recruit Sailors, half a world away conflict was brewing in a place many Americans couldn't find on a map: Korea.

Opposite page (top): 1948-First six WAVEs to re-enlist into the regular Navy thanks to the Women's Armed Services Integration Act.

Opposite page (bottom): Naval Reserve Emergency Communications Van.

Below: Recruiting Posters.

ENROLL IN THE NAVAL RESERVE (V6)
OBTAIN THESE ADVANTAGES BY JOINING NOW

- Keep your rate.
- Get expert training.
- Stay eligible for advancement and longevity.
- Have an opportunity to attend drill with pay and take summer cruises.

ACTIVE DUTY ONLY WITH YOUR CONSENT EXCEPT IN A NATIONAL EMERGENCY
EX-REGULARS AND RESERVES ELIGIBLE (ALNAV 261)

For full information

See Your Nearest Navy Recruiting Station

Come Aboard

351

NAVAL RESERVE

6 KOREA

(1950-1953)

The North Korean invasion on June 25, 1950, to seize the whole Korean peninsula not only caught the United States by surprise, but caught the limited naval forces it had deployed in the wrong ocean. As the American-Soviet relationship changed from wartime allies to peacetime foes competing for influence, initially in Europe, America's strategic focus took a pivot to the Atlantic, despite the fall of mainland China to the Communists in 1949. With Soviet armies positioned in Eastern European countries, and strong Communist parties in Italy and France, the United States rushed aid to Europe under the plan named for President Truman's secretary of state, retired General George C. Marshall. Militarily, the United States and 11 other nations acted to confront the Soviets by forming a collective security alliance in 1949 that would be called the North Atlantic Treaty Organization (NATO).

1951 Navy Fleet Marine Force Corpsmen recalled to active duty.

Thus as the North Koreans rolled south armed with T-34 tanks, there was little in the way of land, air, and naval power to interdict them. Japan-based U.S. Air Force jets only had enough range for short missions over the battlefield, American troops flown in from Japan were inexperienced and under-equipped, and the Navy had only one aircraft carrier, *Valley Forge*, in the western Pacific.

Fortunately, with the help of other regional forces, including the United Kingdom, which provided the carrier *Triumph*, a defensive toehold was established around the southern port of Pusan. For the invading North Koreans, victory could be achieved if they could dislodge the remnants of the South Korean and American ground forces before help could arrive from across the Pacific.

PULLING THE FLEET (AND SAILORS) OUT OF MOTHBALLS

In New York, the United Nations Security Council approved a resolution declaring North Korea an aggressor and resolved that member nations should work together to restore South Korea's territorial integrity. Thus, the United States would lead a coalition military response with General Douglas MacArthur in overall command. In Washington, Congress extended the Selective Service Act. A provision of the act authorized the involuntary activation of retirees and reservists. With the Navy rushing to pull ships out of inactive status, on July 8, the Bureau of Personnel offered a voluntary recall for reservists who were qualified for afloat billets. Eleven days later, the services were granted permission to begin involuntary recalls.

To fill the projected number of hulls being pulled out of mothballs, the Navy needed to add an additional 22,873 officers and 181,450 enlisted men by June 30, 1951—a 50 percent increase in manpower. With no formal declaration of war, the situation in the Far East was defined as a crisis that placed some restrictions on the scope of the recall. Initially, the Navy sent recall notices to 7,200 officers and 49,000 members of the Organized Naval Reserve, about a third of the force. Given the potential Soviet threat in Europe, the Navy wanted to maintain a reserve of its Reserve.

Such was the rush to get current combatants to wartime manning and re-commissioned ships over to the western Pacific, that recalled reservists, most of whom had not seen a day at sea since just after the end of World War II, were sent to sea without any refresher training. A report from Commander Cruiser Destroyer Forces, Pacific reported: "These men have partially 'lost their hand' and require a short time to become reoriented."

Fortunately, in the budget-cutting frenzy that marked the years following World War II, one area where the Navy did not skimp on was inactive ship maintenance. Using new paints and protective coatings as well as extensive use of dehumidifiers, the Bureau of Ships aimed to lose the mothballed fleet to obsolescence before material deterioration.

In 1950, most of the laid-up World War II vintage warships had good hull life left and needed little modernization. In short order, the Navy brought back

An F9F-2 Panther aboard the
aircraft carrier *Valley Forge.*

The cruiser *Saint Paul* conducting naval gunfire support off Korea.

to life ten aircraft carriers and two battleships along with numerous other combatants. In one year the number of combatant ships in the fleet jumped from 245 to 358. To provide manning for all of these ships, by June 1951, 182,000 naval reservists had been recalled—approximately 70 percent of these Sailors deployed on ships.

Whereas during World War II it took nine months to a year to build up sufficient combat strength to move from defensive to offensive operations, during the Korean War the American-led United Nations forces were on the attack within three months. With Naval Reserve Sailors operating many of the amphibious assault ships, MacArthur executed his masterful counterstroke of landing Marines at Inchon on Korea's west coast on September 15, 1950.

NAVAL RESERVISTS JOIN THE FIGHT

As the Marines advanced to Seoul, cutting off North Korean troops around Pusan from their logistical support, the tide of the war had changed. Thus, the Navy now had the luxury of detailing crews to ships being placed back in service thirty days in advance of the re-commissioning to allow for training. A difference between World War II and Korea was the Navy did not hesitate to assign recalled Sailors to ships having far greater tonnage than the amphibious warfare ships and destroyer escorts crewed in the previous war. For example, one of the carriers brought back to life, the

Essex-class aircraft carrier *Princeton*, which returned to service on August 28, had nearly an all-Naval Reserve crew. After an intense period of refresher training, *Princeton* steamed across the Pacific and arrived at a critical juncture following the massive Chinese intervention. Joining the fleet carriers *Philippine Sea* and *Leyte*, the *Princeton* provided vital close air support to enable Marines to fight their way out of the Chosin Reservoir and covered a successful evacuation of ground forces and civilians at Hungnam.

Included in the offshore surface fleet providing gunfire support for the Hungnam evacuation was the battleship *Missouri*, which stayed in commission throughout the post-war period with a citizen from the "Show-Me State" serving as commander in chief. The Navy scrambled to bring the other three *Iowa*-class battleships back in commission with, the lead ship of the class placed back in service on August 25 1951. Meanwhile back in Washington, recruiting officer Lieutenant Sam Gravely desired to go back to sea. His request granted, he attended Communications School in Monterey and then reported to the *Iowa* as the battleship's radio officer just as she deployed to Korea in March 1952. For Gravely, having limited at sea experience in Patrol Craft, the tour in Seventh Fleet flagship exposed him to the big-ship Navy way of doing things. After a successful tour in *Iowa*, Gravely detached to be a communication officer on the cruiser *Toledo*.

Iowa off the coast of Korea, 1952. In addition to *Missouri,* which was in service at the start of the Korean War, the Navy brought back *Iowa, New Jersey* and *Wisconsin* to bombard enemy positions beyond the coastline.

Weather challenged flight operations off Korea.

While Naval Reserve-manned surface ship guns savaged enemy forces trying to move along the coasts, naval aircraft, often piloted by reservists, struck at enemy positions in the interior, providing close air support to U.N. ground forces and striking at North Korea's logistical infrastructure.

THE TRANSITION TO JET AIRCRAFT

The extensive activation of Naval Reserve aviation assets began on July 19, 1950, when the CNO, Admiral Forrest P. Sherman, alerted 42 squadrons to stand by for activation. Within a week, half of the squadrons were activated for assignment to Commander, Air Forces, Pacific Fleet. By the end of August, hundreds of reserve aviators and maintenance crews had arrived at Naval Air Station San Diego to form up Reserve Carrier Air Groups 101 and 102. On September 2, the deputy CNO for Air, Vice Admiral John H. Cassady, reported during an appropriations hearing on Capitol Hill that he anticipated the reserve aviators would be ready for combat in an "amazingly short period of time." What made Cassady's statement even more amazing was that many of the fighter pilots had to transition to F9F-2 Panthers before they deployed. As critical as it was for the pilots to master flying the new fighters, it was also vital for enlisted maintenance crews to become proficient in jet engine technology.

Of the air groups assigned to the front line carriers, half of the pilots in the ready rooms in *Princeton* were Naval Reserve. On *Boxer* the number was 90 percent; on *Bon Homme Richard*, 100 percent. On *Boxer,* for example, the squadrons embarked had formerly flown from Naval Reserve air stations in Glenview, Illinois; Olathe, Kansas; Memphis, Tennessee; and Dallas, Texas.

ENSIGN JESSE L. BROWN

During the struggle to extract the Marines from the Chosin Reservoir, enemy gunfire apparently brought down an F4U Corsair piloted by Ensign Jesse L. Brown. He survived the impact but died in the cockpit, despite the efforts of Lieutenant (Junior Grade) Thomas Hudner, who crash landed his fighter plane in an attempt to rescue Brown. Hudner would later receive the Medal of Honor for his efforts. As a student at Ohio State, Brown earned his commission in the Navy through the Naval Reserve V-5 Aviation Cadet Training program and participated in the NROTC program at the school. After initial training at Glenview Naval Air Station flying a Stearman N2S trainer aircraft, he earned his Wings of Gold on October 21, 1948, and would be commissioned on April 26, 1949. At the time of his commissioning, he was believed to be the first black pilot in the history of the Navy.

At the time of the shootdown Brown was assigned to VF-32, which had deployed on the carrier *Leyte.*

LSTs (landing ship tanks) of the U.S. Navy 7th Fleet disgorge their freight of military vehicles at Blue Beach, Wonson, Korea in November 1950.

Reservists muster at the Naval Reserve Training Center in Pontiac, Michigan.

6,000 of 8,000 missions flown off of carrier flight decks. *Naval Aviation News* observed that even after throwing Air Force and other nations' air assets in the mix, Navy and Marine Corps reservists were flying a third of the combat missions over Korea.

Following the return of the aircraft carrier *Antietam* from her second combat deployment with an all-reserve air group in April 1952, the Commander, Air Forces, Pacific Fleet Vice Admiral Harold M. Martin wrote to the chief of Naval Air Reserve Training a laudatory letter describing the performance of the reservists as outstanding, commenting that they had been so aggressive that at times they had to be directed to exercise more caution. Later in the year, three Naval Reserve pilots from VF-781 off *Oriskany* demonstrated they could hold their own when jumped on by four to seven Soviet MiG-15 fighters over the Sea of Japan. While one of the F9F-5 Panthers was lost to the Soviets, the USNR pilots claimed two MiGs and damaged a third.

COMBAT SUPPORT SERVICES

While much of the naval air power over Korea flew off of the flight decks of carriers, some of it was land-based, with airstrips built and maintained thanks to the work of the Navy's mobile construction battalions. As with the fleet, the post-war demobilization left the Seabees at but a fraction of their World War II strength. Only 3,300 were on active duty at the time of the North Korean attack and some 10,000 men came on active duty to go ashore at Inchon, where Seabees helped build causeways to get supplies ashore. With Marines serving as a major component of the ground combat

In addition to the carrier air groups, the Navy recalled two reserve patrol squadrons for duty in the Pacific. In November VP-812 deployed to Alaska and VP-892 deployed to the western Pacific.

As the Chinese offensive drove U.N. forces back over the 38th parallel in early 1951, placing Seoul again in communist hands, the Navy's recall of Naval Reserve squadrons continued. Of note, in March 1951, five recalled squadrons formed Carrier Air Group 8, which would be assigned to the Atlantic Fleet to backfill for squadrons that had been redeployed. Meanwhile in Alameda, California, another five squadrons formed Air Group 15, which would deploy to Korea.

After the first six months of the war, 198,000 naval reservists had been recalled to active duty with a high percentage being shipped to support efforts offshore, in the air and on the ground. With their presence and the arrival of other armed forces, MacArthur's relief as commander of the United Nations forces, General Matthew Ridgway, rallied his forces against the massive Chinese People's Volunteer Army, which was hampered by ever-growing lines of logistical support as it advanced south. Ridgway exploited his airpower advantage to interdict enemy railroads and convoys that left communist troops on the front lines short on food and ammunition. Seoul again changed hands. Overhead, U.N. troops frequently saw Navy aircraft, likely piloted by naval reservists, going after targets beyond enemy lines. At the end of 1951, Naval Reserve pilots would be credited with flying an estimated

1951: Two Reserve Sailors report for active duty for the Korean War.

103

A chief hospital corpsman administers plasma to wounded Marines.

forces, the Seabees kept the "K" fields open close to the front lines as the different airstrips hosted Marine aircraft that could be on scene to provide close air support within minutes.

In addition to construction support, the Marines leaned heavily on Navy Medicine, from Navy corpsmen on the front lines to more extensive hospital facilities in the rear and at sea. For the at-sea component the Navy sent the hospital ships *Consolation*, *Repose*, and *Haven*. *Consolation* was first to depart, leaving Norfolk on July 14, 1950, to arrive in time to support the Inchon landings. She was to have been joined by the San Francisco-based *Benevolence*, but tragedy struck on August 25, 1950, when outside of the foggy Golden Gate, the freighter *Mary Luckenbach* collided with the hospital ship, which sank, killing 23 crew members. *Repose* made the trip west and arrived off Pusan on September 20, 1950, as the United Nations forces in the defensive perimeter went on the offense against

a fleeing North Korean army following the Inchon landings to the north. The *Haven* would serve as a third hospital ship to provide care for the wounded. Naval Reserve doctors, dentists, nurses and corpsmen made a substantial contribution on these ships and on other units afloat and ashore. To obtain the necessary support, the Navy recalled female petty officers with the corpsman rating. In addition to healing wounds, naval reservists healed souls as over 400 naval chaplains were recalled during the war.

THE BIRTH OF OCS

As was the case in the two previous wars, the one thing that the Naval Reserve could not provide at the onset of mobilization was junior division officers to fill junior officer billets at sea and ashore for a fleet that was quickly expanding. Whereas during World War II colleges and universities welcomed the opportunity to set up officer training programs for the Navy in view of dwindling student bodies, the post-World War II

GI Bill gave millions of young men the opportunity to go to college and schools rushed to build new dormitories and expand facilities. So the Navy decided to move its V-7 program off campus to Newport, Rhode Island, where it transitioned to open as the Officer Candidate School (OCS) in June 1951. Since that time, OCS has provided the Navy a capability to produce junior officers at an adjustable rate to meet manning needs. In 1953, the final year of the Korean War, OCS graduated 5,000 newly commissioned ensigns. A year later, following the truce signed on July 27, 1953, OCS throttled down to 1,000 graduates.

As with World War I and World War II, the majority of those who fought for the Navy in Korea were citizen-Sailors. However, in the previous two wars tens of thousands of young Americans entered directly into the service and received training and their assignments to support the Navy's war effort. Only a minority of these reservists had been affiliated with an organized reserve activity before the war. Since the nature of the service was temporary through the duration of the conflict, these men and women were placed with the Naval Reserve Force (World War I) or the Naval Reserve (World War II). Some of these reservists would affiliate with reserve units after the conflict—especially after World War II.

Three U.S. Navy officer candidates with their reading assignments.

What makes Korea unique is that the majority of the naval reservists who carried the fight to the enemy were experienced Sailors, many of whom had affiliated with units following World War II. With this prior training, the Navy was able to respond. South Koreans can be thankful for their freedom in part due to those Americans who fought not one, but two wars as members of the Naval Reserve.

7 THE GROWING SOVIET THREAT
AND THE NAVAL RESERVE RESPONSE

(1954-1962)

oming on the heels of World War II, the Korean War presented a unique set of circumstances in which the nation benefited from a vast array of relatively recently built ships and aircraft, as well as a large body of reservists who had been battle tested in the Atlantic and Pacific against the Axis foes.

However, there were political repercussions as a result of decisions to draw on non-drilling as well as drilling reservists for duty in the Korean War instead of obtaining new draftees through Selective Service. Of the approximately 980,000 reservists from all services who were recalled between 1950 and 1953, some 60 percent of the officers and 72 percent of the enlisted were World War II veterans, many of whom dubbed themselves "two-time losers." In the meantime, nearly 1,600,000 young men came of military age after World War II and were able to avoid military service. What made matters worse for those in the reserves was that their civilian jobs were not legally protected—many employers simply fired their veterans given their potential for recall. One solution that had received support in many quarters was the concept of universal military training (UMT), which would require all men to undergo six months of training followed by a variable commitment of active/reserve duty for a period of up to seven and a half years. However, the concept ran into fierce opposition in the Senate, where opponents called UMT undemocratic and compared it to the compulsory service that German men faced during the Nazi regime.

ARMED FORCES RESERVE ACT OF 1952

Because UMT was never adopted, the Naval Reserve organization that had been put in place prior to World War II remained fairly intact following passage of the Armed Forces Reserve Act in 1952. What is remarkable about this legislation is that its roots were planted after V-J Day, when Navy Secretary James Forrestal appointed Rear Admiral John Roper to head a board that would re-evaluate the structure of the Naval Reserve. Following the creation of the National Military Establishment in 1947 (renamed the Department of Defense two years later), Forrestal became the nation's first secretary of defense. When the Roper Board's proposed Naval and Marine Corps Reserve Act reached his desk, he determined that the legislation should serve as a model for all of the services. The outbreak and ramifications of the Korean War delayed the introduction of the act until July 18, 1951. The Armed Forces Reserve Act was passed nearly

a year later as Public Law 82-476 on July 9, 1952, to become effective on January 1 of the following year.

The law directed the Defense Department to create Ready and Standby Reserves using an echelon approach to determine a reservist's likelihood to be recalled to service. One distinction between the two groups was that Ready Reserves could be called up after a declaration of war or declaration of national emergency by either the president or Congress. With the Standby Reserves, only Congress could authorize their recall through either a war or national emergency declaration. Four categories of Ready Reserve were established, with all having a two-week annual training requirement. The difference was in drill requirements:

Category A—48 drills   **Category C**—12 drills

Category B—24 drills   **Category D**—No drills

Presentation of best Naval Reserve Center plaque in the 9th Naval District for 1954 to Naval Reserve Center Pontiac, Michigan.

In advocating for the legislation, George C. Marshall, who became secretary of defense in 1951, argued the new system would provide "reservists and their employers much more definite knowledge than they had in the past of the circumstances which they could be called to active duty."

Appointment as Lieutenant (j.g.) in the Naval Reserve on June 15, 1942, Richard M. Nixon received aviation indoctrination training at the Naval Training School, Naval Air Station in Quonset Point, Rhode Island. Following an assignment to Naval Reserve aviation base in Ottumwa, Iowa, Nixon volunteered for sea duty and reported to Commander Air Force, U.S. Pacific Fleet, where he was assigned as Officer in Charge of the South Pacific Combat Air Transport Command at Guadalcanal and later at Green Island. His unit prepared manifests and flight plans for C-47 operations and supervised the loading and unloading of the cargo aircraft. Promoted on October 1, 1943, Lieutenant Nixon served with Fleet Air Wing EIGHT and then returned to the states for Bureau of Aeronautics tours in Washington, D.C., and New York City. He was released from active duty on March 10, 1946.

The implementation of the Armed Forces Reserve Act had little immediate impact on drill decks around the nation. A more significant impact would be felt following the inauguration of President Dwight D. Eisenhower on January 20, 1953. Of note, one of the naval officers who was placed into the new Standby Reserve category was the newly sworn in vice president, Lieutenant Commander Richard M. Nixon, USNR.

THE NEW LOOK

A truce that would remain in effect into the twenty-first century ended combat in Korea on July 27, 1953. Reflecting in his memoirs, Eisenhower viewed the Korean War as a costly conflict that ate up manpower resources. Wars of manpower attrition placed the United States at a disadvantage. Eisenhower directed a re-evaluation of the national strategy against the Communist bloc led by the Soviet Union and the Peoples Republic of China. The result of the review, dubbed "Project Solarium," was the "New Look"—a national security strategy that emphasized an investment in technology, especially high-tech systems that employed and delivered nuclear weapons. Under Eisenhower, the Air Force received more than 40 percent of defense funds in 1954 to build bomber forces to deliver hydrogen bombs.

The costs associated with this strategy would be covered by reductions in the military manpower component, active and reserve.

One result of the Korean War was the number of officers who had earned their commissions during World War II had become more senior in rank. During fiscal 1954, a board led by Rear Admiral Ellery W. Stone, USNR, involuntarily separated 2,000 officers from the service. The following year, a board led by Rear Admiral Charles L. LaBarge screened the records of 8,000 reserve officers on active duty to eliminate another 1,000 officers. Inactive Naval Reserve officers were also removed with 45,000 officers terminated in 1954 and another 16,500 in 1955.

One of the officers who survived the cut was Lieutenant Commander Nixon. Initially, the Navy declined to promote Nixon to commander in 1953, citing his failing to keep up his correspondence coursework. However, when it was discovered that Nixon had completed the coursework, he was retroactively promoted.

While Nixon retained his commission, many others had not and the voice that represented Naval Reserve officer interests before World War II had faded from the scene. At the end of World War II, Forrestal supported the creation of the Reserve Officers of the Naval Service (RONS), which was made up of Navy, Marine Corps and Coast Guard reserve officers. In 1946, RONS combined with the Naval Reserve Officers Association to form RONS-NROA. In 1948, RONS-NROA merged into the older all-services Reserve Officers Association (ROA). However, following the Korean War, many Naval Reserve officers felt that the Army-Air Force dominated ROA was an ineffective voice. In 1954, with encouragement and support from many senior regular Navy officers, forty-three Naval Reserve officers founded the Naval Reserve Association.

Three years later, two Naval Reserve chief enginemen, Joe Wasson and Thomas Patten, who drilled at the Washington Navy Yard, created a parallel organization to represent enlisted reserve interests. Founded on March 25, 1957, the Naval Enlisted Reserve Association had hoped to quickly grow given there were some 70,000 enlisted reservists. However, the organization attracted only a few hundred members for its first few years. A decade later, recruiting efforts bore fruit and by the 1980s there would be some 16,000 members.

The Naval Reserve Association and Naval Enlisted Reserve Association often played a supportive role to the official Navy hierarchy by spreading the word about the purpose of the Naval Reserve, manpower

NAVY RESERVE SEABEES

By Master Chief James L. Leuci
U.S. Navy Reserve

Today, the sight of Sailors building roads, bridges, and buildings is nothing new—that is what Navy Seabees do. It hasn't always been that way. Prior to World War I, naval officers of the Civil Engineer Corps (CEC) generally planned and oversaw construction projects performed by civilians. The sudden expansion of Navy in World War I required the rapid construction of new facilities. Naval Reserve Sailors were the solution.

The Twelfth Regiment (Public Works) was organized at Great Lakes Naval Training Station and commanded by Commander Walter H. Allen, CEC, USN. Over 6,000 construction specialists and artisans, enrolled in the Naval Reserve Force to form in the regiment. In March 1918, 350 men were sent to France to help construct an aviation base at Pauillac and to build radio towers. Others went to work assembling and operating the trains of the naval railway batteries on the Western Front. When the war ended the Twelfth Regiment was disestablished. However, the concept of having skilled workers who were reserve Sailors was not forgotten.

In 1941, prior to the U.S. entry into World War II, the Navy began recruiting skilled construction workers, as enlisted men, into the Naval Reserve to form Headquarters Construction Companies. After the United States entered World War II, the demand for naval construction personnel dramatically increased. The first Sailors of the construction battalions, popularly known as Seabees, had an average age of 37. As the war progressed, younger, less experienced Sailors became Seabees.

Seabees served in the Asiatic and European Theaters. They built airfields and bases in the South Pacific and Alaska. Seabees participated in the amphibious assaults on the beaches of North Africa, Salerno and Anzio in Italy, Normandy, and across the Rhine River in Germany. When the war ended, nearly 300,000 officers and enlisted men had served in the Seabees. Nearly all were demobilized by the end of 1946. Only 5,000 Seabees remained on active duty as part of the post-war Navy.

Nearly 250,000 demobilized Seabees joined in the Volunteer Naval Reserve after the war. By the end of 1947, Civil Engineering Corps Volunteer Reserve units had been established in over 175 cities. In 1948, Seabee units became part of the Organized Reserve.

Over the following decades, reserve Seabee units trained to perform missions in extreme cold weather and harsh desert environments. Seabees mobilized and served on active duty during the Korean War. The following decade, in 1968, two reserve Seabee battalions mobilized and deployed to South Vietnam for a year.

In 1990-91, Naval Reserve Seabees units deployed to Southwest Asia for Operations Desert Storm and Desert Shield. Ten years later, the September 11, 2001, terrorist attacks prompted the largest mobilization of the Naval Reserve Sailors since the Korean War. For more than ten years, activated reserve Seabees have conducted operations in Iraq and Afghanistan.

Today, reserve Seabees are one of the most in-demand assets utilized by the U.S. Navy. Whether constructing roads, bridges, and buildings in war-zones or conducting humanitarian or disaster relief operations in the U.S. and abroad, reserve Seabees live up to their motto: "Can Do."

Seabees working in Vietnam.

issues, and promotion opportunities. With numerous institutional changes occurring in the mid-1950s, such interpretive services were valued.

REFOCUSING THE MISSION

William H.P. Blandy would conduct a comprehensive review of the Naval Reserve.

With the appointment of retired Admiral William H.P. Blandy to head a newly created Naval Reserve Evaluation Board in October 1953, changes would be coming in the post-Korean War organization. The board was meticulous. Not only did the board interview 426 individuals from flag officers to disgruntled ex-enlisted, but it consulted with representatives of other services' reserve organizations as well as the Royal Navy.

One of the first challenges confronting the board was to define the mission of the Naval Reserve beyond the concept of an augmentation force. The board found the existence of six mission statements. An amalgamated version would become one of the 105 recommendations that would be submitted to Secretary of the Navy Charles Thomas in August 1954. Thomas accepted ninety of the recommendations. One recommendation not approved had called for the establishment of the Deputy Chief of Naval Operations for Naval Reserve Affairs. The Chief of Naval Operations, Admiral Robert B. Carney, argued that the creation of another deputy chief would provide the reserves an emphasis that was not warranted at the time.

Accepted recommendations and other changes brought about due to the Reserve Forces Act of 1955 resulted in closer Navy-Naval Reserve integration. Passed on August 9 as public law 84-305, the Reserve Forces Act increased the overall ceiling of Ready Reservists for all services from 1.5 million to 2.9 million. One of the

programs authorized by the legislation was the "2x6" program, which called for a recruit to serve two years of active duty and then four years in Ready Reserve status by attending 48 drills a year and meeting annual training requirements.

Naval Reserve aviation, following its tremendous contribution in Korea, continued to lead the way in working with their active-duty counterparts. Captain J.L. Counihan, USNR, as the commanding officer of the Naval Reserve Training Unit in Jacksonville, recommended real-world overseas training for reserve air squadrons. Subsequently, in the summer of 1954, a patrol squadron, VP-741, flew to the Azores, to Morocco, and on to the Aegean Sea, where it participated in the Sixth Fleet mining exercise. A year later, two patrol squadrons deployed to the Mediterranean and one to the western Pacific. A dozen patrol and reconnaissance squadrons deployed overseas in 1956. As the decade proceeded, patrol squadrons began replacing World War II-era aircraft, receiving the P2V-3 Neptune and S2F Tracker.

ANTISUBMARINE WARFARE

Naval Reserve aviation emerged from the Korean War as a balanced air force operating 1,500 aircraft, including fixed-wing, single- and multi-engine jet and propeller airplanes, helicopters, and lighter-than-air craft. Some 36,000 officer and enlisted naval aviators drilled at and operated from 21 reserve air stations and six Naval Air Reserve training units. However, the nature of the threat dictated an evolution in emphasis. With the death of Soviet leader Joseph Stalin in 1953, plans for a big surface navy were buried with him. With the emergence of Nikita Khrushchev as the Soviet premier and Admiral Sergei Gorshkov as the commander of the Soviet Navy, the submarine was given capital ship status. Soviet shipyards produced Whiskey- and then Foxtrot-class submarines at a pace that would have caused envy in World War II Germany. Following the 1954 launch of the USS *Nautilus*, the world's first nuclear-powered submarine, the Soviets began to deploy their own nuclear submarines as the decade drew to a close.

Thus, anti-submarine warfare would become a Naval Reserve aviation specialty as reserve patrol squadrons stationed on the East and West Coasts could search for submarines offshore as operational training that contributed immensely to the nation's defense. Naval Reserve aviation also contributed to the defense of

P2V-3 Neptune aircraft.

The Soviets produced more than 60 Foxtrot-class diesel submarines.

the nation from Soviet bombers. As the fighter pilots systematically traded in their propeller planes for jets, they were also available to be called to perform interceptor duties under the cognizance of the Air Force-led Air Defense Command. A joint-command, Air Defense Command employed Naval Reserve officers with various Air Wing staffs to coordinate the employment of tactical Navy fighters in the skies over North America.

One challenge the Naval Air Reserve faced in the 1950s was air station closures. In some cases, such as the air stations in Squantum, Massachusetts, and Anacostia in the District of Columbia, the growth of nearby commercial airports forced a local transfer. In Massachusetts, the Navy reactivated a World War II lighter-than-air base at South Weymouth to accept the twenty-five Naval and Marine Corps Reserve squadrons that had flown from Squantum. In Washington, the Navy would establish an air facility at Andrews Air Force Base in nearby Maryland. However, while the closure of ten other Naval Reserve air activities located in more remote areas in the 1958-1959 timeframe saved operational overhead through unit consolidation, highly trained reservists who could not travel to the squadron's new distant location had to resign from the program. To fill these manpower voids, the Naval Air Reserve offered a program to 1,500 enlistees to come on active duty for

six months and then serve an eight-year obligation at a Naval Air Reserve installation.

Whereas Naval Reserve aviation had established an administrative chain of command immediately following World War II, non-aviation reservists had been administered by active-duty counterparts, with training the responsibility of the various naval district commandants. That changed on July 1, 1956, with the establishment of the Naval Reserve Training Command, headquartered in Omaha, Nebraska. While the training responsibilities were retained by the naval district commandants, the commander of Naval Reserve Training Command reported to the chief of naval operations through the deputy chief of naval operations for personnel.

One of the criticisms of the Blandy Board for the post-war structure of the non-aviation reserves, which emphasized technical training to prepare reserve Sailors to plug needed holes as required, was that the reserve centers had taken on the feel of "night schools" and seamanship skills had suffered. A reorganization occurred on the drill decks with the pre-war fleet division structure being reinstituted. By mid-1957, fifty-three units were created with a mission to augment crews of destroyers to bring them up to full manning in a time of national emergency.

Above: Naval Reserve recruiting poster.

Opposite page: John F. Kennedy as a Naval Reserve Lieutenant (top) and as Commander in Chief (bottom). Commissioned in the Naval Reserve in September 1941, Kennedy was initially assigned to the Office of the Secretary of the Navy, sought combat duty following the Japanese attack on Pearl Harbor. Assigned to motor torpedo boats, Kennedy earned the Navy & Marine Corps Medal for his heroic conduct associated with the loss of *PT-109* in August 1943.

With the growing Soviet submarine force, units and individuals in aviation and non-aviation components having an ASW mission would be given priority for training funding. In a directive signed by Chief of Naval Operations Admiral Arleigh Burke on February 13, 1958, reservists having such a mission would be designated as Selected Reservists. Thus the term "SelRes" entered the Naval Reserve lexicon. So that these reservists could be quickly recalled in the event of emergency, they were provided with pocket-size pre-cut orders to their active-duty command that would be honored by commercial transportation operators.

Such was the focus on the emerging undersea threat that on May 1, 1958, the Navy provided the Naval Reserve four destroyer escorts that were to be laid up. Assigned to various naval districts under the cognizance of the Naval Reserve, these ships were placed in a decommissioned "in-service" status and were crewed by a mix of active-duty and Selected Reservists. A year later another thirty destroyer escorts and six destroyers were placed in this status. For destroyers, the ships had 118 active duty and 187 Selected Reservists assigned. For the destroyer escorts, approximately 83 percent of the 210 man crew were SelRes. Not all of these ships were decommissioned. All of the destroyers and some destroyer escorts stayed in commission, ready to deploy on short notice.

READINESS

The Korean War demonstrated that submarines were not the only underwater threat. An amphibious attack on Wonsan had to be delayed for five days as primitive mines had to be removed by Naval Reserve-crewed minesweepers. In 1960, eleven of these Korean War vintage sweepers were assigned to naval districts to be manned by Selected Reservists.

With the naval district commandants taking charge of these ships, the manpower organization within the Selected Reserve to provide crews had evolved into two categories. Category (A) envisioned 135,000 SelRes who would be ready on mobilization day (M-Day) to go to sea on fully equipped reserve-manned ASW ships and minesweepers as well as augment active fleet units to wartime manning levels. Other Category (A) reservists would be assigned fleet support and vital shore establishment duties.

The 117,000 SelRes placed in Category (B) status were expected to be available 30 days after mobilization (M+30) as they activated ships in the reserve fleet and provided additional support to the fleet and shore establishments.

Admiral Arliegh Burke conducting an inspection of naval reservists at Naval Reserve Aviation Training Unit Anacostia, Washington D.C. During his six year tenure as Chief of Naval Operations, Burke oversaw the introduction of emerging technology into the fleet.

One concern expressed by studies conducted in the early 1960s was about readiness. Both the General Accounting Office and the Naval Reserve Evaluation Board found issues with the quality of training and hence, readiness. Technological advancements such as nuclear power, missiles, and advanced electronics, simply could not be addressed at reserve centers. At the end of 1960, the eighty-eight ships assigned to the Naval Reserve still maintained much of their World War II-era hardware. The situation was not as extreme with the Naval Air Reserve, as a rapid turnover of front-line aircraft meant the hand-me-downs were not that antiquated.

Many naval reservists such as Grace Hopper were contributing to the advancement of technology in their civilian jobs. Hopper, who worked for the Philadelphia-based UNIVAC division of Remington Rand, drilled as an ordnance officer with Volunteer Ordnance Unit 4-3, assigned to the Fourth Naval District. For active duty, she found herself troubleshooting and performing programming work at such locations as the Naval Proving Grounds, at Dahlgren, Virginia, and the Philadelphia Naval Shipyard. Other assignments she accomplished on active duty included writing programs for rocket trajectory and resolving turbine problems. Promoted to commander in 1957, her reputation within the Bureau of Ordnance and the Bureau of Ships was enhanced by the numerous talks she gave to various active-duty and reserve audiences explaining the new technology. Unfortunately for Hopper, the Women's Armed Services Integration Act of 1948 capped the number of women who could attain the rank of captain to one: the Assistant Chief of Naval Personnel for Women. It seemed that Hopper would retire as a commander when she reached the mandatory retirement age of 60 in 1966.

FLEXIBLE RESPONSE

Thanks to pioneers like Commander Hopper, technology became a focus of the first former Naval Reserve officer ever to attain the rank of commander in chief: John F. Kennedy. In 1961, four years after the Soviets placed the Sputnik satellite in orbit on October 4, 1957, President Kennedy challenged the nation to place a man on the moon by the end of the

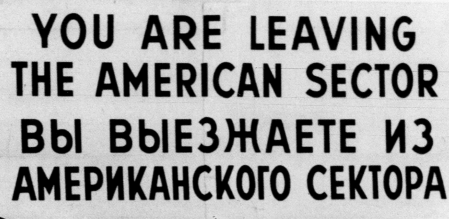

Three of 172 Naval Reserve Sailors that traveled to West Berlin serving on four Naval Reserve Force combatants deployed to Northern Europe during the Berlin crisis.

decade. The former skipper of *PT-109* also sought to use technology to enhance the conventional capabilities of the armed forces. As crises in Southeast Asia, Suez, the Taiwan Straits, Lebanon, and Cuba evolved, a peacetime Navy found itself operating at more than a peacetime operational tempo. To address these situations, Kennedy wanted more options than to threaten nuclear annihilation. Reserve forces would serve as a component of a new strategic vision that would be dubbed "Flexible Response."

Kennedy's strategic vision would be immediately tested in Berlin. As with the rest of Germany following World War II, the victorious Allies split the German capital into occupation zones. Since the divided Berlin was located deep in the Soviet-occupation zone, the American-British-French-occupied West Berlin became a democratic oasis surrounded by a totalitarian desert known as the German Democratic Republic, or East Germany. In the decade and a half following the defeat of the Nazis, some 3.5 million Germans who had lived in the Soviet zone had fled to the West. By 1953, an extensive "Iron Curtain" of barbed-wire fences stemmed direct border crossing into West Germany. By the summer of 1961, West Berlin served as the last avenue of escape for East Germans fleeing Communist oppression and the Soviets demanded that the United States, Britain, and France withdraw their token forces. Reacting to Soviet threats, Kennedy addressed the nation on July 25 to signal his intent to meet Soviet aggression through a large increase in appropriations for conventional forces. In addition, Kennedy announced a doubling of the monthly draft call to provide more Soldiers for the Army and the activation of upwards of 250,000 Reservists and National Guardsmen.

THE BERLIN CRISIS

The Soviets responded by allowing the East Germans to wall off the West Berlin enclave. Fearing that the Soviets might impose another blockade on the city similar to the one in 1948 (which was met by the Berlin Airlift), Kennedy prepared for an armed confrontation that would require the transport of thousands of Army troops to Europe. While troops could be airlifted to Europe, most of their armaments needed to be transported across the North Atlantic on cargo vessels that could be vulnerable to submarine attack. The Navy's role to assure the safe arrival of these materials would be critical, and on August 25, the Navy recalled

The NRF destroyer *Robinson*, shown here, and the *Hunt*, *Miller*, and *Remy* deployed to Northern Europe during the Berlin Crisis.

6,400 Selected Reservists who had drilled with anti-submarine warfare air and surface units. On the air side, the Navy placed thirteen carrier-based ASW squadrons and five land-based patrol squadrons. To bolster the surface fleet, the Naval Reserve manned up thirteen destroyers and twenty-seven destroyer escorts. The period of the recall would be twelve months.

Senator John Stennis of Mississippi observed, "The greatest importance lay in the fact that these men were trained, that they were ready in units, and that they were ready to go on short notice."

For the most part, Stennis was correct. Thanks in part to the naval air station consolidation of the late 1950s, the eighteen Naval Reserve air squadrons recalled were short on manning, which was resolved with an additional recall of 213 officers and 1,744 enlisted on September 13. In addition, not all of Naval Reserve ASW combatant ships were able to put to sea. Five of the nine destroyers and two of the twenty-seven destroyer escorts were undergoing overhaul at the time of the recall. For the other ships, it took three to four months to make them deployment-ready, which taxed morale. However, once at sea the adage "underway Sailors are happy Sailors" kicked in.

The Naval Reserve recall for the Berlin Crisis represented a fraction of the 156,000 Reservists and National Guardsmen brought on active duty as part

Naval Aviators typical of men from three Naval Air Reserve aviation squadrons, VS-872, VS-873, and VP-872, which were recalled to active duty from October 1961 through August 1962 as a result of the Berlin Crisis.

of the Kennedy administration's attempt to show resolve and assure America's allies in the face of Soviet belligerence. Overall, the call-up impressed upon the Soviets that America would not give up Berlin without a fight and they decided to withdraw an end-of-year ultimatum demanding a removal of U.S., U.K., and French forces. West German Chancellor Konrad Adenauer observed that "the prime factor influencing Khrushchev in his slowdown was the swift, decisive buildup of the American forces."

Not seeing the big picture, however, many reservists questioned the need to be recalled for situations short of war. One Army Reserve major general following the crisis testified that the government should not "call up the Ready Reserves again to support diplomatic offensives in a Cold War that may last a generation."

For those naval reservists who had been recalled, the concerns about being dragged back repeatedly as pawns in future diplomatic shows of force prompted half of the enlisted men and a quarter of the officers to leave the Selected Reserve at the first opportunity. Within the overall Naval Reserve force structure the losses were negligible. However, similar trends among the other service Reserve and National Guard forces caught the attention of politicians. Senator Richard Russell of Georgia expressed disdain for "summer soldiers" who were willing to accept reserve pay and benefits but jumped ship when duty called.

In the reservists' defense, Chief of Naval Personnel Vice Admiral William R. Smedberg III pointed out

that employers may be reluctant to employ Sailors who could be subject to repeated recalls.

As a result of the Berlin Crisis recall, national leadership became gun-shy about the prospect of declaring states of national emergency to recall Reservists and National Guardsmen. Two months after releasing the citizen Soldiers, Sailors, and Airmen from active duty (no Marines were recalled), the United States faced its greatest threat during the Cold War—the installation of Soviet nuclear-tipped medium and intermediate range surface-to-surface missiles in Cuba.

Some 14,000 Air Force Reservists responded to a recall notice for what became a one-month tour of active duty. However, having just released Navy Reservists two-months prior, Chief of Naval Operations Admiral George Anderson did not want to hit the formal recall button. Instead, Anderson extended enlistments and recalled a minimal number of reservists to fill critical billets.

Testifying before the Senate Armed Services Committee, Secretary of Defense Robert S. McNamara argued he needed military capabilities to respond "immediately" to challenges posed by the Soviet Union. Rather than turn to the reserves to shore up the active forces in future crises, McNamara recommended enlarging the active force component. Thus, unlike World War I, World War II, and the Korean War, the conflict in Southeast Asia that would place over a half million "boots on the ground" in Vietnam by 1968 would relegate the Naval Reserve to an underutilized status.

1962: Fleet Admiral Chester W. Nimitz inspecting naval reservists prior to their release from active duty.

8 VIETNAM
AWAITING THE CALL (1963-1968)

The destroyer escorts *Edmunds*, *Walton*, *McGinty*, and *Whitehurst* had much in common. All shared a similar displacement between 1,350 and 1,400 tons. All were built in the middle of World War II and saw service in the western Pacific. All were decommissioned after World War II. All four were re-commissioned following the outbreak of the Korean War. Manned with recalled naval reservists, the four escorts supported Seventh Fleet operations off Korea, performing bombardment and patrol duties. Following that conflict, the four small combatants remained on active duty. In 1958 and 1959 the ships were assigned to naval districts on the West Coast to serve as Naval Reserve training platforms. *Edmunds* and *McGinty* went to Portland, *Whitehurst* remained at her homeport of Seattle, and *Walton* was based out of San Francisco.

The destroyer escorts *Walton (top)* and *Whitehurst.*

Walton illustrated the high operations tempo maintained by reserve ships by conducting weekend and two-week cruises to hone the seamanship skills of the embarked Selected Reservists. Two-week training cruises took *Walton* to ports all along the West Coast as far south as Mazatlan, Mexico, and north to Esquimalt, British Columbia. While at sea, the ship participated in anti-submarine warfare exercises, underway refueling, gunnery exercises, highline transfers, and general quarters drills. Such was the professionalism of *Walton*'s reserve bluejackets, the ship earned its reserve escort destroyer squadron's coveted Battle "E" award in both 1959 and 1960.

The other common tie among the four West Coast reserve escorts was that the Navy turned to them and their SelRes crews for duty with the fleet as a result of President Kennedy's reserve call-ups to respond to the Berlin Crisis. *Walton*'s command historian wrote that "her shuttling about the West Coast was ended for the time-being."

THE COMMUNIST THREAT IN SOUTHEAST ASIA

While the show of reserve muscle was intended primarily to send a direct message to Moscow and reassure American allies in Europe, Kennedy also wanted to demonstrate a commitment to friends in Asia. For example, on November 22, 1962, the president directed that the U.S. Embassy in Saigon inform the South Vietnamese government that the United States would be willing to play a more aggressive role in supporting maritime operations to interdict and deter North Vietnamese shipments of troops and armaments to the communist insurgency in the South. Thus, of the 40 destroyers and destroyer escorts brought back on full-time active duty, thirteen had Pacific Coast homeports. For these ships, a "WestPac" deployment would take the Reserve Sailors away from home for seven or eight months.

For the four reserve destroyer escorts, South Vietnam would be added to the overseas assignment. Initially the Navy based five minesweepers in December 1961 at Danang to train and support South Vietnamese Navy interdiction efforts. Lacking speed and endurance, the minesweepers were not the best platforms to meet the mission. Secretary of Defense Robert McNamara pushed for more capable ships. *Edmunds* and *Walton* arrived at Danang in late February. Later joined by *McGinty* and *Whitehurst*, the American reserve destroyer escorts capably performed their duties and departed Southeast Asia for return voyages back to the West Coast.

Lyndon B. Johnson in his service dress blues during the early months of World War II. A congressman from Texas who sat on the Naval Affairs Committee, Johnson received a commission as a Lieutenant Commander three days after the attack on Pearl Harbor and after inspecting shipyard facilities along the Gulf of Mexico and the Pacific, joined a three-person survey team to evaluate operations in the Southwest Pacific. He left active duty after six months following a decision by President Roosevelt not to have legislators serve on active duty. As with Richard Nixon, Johnson had retained his Naval Reserve commission as vice president, so when he became president following the assassination of President Kennedy, Johnson theoretically could have mobilized himself for active duty!

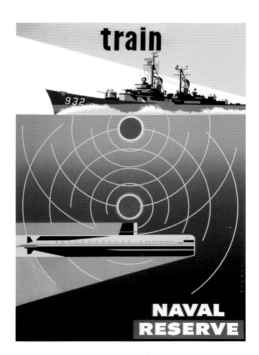

A Naval Reserve poster featuring a *Forrest Sherman*-class destroyer.

The services provided by the SelRes crews embarked in those four escorts could have served as a template for future Naval Reserve involvement over the next decade as the United States became increasingly engaged in Vietnam. Instead, the national leadership decided to prosecute the war mostly using active-duty forces.

TO MOBILIZE OR NOT TO MOBILIZE?

America's involvement in Southeast Asia during the 1960s until 1975 would be controversial on many levels. The decision not to extensively employ the nation's reserve forces had repercussions for decades. The internal debate during the administration of the first Naval Reserve officer to become Commander-in-Chief, Lyndon B. Johnson, typically pitted Secretary of Defense McNamara against the military's uniformed leadership. Johnson, who resigned his commission as a USNR commander on January 18, 1964, a month and a half into his presidency, typically supported his defense secretary in resisting the recall of reservists, as did two prominent congressmen who also saw service as Naval Reserve officers during World War II: Gerald R. Ford of Michigan and Melvin R. Laird of Wisconsin.

As the conflict expanded, the arguments for and against employing reserve forces evolved. The arguments against reserve call-ups included:

Imminent danger:
Following the Berlin Crisis many questioned the need to recall reserve forces to meet a perceived threat, and the insurgency in South Vietnam did not constitute a direct threat to the American homeland.

Other contingencies:
Employing reserve forces in Southeast Asia could embolden the Soviet Union, Communist China, or other communist surrogate nations to take military initiatives.

Fairness:
The Korean War "two-time loser" stigma, where some citizens served their nation twice while others were able to avoid active duty, still resonated only a decade after that conflict. Instead, the government expanded the number of young men procured through Selective Service.

Domestic political concerns:
Johnson had an extensive domestic agenda to pursue and did not want to alienate potential legislative allies. While the Senate was supportive and voted 56 to 21 on August 17, 1966, to call up reserve forces, eight days later the House, facing mid-term elections, voted by a margin of 378 to 3 against giving the president recall authority.

Not calling on reserve forces led to some unfortunate consequences. The draft hardly turned out fair as the sons of elites took advantage of educational and other exemptions to avoid service overseas. In addition, once it became obvious that reserve forces were not going to be subjected to call-up, those forces were seen as havens for young men who wanted to avoid the draft. As a result, a disproportionate percentage of minorities and individuals from lower socio-economic groups were sent to Vietnam.

Reserve readiness also suffered. Rather than purchase new equipment, Secretary McNamara raided the reserve forces to acquire replacement guns, aircraft and equipment to sustain the war effort overseas. For members of the Naval Reserve Association attending the October 1967 annual meeting, the deteriorating condition of destroyers and destroyer escorts assigned as training platforms and the obsolescence of aircraft seemed to be recurring topics of conversation. A month later Naval Reserve aviation readiness received another blow when the number of annual flying hours was cut from between 100 and 130 to a maximum of 75. Thus, one more argument emerged against mobilization: The reserve forces were underequipped and undertrained.

In March 1967, the overall commander in Vietnam, General William C. Westmoreland, asked for additional forces and called for the mobilization of reserve forces. For gunfire support, Westmoreland wanted the Navy to provide an additional five destroyers and a cruiser. In considering the request, the Joint Chiefs looked to activate fifteen Naval Reserve destroyers as well as the 4th Marine Division. To support the recall of the Marines, several supporting Naval Reserve units, such as the Seabees and medical units, would need to be activated. Wary of the congressional and public debate over mobilizing reserve forces as well as a potential $10 billion price tag for fiscal 1968, McNamara rejected the request.

THE SEIZURE OF *PUEBLO* AND TET

Events in 1968 finally caused Johnson to relent—somewhat. On January 23, 1968, North Korean gunboats seized USS *Pueblo*, which was conducting electronic intelligence collection off Wonsan. This, along with other North Korean aggressive actions, raised concerns of a second Korean War at a time when the Soviets were believed to be contemplating moves against West Berlin. A week after the seizure of *Pueblo*, the other shoe dropped with the massive attacks conducted throughout South Vietnam by North Vietnamese and Viet Cong troops in conjunction with the Tet holiday.

NAVAL RESERVE

NAVPERS MCNPB 30,906

Naval Reserve bumper sticker.

able ··· ready ··· willing

NAVAL RESERVE

The Naval Reserve was able, ready, and willing, but the nation's leaders were not.

In response to North Korea, a task group centered on the nuclear aircraft carrier *Enterprise* conducted an at-sea show of force and six active tactical air squadrons were quickly deployed to bases ashore in the Far East. At the direction of President Johnson, Chief of Naval Operations Admiral Thomas H. Moorer mobilized three fighter and three attack Naval Air Reserve squadrons to replace aircraft and aircrews that had been sent to the western Pacific. In addition, $2.4 million of the $4.5 million that had been cut from the Naval Air Reserve training budget was restored to enable pilots to regain the needed hours to remain proficient.

The mobilization exposed two problems. First, the thirty-six F-8 Crusader and thirty-six A-4 Skyhawk aircraft were earlier models with avionics that were not compatible for aircraft carrier operations. Thus the six squadrons remained stateside during the nine months they were on active duty. Second, the squadrons had an authorized manning level of 1,115, but had only 593 SelRes available for recall; therefore the Navy needed to find an additional 524 individuals from other sources to fill the vacant billets. Eventually, the Navy would replace the aircraft in these squadrons with carrier-compatible planes.

In Vietnam, South Vietnamese and American forces absorbed the brunt of the Tet Offensive and inflicted heavy casualties on the enemy. Because the communist forces had expended much blood and material, Westmorland sent a cable to Washington on February 12 urging the call-up of reserve forces to enable offensive operations that could end the war.

LIMITED MOBILIZATION

Back in Washington, during McNamara's last two weeks in office as secretary of defense, Westmoreland's request again caused strong debate within the Pentagon and the White House. On March 3, following the departure of McNamara, the Joint Chiefs proposed recalling 262,000 reservists from all of the services. McNamara's replacement was Clark Clifford, who had served in the Truman White House as an assistant naval aide after receiving a reserve commission in World War II. Ten days later, Johnson opted to recall

13,500 reserve personnel to support operations in Vietnam and to bring another 48,500 reservists on active duty as a strategic reserve. In his March 31 speech to the nation announcing the cessation of the aerial campaign over North Vietnam and his decision to not seek re-election, Johnson mentioned the recall. When Clifford fully detailed the plan, the tally amounted to about 24,000 reservists. Of those, less than half would travel to Vietnam.

For the Navy, approximately 1,000 Seabees dressed out in uniform. Activated in May 1968, Reserve Naval Mobile Construction Battalions 12 and 22 conducted pre-deployment training at Gulfport, Mississippi, before arriving in Vietnam late in the summer for an eight-month tour in-country. Following their return, the Navy released the Seabees from active duty, marking the only activation of Naval Reserve units to support the war effort.

COMBAT SUPPORT

While the nation's leadership decided against mobilizing USNR units to fight in Southeast Asia, naval reservists were present in the war zone or provided support from afar. For example, in May 1965, the Commander in Chief, Pacific, requested volunteer crews of the Naval Air Reserve to assist with the airlift of high priority items to Southeast Asia. A *Navy Times* article described one such eight-day mission in late 1967 when a Naval Reserve C-118 airlifted aircraft parts and helicopter engines to Danang and during the return trip ferried to basic training thirty-seven Filipinos who had enlisted in the U.S. Navy. As Naval Air Reserve

Left: Two Naval Reserve Mobile Construction Battalions, 12 and 22, were activated in May 1968.

Below: Naval Reserve logistics squadrons, flying aircraft such as the Douglas C-118, flew missions to South Vietnam throughout the conflict to support the allied in-country effort.

GLENN FORD

Another Hollywood star who served in the Naval Reserve was Glenn Ford. During World War II, Ford served with the Marine Corps performing film and radio duties domestically. Following the production of the movie *Don't Go Near the Water* with Ford playing the role of a Navy public affairs officer, fiction became reality as the actor received a commission in 1958 as a lieutenant commander.

During his annual training Ford promoted the Navy through various media. In 1967, he traveled throughout South Vietnam with a Combat Camera film crew and earned a Navy Commendation Medal. The following year he was promoted to captain.

C-118 pilots shuttled back and forth across the Pacific, Naval Air Reserve intelligence units handled other tasks to support forces overseas. For instance, the Norfolk-based Naval Air Reserve Intelligence Unit 861 earned a Meritorious Unit Commendation for conducting detailed studies of the coastlines and landing beaches in Vietnam.

In July 1965, Secretary of the Navy Paul Nitze authorized a recall of Naval Reserve officers, seeking volunteers of various ranks to come on active duty from the Medical Corps, Supply Corps, Chaplain Corps, and Civil Engineering Corps, as well as unrestricted line officers below the rank of lieutenant commander. For those who responded, there may have been some surprise when they arrived in Vietnam and realized how many others in-country were USNR. At the time over 100,000 serving on active duty had entered the Navy through reserve officer commissioning programs or enlisted recruitment programs that required two years of active duty. Many of these active-duty reservists served with distinction off the coast, in the skies, and on the rivers of South Vietnam. Some would be highly decorated for their heroism. Sadly, many would also have their names memorialized on a black granite wall that would later be placed in the nation's capital.

In his book, *Citizen Sailors: The U.S. Naval Reserve in War and Peace,* published in 1969 with the support of the Naval Reserve Association, William R. Kreh offered a snapshot of just how many reservists were fulfilling their active-duty obligations off Vietnam

on August 2, 1964, when the destroyer *Maddox* came under attack in the Tonkin Gulf by North Vietnamese patrol craft. Kreh noted that seventeen members of 255-man crew were naval reservists, including the communications officer, Combat Information Center officer, and damage control assistant. On that day, North Vietnamese patrol boats, speeding toward the *Maddox* in the early afternoon, responded to warning shots by unleashing a torpedo attack. As *Maddox* swung hard to port to evade the torpedoes, she opened up with her 5-inch and 3-inch batteries. At some distance over the horizon, the aircraft carrier *Ticonderoga* and four escorting destroyers received *Maddox*'s radio report of the attack. Included in *Ticonderoga*'s crew and air wing were 287 reservists. The four escorting destroyers had 107 USNR Sailors among them. To the south, the destroyer *Turner Joy*, with twenty-seven reservists embarked, changed course to close on *Maddox*. Four F-8 Crusaders launched from *Ticonderoga* streaked to help defend *Maddox* and drive off the North Vietnamese. The incident canceled Hong Kong liberty for the aircraft carrier *Constellation* and her three escorts. Among the crews of the four ships, Kreh noted there were 403 USNR Sailors.

Kreh also wrote of the second incident on the night of August 4 when radarmen in *Maddox* detected approaching blips. Joined by *Turner Joy*, the *Maddox* again went to general quarters as the two destroyers met the perceived threat with steady gunfire. In the aftermath, the author noted that *Turner Joy*'s gunnery

A-4 launching: The Douglas A-4 Skyhawk served as the Navy's frontline attack aircraft in Vietnam. Many were lost to enemy gunfire and missiles.

officer, "a 26-year-old Naval Reservist from Bridgeton, Missouri, named Lieutenant (jg) Charles S. Monia" would receive a commendation from the Secretary of the Navy as his guns "sank two of the Red boats and damaged two others." Unfortunately, historical analysis has not been kind to those two destroyers on that night. Steaming in heavy seas, the two destroyers' radar targets were later determined to be false.

Acting on the belief that a second attack had occurred, President Johnson directed that Navy carrier aircraft attack four communist PT boat bases and an oil-storage facility. On the morning on August 5, the carriers *Ticonderoga* and *Constellation* launched air strikes. The American attacks met their intended objectives with the destruction or damage of some twenty-five PT boats, elimination of seven anti-aircraft installations, and leveling 90 percent of the oil storage facility at Vinh. However, two aircraft off *Constellation* that were flown by USNR officers failed to return. Lieutenant (Junior Grade) Everett Alvarez Jr., who had earned

Lieutenant (j.g.) Richard C. Sather.

Lieutenant Commander Everett Alvarez Jr. after his release in 1973.

his Naval Reserve commission through the Aviation Officer Candidate program in 1960, was forced to bail out after enemy anti-aircraft fire crippled his A-4 Skyhawk. Fished out of coastal waters, Alvarez began over eight years in captivity in North Vietnam. Lieutenant (JG) Richard C. Sather, who followed Alvarez through the Aviation Officer Candidate program, earned his commission a year later and flew a propeller-driven A-1 Skyraider of Korean War fame. Unfortunately for Sather, his aircraft took a direct hit from which he did not escape. His name is among those on the black granite wall in Washington, D.C.

Other chapters in Kreh's book spotlighted naval reservists serving on off-shore destroyers and cruisers conducting naval gunfire support during Operation Sea Dragon, which aimed to disrupt the movement of enemy supplies along the Vietnam coastline. To help spot enemy targets, naval aircraft worked closely with the offshore gunships. Kreh estimated a third of the pilots flying off carriers stationed in the Tonkin Gulf held Naval Reserve commissions. Additionally, 20 percent of the LSMR rocket ship crews and a third of the Swift Boat crews operating in the southern part of the country as part of the Operation Market Time interdiction effort were naval reservists fulfilling their active duty obligations. A similar proportion of naval reservists crewed PBRs (Patrol Boat Riverine) that fleshed out Viet Cong positions in the waters of the Mekong Delta as part of Operation Game Warden. Among the naval reservists highlighted were Lieutenant Harold D. Meyerkord. Meyerkord fought valiantly when the enemy ambushed his PBR. He received the Navy Cross posthumously. Kreh's narrative also covered other contributions made by reserve Seabees, chaplains, SEALs, and doctors.

Riverine operations: Many Sailors who served with on riverine craft had Naval Reserve commissions or enlisted into the Naval Reserve.

CHAPLAINCY IN THE NAVY RESERVE

By Commander J. Travis Moger
Chaplain Corps, U.S. Navy Reserve

Reserve chaplains have served in every major conflict since World War I. Enlisted chaplain assistants called religious program specialists (RPs) have served in every major conflict since the establishment of the rating in 1979. The First World War proved the value of Naval Reserve personnel, including chaplains, augmenting the active component during wartime. The Chaplain Corps ranks swelled from forty to over two hundred by war's end thanks to reservists such as Henry van Dyke, the celebrated educator, author, diplomat, and Presbyterian clergyman who wrote the words to the hymn "Joyful, Joyful, We Adore Thee."

At the outbreak of World War II in 1939, there were sixty-three Naval Reserve chaplains. Over 2,800 clergymen entered the Chaplain Corps as reservists during the United States' participation in the war from 1941 to 1945. By the end of the war, over 96 percent of chaplains on active duty were reservists, and nine out of thirteen killed in action were reservists. Father Joseph T. O'Callahan was awarded the Medal of Honor for heroism during a Japanese air attack on the USS *Franklin* in 1945. Chaplain O'Callahan worked tirelessly to rescue the injured and trapped, administer last rites to the dying, and put out fires on board the ship. After his release from active duty in 1946, Chaplain O'Callahan continued to serve in the Naval Reserve, retiring with the rank of captain in 1953.

When the Korean War began in 1950, twenty-one Naval Reserve chaplains were mobilized to active duty along with the various Marine Reserve units across the country to which they were assigned. The need for more chaplains during the conflict caused the chief of Navy chaplains to recall reserve chaplains involuntarily. Over 400 reserve chaplains were recalled to active duty in the course of the war, 119 involuntarily. In addition to mobilized chaplains serving on active duty, there were at least three inactive reserve chaplains serving in the Far East at the time. One of these was Stanton R. Wilson, who served as a missionary of the Presbyterian Church (USA) in Korea.

In a departure from the Korean War model, during the Vietnam War there was no request made of reserve chaplains to mobilize for active duty, voluntarily or involuntarily. However, reserve chaplains did serve with distinction. Father Vincent Capodanno, a lieutenant in the Naval Reserve, received the Medal of Honor posthumously for ministry to wounded and dying Marines while under enemy fire during Operation Swift in 1967. In 2001, the Catholic Church opened his "cause for canonization," a step toward making him a saint.

By the late twentieth century, the Navy Chaplain Corps was becoming increasingly diverse. Reverend Dianna Pohlman became the first female chaplain in the U.S. armed forces when she was commissioned a lieutenant (junior grade) in 1973. Another sign of diversity was increased promotion opportunities for religious minorities. In 1975, Rabbi Bertram W. Korn was promoted to the rank of rear admiral in the Naval Reserve, becoming the first Jewish chaplain to attain a flag rank in the U.S. armed forces.

From the terrorist attacks on September 11, 2001, to September 30, 2013, 262 reserve chaplains and 222 reserve RPs were mobilized to active duty, some completing multiple mobilizations. Most of these deployed in support of combat operations in Iraq and Afghanistan, sometimes as part of reserve units, sometimes as individual augmentees. Despite the high operational tempo during this period, the Chaplain Corps was able to recruit and retain high-caliber individuals for its reserve component, including Father Michael C. Barber, ordained Bishop of Oakland, California, by the Catholic Church in 2013.

As we commemorate the 100th anniversary of the Navy Reserve, there are approximately 230 chaplains and 230 RPs in the reserve component.

Father Capodanno in Vietnam.

THE SOVIET THREAT

While there is a historical focus during this time frame on the war in Southeast Asia, often overlooked were broader Cold War and other developments overseas. The deployment of American ballistic missile submarines capable of launching nuclear-tipped missiles thwarted the crisis caused by placement of Soviet missiles in Cuba. As a result, the Soviet Union built its navy into a credible blue water fleet. The U.S. Naval Reserve supported fleet commanders by tracking the potential threat. For example, the Soviets sent trawlers off American coastlines to collect intelligence. Naval Reserve assets, such as the destroyer *Brannon*, tracked the interlopers. In the case of *Brannon*, the American reserve destroyer kept tabs on the Soviet trawler *Arban* off the northwest coast of Washington in May

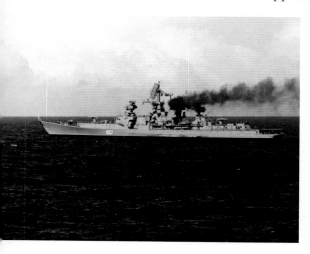

Soviet Kresta II-class cruisers carried surface-to-surface and surface-to-air missiles.

1965. While spy trawlers and regular commercial fishing fleets became regular fixtures off the American shorelines, the Soviets also expanded their presence under and over the nearby high seas. On a continuing basis, Naval Reserve S-2 Tracker and P-2 Neptune aircraft off the East and West Coasts routinely searched for Soviet submarines, such as the Yankee-class ballistic missile boats that began entering service in 1968. Meanwhile, off the East Coast, Soviet Tu-95 Bear maritime patrol aircraft often made patrol runs to and from an air facility in Cuba to monitor American naval activity. Naval Reserve F-8 Crusader and later F-4B Phantom fighters occasionally joined up to provide escort.

There were other events where the Naval Reserve pitched in to help make a difference. During the massive East Coast blackout of November 1965, the reserve destroyer *Bristol* steamed out of the Brooklyn Navy Yard and headed to Astoria, Queens, to dock next to a power plant, where she provided power to the critical facility until the electric grid could be restored the following day. In another example of Good Samaritan work, the destroyer escort *Greenwood*, en route from Tampa to training at Guantanamo Bay, picked up three survivors of the capsized yacht *Lake St. John* off the northern coast of Cuba.

F. EDWARD HÉBERT

The institutional stature of the service reserve components grew during this period due to the advocacy of Congressman F. Edward Hébert of Louisiana. Hébert, who would chair the House Committee on Armed Services between 1971 and 1975, pushed through the Reserve Forces Bill of Rights and Vitalization Act of 1967. Signed into law on December 1, 1967, the legislation established the Office of Assistant Secretary of Defense for Manpower and Reserve Affairs and created similar positions within each service hierarchy. On April 3, 1968, President Johnson nominated Randolph S. Driver to be the first Assistant Secretary of the Navy for Manpower and Reserve Affairs.

Additional legislation passed in May 1968 provided portal-to-portal coverage for reservists who were injured, got sick, or died en route to or from drills and established civilian re-employment rights for reservists called to active duty.

THE ANTI-WAR MOVEMENT

The publication of *Citizen Sailors* in 1969 must be appreciated in the context of an era when public support for the war effort following the Tet Offensive in January had waned. Sadly, many who opposed the war not only attacked the government's strategy to contain communist expansion, but were contemptuous of those who served in the nation's armed forces. As a growing anti-war protest movement spread across college campuses, ROTC programs, which often represented the face of the military on campus, were targeted for removal by student protesters and many faculty members. In February 1968, arsonists set fire to the NROTC building at Stanford University. A year later, in May 1969, an NROTC classroom at Harvard was set ablaze. Five months later a protester threw a Molotov cocktail through a barred window at the Columbia University NROTC office.

By that time the protest movement had accomplished its objective at Ivy League campuses. One by one the schools voted not to give academic credit to NROTC courses taught on campus. On September 3, 1969, the Navy announced it would phase out NROTC classes at Harvard, Columbia, Brown, Dartmouth, Tufts, and Stanford.

Naval Reserve facilities were not immune from the unrest. On September 29, 1968, saboteurs used explosives to set fire to vehicles stored at the Naval and Marine Corps Reserve Center in Eugene, Oregon.

The attack in Oregon was just one of several violent episodes in a tumultuous year that saw the tragic assassinations of Martin Luther King Jr. and Robert F. Kennedy. In the case of Kennedy, who represented New York in the Senate, an assassin's bullets in a Los Angeles hotel ended the presidential aspirations of yet another former Naval Reservist. Unlike his elder

Monday, May 4, 1970, Ohio National Guardsmen fired rounds into a crowd of student protesters and bystanders, killing four students and wounding nine others at Kent State University. The shootings inflamed further anti-war sentiment across the country.

brothers, "Bobby" opted out of the V-12 program he was attending at Harvard to request an enlisted assignment to the newly commissioned destroyer *Joseph P. Kennedy Jr.*—named for his eldest brother, who died on an August 12, 1944, Operation Aphrodite mission that required him to pilot an explosive-laden remote-control bomber into the air before bailing out. Unfortunately, the bomber exploded prematurely, killing Lieutenant Kennedy and co-pilot Lieutenant Wilford Willy.

The Navy honored the request and the younger Kennedy reported to *Joseph P. Kennedy Jr.* on February 1, 1946, as a seaman apprentice for the ship's shakedown cruise. After four months, Kennedy received his honorable discharge. With Kennedy's death, the Democratic nomination for president at the Chicago convention went to the sitting vice president, Hubert H. Humphrey. In the general election he faced another former vice president, Richard M. Nixon. The election of Nixon would place yet another former Naval Reserve officer in the White House.

Members of the Kennedy family at the July 26, 1945 launching of the destroyer *Joseph P Kennedy Jr.* From left, Edward Kennedy, Eunice Kennedy, Rose P. Kennedy, Jean Kennedy, Robert Kennedy, Pat Kennedy, and Joseph P. Kennedy Sr.

VIETNAM NAVAL RESERVE MEDAL OF HONOR RECIPIENTS

Vincent Robert Capodanno served as a chaplain with the 3rd Battalion, 5th Marines, 1st Marine Division, in Vietnam. On September 4, 1967, Lieutenant Capodanno followed Marines involved in an assault on a North Vietnamese position close to the demilitarized zone. Pinned down, Capodanno left the safety of his position to aid and administer to wounded and dying Marines. Wounded by a mortar round, Capodanno aided several other Marines, shielding a wounded corpsman when enemy bullets ended his life.

Thomas R. Norris served with the Navy SEALs in Vietnam. In April 1972, Lieutenant Norris led a South Vietnamese commando team to attempt a rescue of two airmen. Evading enemy patrols, the team first recovered Air Force Lieutenant Mark Clark. A few days later Norris, assisted by petty officer Nguyen Van Kiet, extracted Lieutenant Colonel Iceal Hambleton, evading enemy machine gun fire with the help of air cover.

Joseph Robert Kerrey joined the Navy SEALs and upon arriving in Vietnam in 1968, took on several challenging assignments. On March 14, 1969, Lieutenant (Junior Grade) Kerrey led a SEAL team to attack a Viet Cong-held island off the coast of South Vietnam. Ascending a 350-foot cliff, Kerrey split his team and attacked the enemy camp from two directions. During the fierce firefight Kerrey had his right leg shattered beyond repair by an exploding grenade. Yet he was able to organize an extraction site and helicopters arrived to airlift his team and prisoners out.

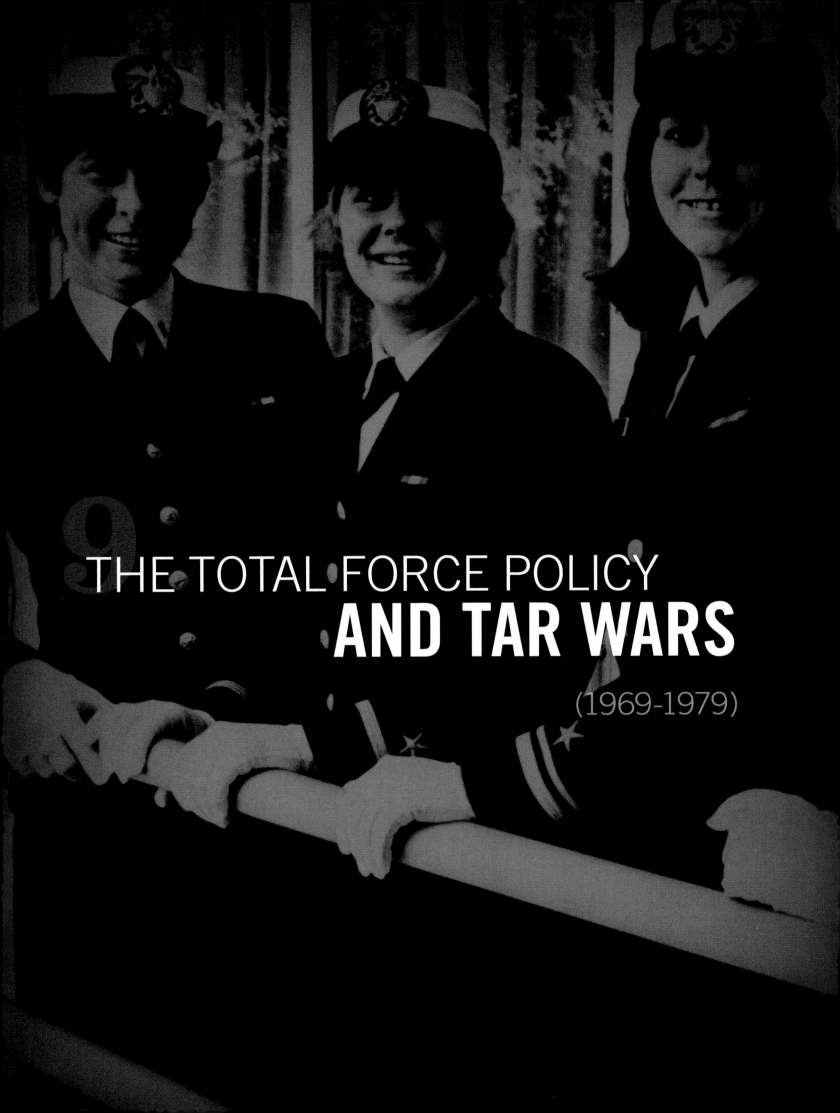

9

THE TOTAL FORCE POLICY
AND TAR WARS

(1969-1979)

Upon taking the oath of office, the 37th president of the United States, Richard M. Nixon, took on the unenviable challenge of leading a nation that was divided on such issues as the war in Southeast Asia and the advancement of civil rights for minorities and women.

Fortunately for Nixon, an event occurred in the summer of 1969 that temporarily, at least, unified the nation: the fulfillment of John F. Kennedy's pledge to land a man on the moon by the end of the decade. Answering the president's "most historic phone call" from the White House approximately a quarter million miles away was astronaut Neil Armstrong. Armstrong received his Naval Reserve commission through the Naval Aviation College Program that had been introduced in the late 1940s as part of "the Holloway Plan."

Armstrong's journey to the moon started after two years of undergraduate studies at Purdue University. He reported for flight training at Naval Air Station Pensacola in 1949 and earned his Wings of Gold the following summer as a flying midshipmen. Trained to fly jets, Armstrong earned his Navy commission in January 1951. Assigned to VF-51 embarked in the aircraft carrier *Essex*, Armstrong flew F9F Panthers into combat over Korea and was credited with 78 missions. He left active duty in August 1952 to finish his undergraduate education and remained in the Naval Reserve until resigning his commission on October 21, 1960. By then he had established a reputation as a civilian test pilot and was far along on his journey to Apollo.

ADVANCING CAREERS

For Armstrong and numerous other astronauts/ mission specialists, Naval Reserve aviation commissioning programs had provided the foundation for later journeys into space.

Reserve commissioning programs opened doors to others. In the spring of 1971, the guided missile frigate *Jouett* returned from duty off Vietnam and pulled into Pearl Harbor for liberty. After calling on Commander Cruiser Destroyer Flotilla Five, *Jouett*'s commanding officer returned to hear, "bong bong, bong bong, bong bong, *Jouett* arriving." Captain Gravely recalled: "I got out of the car and I walked up the gangway, and there were all my officers lining the quarterdeck—six side boys and the whole bit. As I stepped up my exec,

A young Neil Armstrong in uniform.

A year before his death, Armstrong visited the Navy Museum, in Washington, D.C., to admire a model of the F9F Panther he flew in Korea. Armstrong had underwritten the model's construction.

Commander Newcomb, grabbed my hand and shook it and said, 'Congratulations, Admiral. You made it, you made it.'"

Having augmented to the regular Navy in 1955, the V-7 commissioned Gravely became the first black officer to command a ship in 1961 when he received the destroyer *Theodore E. Chandler*. Subsequently, he commanded the destroyer escort *Falgout*, and the destroyer *Taussig*.

Above: Commander Grace Hopper at her office in the Pentagon.

Top left: A product of the World War II V-12-V-7 programs, Sam Gravely became the Navy's first African American admiral.

Top right: Captain Robin Quigley served as the Assistant Chief of Naval Operations for Women.

Opposite page: In March 1973 at NAS Pensacola, Lieutenant(j.g.) Barbara Allen, Ensign Jane M. Skiles, Lieutenant (j.g.) Judith A. Neuffer, and Ensign Kathleen L. McNary entered flight training.

As the first African American to be selected to O-6, Captain Gravely continued to cherish his time at sea in *Jouett*. Upon returning to San Diego, the ship and her admiral-selectee received tremendous media attention. Gravely received over 1,500 congratulatory letters. He left *Jouett* in June 1971 with orders to return to Washington as Commander, Naval Communications Command.

Also assigned to duty in Washington at the time was Commander Grace Hopper. After being retired in 1966 at the age of 60, the Navy still needed her pioneering expertise as the service was a leader in the use of computers. Hopper initially received orders to come out of retirement for six months. Those orders kept getting extended. For ten years Hopper worked in the Navy's Office of Information Systems Planning, directing the Navy Programming Languages Group.

Hopper, whose earlier work at Remington Rand led to the development of the standardized computer programming language COBOL (COmmon Business-Oriented Language), played a central role in establishing programming standards to be met by vendors who sought the Navy's business.

While the barriers to promotion for minorities were being broken down by Gravely, institutional barriers continued to block women such as Hopper from advancement. While the Women's Armed Services Integration Act of 1948 enabled women to serve in

the regular Navy, the provisions only allowed for one female to serve at the rank of captain as the Assistant Chief of Naval Operations for Women. Although the law ended the WAVES program, the term stuck in the media as Hopper was often identified as a WAVE ordnance officer well into the 1950s.

Admiral Elmo R. Zumwalt, the Chief of Naval Operations in the early 1970s, recounted in his memoir *On Watch* that his Assistant Chief of Naval Operations for Women, Capt. Robin Quigley, argued for the elimination of her position atop the female stovepipe if women were going to be treated as equals. Quigley's request was mostly met, though some of her former duties were passed on to another female officer in the Bureau of Personnel. Subsequently, Zumwalt sent out one of his trademark Z-Grams—Z-116—on the subject of integrating women into fleet functions as much as legally permissible given congressional restrictions, to include promotions to flag rank. Alene B. Duerk became the first woman to achieve flag rank in June 1972. As with Gravely and Hopper, Duerk earned her commission in the Naval Reserve, where she began as an ensign in the Nurse Corps during World War II. Released from active duty in 1946 after a tour on board the hospital ship *Benevolence* in the western Pacific, Duerk affiliated with the Naval Reserve in 1948 and was called to active duty in 1951. As with Gravely, she never left active duty until retirement, augmenting to the regular Navy in 1953.

A year after Duerk pinned on her one star, the 67-year-old Hopper finally earned her eagle collar insignia. Hopper was promoted to commodore (rear admiral, lower half) in 1983 and retired for the last time in 1986. In the late 1970's before a group of NROTC midshipmen at Penn State, she was asked about Navy careers for women: "I'm considering it."

The promotions of Gravely, Duerk, and Hopper were positive manifestations of changes that needed to occur as a result of the tumultuous 1960s. To implement change, President Nixon selected a vice admiral who commanded the U.S. Naval Forces in Vietnam, the aforementioned Zumwalt.

To address societal demands, Zumwalt set about to make the Navy more inclusive and to create opportunities for minorities and women that would pay repeated dividends to the service for decades to come. However, some changes, such as a transition away from the traditional enlisted jumper uniform to a bus-driver style jacket and pants, would quickly be regretted. Over 31,000 of the new uniforms would go to enlisted reservists beginning in October 1973.

One of Zumwalt's greatest challenges was addressing the manpower needs of the service as the United States withdrew forces from Southeast Asia and shifted to an all-volunteer force.

What was good in the Navy is great in the Naval Reserve.

Naval Reserve poster from 1972.

THE TOTAL FORCE POLICY—ONE NAVY CONCEPT

The reduced numbers of young men being conscripted as the United States withdrew from Vietnam meant there was less incentive to join a reserve component as a means of avoiding the draft. In 1973, Secretary of the Navy John Warner estimated that 40 to 45 percent of non-prior-service enlistments were draft avoidance motivated. The numbers began to decline between 1969 and 1970 as the number of Selected Reservists dropped from 133,000 to 124,500. To retain SelRes manning levels, the Naval Reserve would need to aggressively recruit Navy veterans, emphasize skill-training benefits to attract first-timers, and overcome the negative attitude that the general public had about the military as a result of the Vietnam War.

Sailors who left active duty to affiliate with the Naval Reserve may have been surprised to return to their old ships. But, in 1969 and 1970, the Navy decommissioned many of its World War II-era reserve destroyer escorts and destroyers and replaced them with more updated World War II-vintage combatants that were suited for fleet operations. In 1972, two of these destroyers actually steamed to the Mediterranean Sea to participate in ASW exercises. On the other side of the world, a dozen of the modernized reserve destroyers participated in Pacific Fleet exercises. In addition to the updated destroyers, the Naval Reserve received nine minesweepers, placing the Navy's minesweeping capability in Naval Reserve hands.

A similar transfer of fleet-compatible aircraft continued to modernize Naval Air Reserve squadrons following the lessons learned from the *Pueblo* incident call-up. Anti-submarine warfare continued to be a mission area where naval reservists worked side-by-side with their active-duty counterparts. In early 1972, Rear Admiral Howard E. Greer,

Hand-painted ship emblem once displayed on the Seattle-based Naval Reserve Force destroyer *Epperson*.

1970 NAVAL RESERVE MOBILIZATION

Enraged when Congress rewarded itself with a 41 percent salary boost while limiting the New York-area postal workers to a 4-percent raise, the workers went on a wildcat strike on March 18, 1970. In response, President Nixon, after exhorting the workers to return to their jobs, declared a national emergency on March 23 that enabled him to call on members of the Army and Air National Guards, as well as Army, Navy, and Air Force reservists, to serve as mail sorters and letter carriers. Nearly 3,900 naval reservists who drilled in the New York area were ordered to report to their reserve centers. The recall ended three days later as postal workers agreed to return to work.

Commander, Naval Air Reserve Force, noted how reserve patrol squadrons rotated out of Rota, Spain, to support efforts to track Soviet activity in the Mediterranean Sea and the North Atlantic Ocean.

In an unconventional use of ASW assets, in late June 1972 aircraft from two Naval Reserve helicopter squadrons based in Rhode Island and New Jersey joined with other Navy and Army helicopters to help evacuate some 1,790 civilians who were trapped along the Susquehanna River and its tributaries by flood waters caused by Hurricane Agnes.

The Vietnam drawdown and subsequent manpower challenges and equipment issues influenced the shape of the future U.S. military. Defense Secretary Laird in 1970 expressed confidence in an all-volunteer military supported by reliable reserve components. For Laird, manning, equipping, and employing effective Guard and Reserve forces would be critical. His successor, James Schlesinger, furthered this concept as the Total Force Policy. Retaining the separate

John W. Warner following his tenure as Secretary of the Navy would go on to represent Virginia in the Senate, where he would serve as an advocate for the Navy and the Naval Reserve.

services, Schlesinger pushed to increase the authority of regional unified operational commanders in coordination with allied nations.

Secretary of the Navy Warner envisioned the Naval Reserve's role in the Total Force Policy, dubbed the "'One Navy' concept," as shifting from the traditional augmentation force to providing mission-specific units. In some cases, such as minesweeping and in-shore underwater warfare, the Naval Reserve would assume missions that were formerly conducted by active-duty forces. In addressing a meeting of the Reserve Officers Association in August 1972, the Assistant Deputy Chief of Naval Operations for Naval Reserve, Rear Admiral John B. Johnson, told attendees that he anticipated a "rediscovery" of the Naval Reserve by the Pentagon, and noted how the entire coastal warfare mission would be transferred from the active Navy. Through such mission transfers, the Navy could absorb anticipated budget cuts that typically befall the military during post-war drawdowns while maintaining combat readiness.

The One Navy concept also reflected the reality that in some cases augmentation would no longer be practical. By the 1970s the majority of the Navy's submarine force was nuclear powered, with ballistic missile submarines rotating active-duty crews to maximize time on station. Given that the submarines of the Naval Reserve fleet were World War II

FORMER NAVAL RESERVE TRAINING SUBMARINES THAT ARE MUSEUM SHIPS

SUBMARINE NAME	RESERVE CENTER CITY	CURRENT LOCATION
Batfish	New Orleans, La.	Muskogee, Okla.
Bowfin	Seattle, Wash.	Pearl Harbor, Hawaii
Cavalla	Houston, Texas	Galveston, Texas
Cobia	Milwaukee, Wis.	Manitowoc, Wis.
Cod	Cleveland, Ohio	Cleveland, Ohio
Drum	Washington, D.C.	Mobile, Ala.
Ling	Brooklyn, N.Y.	Hackensack, N.J.
Lionfish	Providence, R.I.	Fall River, Mass.
Pampanito	Vallejo, Calif.	San Francisco, Calif.
Requin	St. Petersburg, Fla.	Pittsburgh, Pa.
Silversides	Chicago, Ill.	Muskegon, Mich.
Torsk	Washington, D.C.	Baltimore, Md.

pre-nuclear vintage, the practicality of keeping submarine Sailors up on current technology was questionable. Thus, these antiquated boats were phased out of naval service. However, many of these submarines remain today as historic ships, having been embraced by local communities as a means to memorialize those who served in the Silent Service.

In addition to the retirement of conventionally powered submarines, the Navy removed small craft from the inventory of waterfront reserve centers as training platforms.

CHIEF OF NAVAL RESERVE ESTABLISHED

With the non-aviation side of the Naval Reserve now centered around destroyers and land-based reserve centers, the title of its leading officer changed from Commander, Naval Reserve Training, to Commander, Naval Surface Reserve, in 1972.

To further oversee the projected integration of the Naval Reserve with the fleet, a new echelon command came into existence on February 1, 1973, with the establishment of Naval Reserve Command, headquartered in New Orleans. Both the Army and Air Force, thanks to Congressman Hébert's 1967 legislation, had created chief of reserve positions for their respective reserve components. Secretary Warner envisioned some modest cost benefits with the functional merger of two Naval Reserve forces— air and surface—under one umbrella. The Chief of Naval Reserve as an operational command would also be dual-hatted as a member of the CNO's staff as Director, Naval Reserve.

The dual-hatted nature of the job would create a small burden for the first and subsequent chiefs of Naval Reserve as much time would be spent traveling between Washington and New Orleans, in addition to the typical visits to reserve activities in the field. To help maintain continuity in Washington, the title of Assistant Deputy CNO for Naval Reserve was changed to Deputy Director of Naval Reserve. Whereas the New Orleans-based Chief of Naval Reserve/Director of Naval Reserve was envisioned to be a vice admiral, his Washington-based deputy would typically be a one-star rear admiral.

Rear Admiral James D. Ramage as the Commander, Naval Air Reserve, still headquartered in Glenview, Illinois, received orders to be the "acting chief" as

Above Left: A Naval Reserve friend in high places, Senator John Tower fought in the Pacific during World War II and remained in the Naval Reserve, retiring as a Master Chief Petty Officer in 1989.

Above Right: Vice Admiral Damon W. Cooper, USN.

Vice Admiral Damon W. Cooper awaited relief in the western Pacific to become Chief of Naval Reserve. Embarked in *Enterprise* as Commander, Attack Carrier Striking Force, 7th Fleet, Cooper had been directing naval air operations off Vietnam since August 1970. A distinguished naval aviator, Cooper had command of the aircraft carrier *Ticonderoga* during the Gulf of Tonkin crisis of 1964 and ordered his aircraft to respond to North Vietnamese torpedo boat attacks. A graduate of the Naval Academy, Cooper earned his Wings of Gold and eventually commanded Torpedo Squadron 24 during the final

Master Chief Richard P. Johnson served as the first Reserve Force Master Chief from 1973 to 1975.

year of the war. He saw additional combat service during the Korean War as an air intelligence officer assigned in *Philippine Sea* and commanded a fighter squadron embarked on *Essex*. Given the dominance of Naval Reserve commissioned aviators operating off flight decks in both wars, Cooper appreciated the capabilities reservists could bring to a fight.

Assuming the position of Chief of Naval Reserve in April, Cooper began the great consolidation. In a press release sent out from the office of Representative Hébert, the Louisiana congressman boasted that 1,700 new military and government employees would be coming to New Orleans. In addition to a command headquarters, the Navy concurrently established the Naval Reserve Personnel Center to be located with the command. The new center represented a consolidation of manpower functions that were being handled in Washington, D.C.; Bainbridge, Maryland; and Omaha, Nebraska.

MODEST REDUCTIONS IN FORCE

Cooper did not endear himself to the drill deckplates when the Navy announced its intention to draw down the number of Selected Reserve billets from 129,000 to 117,000. Testifying before the House Armed Services Committee at the end of May, leaders from the Naval Reserve Association and the Reserve Officers Association protested the proposal. Cooper countered that the Navy needed to balance its manpower and material requirements. Speaking bluntly three weeks later at a Naval Reserve Association gathering, Cooper argued for the need to purge non-producers from the ranks and reiterated the need to cut 12,000 pay billets.

Additional factors came into play besides a desire to remove deadwood to fund force modernization. The Navy maintained 976 ships in 1968, but that number dropped to below 600 by 1974. As the number of ships declined, so did the requirement for SelRes members to augment them. The Naval Reserve also faced an imbalance in the types of ratings. Cooper did not want to fill enginemen billets with yeomen. In the end, instead of removing deadwood, the Naval Reserve cut down non-existent timbers. Some 9,000 of the 12,000 billets removed were actually unfilled due to a lack of qualified Sailors.

With a somewhat reduced Naval Reserve end-strength, a political struggle emerged between the executive branch and Congress on the president's ability to deploy the Naval Reserve and other military

GERALD R. FORD

Nixon's resignation in August 1974 brought yet another former Naval Reserve officer into the Oval Office—Gerald R. Ford. A graduate of the University of Michigan, where he played football, and Yale Law School, where he coached football, Gerald R. Ford enlisted in the Navy after the attack on Pearl Harbor and received his Naval Reserve commission as an ensign on April 13, 1942. Recognizing Ford's talent for teaching, the Navy sent him to instructor school in Annapolis and he subsequently found himself at a Navy preflight training school at Chapel Hill, North Carolina, where he taught such subjects as basic seamanship, navigation skills, ordnance, gunnery, and first aid to prospective naval aviators. By May 1943, now-Lieutenant Ford received orders to the pre-commissioning detachment of the light carrier *Monterey*, where he organized part of the ship's navigation and Combat Information Center teams. After several combat actions, a typhoon took *Monterey* out of action as aircraft in the hangar deck tore loose and collided, bursting into flames. Ford, serving as the general quarters officer of the deck, went below to observe and report back to the captain on the efforts to contain the blaze. With *Monterey* returning to Bremerton, Washington, for repairs, Ford received orders to again employ his teaching and coaching skills at Saint Mary's College of California, and then at the Naval Reserve Training Command at Naval Air Station Glenview. Released from active duty as a lieutenant commander in February 1946, Ford resigned his Naval Reserve commission four months later.

Gerald R. Ford in uniform during World War II.

components into sustained combat. The War Powers Resolution stated that after 60 days, Congress would withhold funds for any military operation initiated by the president if the operation did not receive congressional approval. This resolution, passed in the wake of the end of the Vietnam War at a time when officials in the Nixon administration were being investigated for a break-in at the Democratic National Committee headquarters in the Watergate complex, would factor in decisions to mobilize reserve forces in the ensuing decades.

With a change of leadership in Washington came a change of leadership in New Orleans as Vice Admiral Pierre N. Charbonnet relieved Vice Admiral Cooper as the Chief of Naval Reserve. Another graduate of the Naval Academy who received his commission on the eve of World War II, Charbonnet, as with his predecessor, had a successful active-duty career as a naval aviator.

Charbonnet's four-year tour in command of America's citizen Sailors would not be void of controversy. If President Ford had any loyalty to his former service, it was not apparent in his administration's proposed budget for fiscal 1976. His proposed cuts aimed to reduce the number of SelRes members to 92,000.

Again, voices from the Reserve Officers Association and the Naval Reserve Association were heard on Capitol Hill. In April 1975, the Naval Reserve Association released a position paper that called on the Navy to further define and clarify the role of the Naval Reserve, provide the Chief of Naval Reserve the support to operate a viable reserve, and stop additional billet cuts. In battling the proposed cuts, the two associations actually lobbied Congress to increase SelRes end strength by 20,000 billets. In June the Senate rejected the proposed amendment for a $25 billion defense procurement bill by voice vote, thus defeating the increase.

Given the perceived assault on the Naval Reserve by senior leadership, resentment reminiscent of the 1930s simmered on the drill deckplates. Naval reservists felt further slighted by a Government Accounting Office study that examined the activities of reservists from all services and claimed $1.2 billion of $2.7 billion spent on training was wasted on "needless" activities such as inspections, lectures on drug abuse, equal opportunity efforts, physical fitness, and grooming standards.

Vice Admiral Pierre N. Charbonnet, USN.

The growing friction received national attention when on August 3, 1975, the *New York Times* reported that one retired reserve captain, Paul L. Hummel, a regional president of the Naval Reserve Association, was barred from all Naval Reserve facilities in western states by the commandant of the 11th and 12th Naval Districts after Hummel published a letter challenging statements made by Vice Admiral Charbonnet and calling for a Navy policy statement to favor a strong Naval Reserve.

Hummel's concerns were echoed by some in Congress. Representative Bill Chappell of Florida questioned whether Navy officials truly espoused "solid support for the Naval Reserve program and dedication to the Total Force concept" in view of "an apparent disregard of funding requirements."

Following much jostling in the legislative chambers, the House-Senate conference committee reviewing the fiscal 1976 defense appropriations bill called for a Naval Reserve end-strength of 102,000. In addition, the committee recommended approval of plans for the Naval Reserve to develop a regional readiness command structure based on reservist demographics. One area that received close scrutiny was the coastal warfare mission, as the Coast Guard Reserve program maintained units that performed similar functions.

PROPOSED MASSIVE CUTS

While the Senate and House fleshed out the 1976 appropriations, a change in leadership occurred in the Pentagon. On November 20, 1975, Donald H. Rumsfeld became the 13th Secretary of Defense. Graduating from the NROTC program at Princeton in 1954, Rumsfeld underwent flight training and served three years on active duty as an aviator and flight instructor. He continued his naval aviation career in the Naval Reserve, initially flying ASW

THE ADMIRALS' ADVANTAGE

By Commander Randy Carol Goguen
U.S. Navy Reserve (Retired)

Reservists made significant contributions to Naval Intelligence during both world wars, adapting expertise acquired from civilian professions to support critical Navy missions during times of national emergency. Their demonstrated success influenced the decision to establish permanent officer and enlisted intelligence specialists in the post-war era. As the reserve component of Naval Intelligence evolved through the Cold War and into the twenty-first century, advances in information technology and organizational innovation enabled reservists to integrate effectively with the active component, providing unprecedented levels of real-time production support to gaining commands on a 24/7 basis from Joint Reserve Intelligence Centers (JRICs). Additionally, individual augmentees have deployed forward on extended active duty worldwide to support overseas contingency operations.

In July 1918, only two years after the U.S. Naval Reserve Force was established, three quarters of the officers assigned to the Office of Naval Intelligence (ONI) were members of the USNRF. They also comprised the majority of personnel assigned to naval district and attaché offices. Approximately 90 percent of intelligence officers during World War II were reservists. Schools established by ONI and the Bureau of Aeronautics during the war provided specialized training in operational intelligence, air combat intelligence and photographic intelligence to thousands of reserve officers who were deployed to the fleet and theater commands. Enlisted yeomen provided administrative support. In 1942 the Navy established as one of its wartime emergency ratings Specialist (Intelligence Duties) for enlisted personnel.

The Navy established the restricted line designator 163X for officer intelligence specialists in 1947. The enlisted aviation rating for Photographic Intelligenceman (PT) was established in 1957. In 1968 many unrestricted line air intelligence officers transferred into the expanded special duty 163X community where promotion opportunities were more favorable. In 1972 enlisted personnel with the PT rating and yeomen with the 2505 Navy Enlisted Classification code were merged to create the Intelligence Specialist rating. Drilling reservists provided intelligence production support from their units and were an important source of surge capacity during the Cold War.

The terrorist attacks of September 11, 2001, and the ensuing Operations Noble Eagle, Enduring Freedom, and Iraqi Freedom created high demand for Naval Intelligence reservists to meet emerging and evolving requirements. While Naval Intelligence comprised only 1 percent of the Navy's total force in 2005, it filled nearly 35 percent of all the Navy's individual augmentation requirements. More than 1,700 reservists, nearly 45 percent of the Naval Reserve Intelligence Command, had been mobilized by 2005. With the establishment of the Information Dominance Corps (IDC) in 2010, comprising information-related disciplines of intelligence, cyber, networks, space, oceanography, meteorology, and electronic warfare, the officer designator for Naval Intelligence changed to 183X. As members of the IDC, Naval Intelligence reservists are contributing to an interdisciplinary warfighting methodology that will best serve the Navy in an increasingly complex twenty-first century operating environment.

Navy Reserve intelligence personnel in Iraq, 2008.

aircraft from Naval Air Station Anacostia in the District of Columbia while working on Capitol Hill as a congressional staffer. When he took on a district staff position for a Michigan congressmen, Rumsfeld shifted squadrons to fly S2F Trackers from NAS Grosse Ile, Michigan. Rumsfeld was elected to Congress from Illinois in 1962 at age 30 and served in the House until Richard Nixon appointed him to the first of several administrative positions leading to the Secretary of Defense job. Until being appointed to run the Pentagon, Rumsfeld continued to fly with the Naval Reserve. Obliged to transfer to the Individual Ready Reserve, Rumsfeld would finally retire from the Naval Reserve in 1989 with the rank of captain.

Given his pedigree, Chief of Naval Operations Admiral James L. Holloway III, the son of the noted admiral who was responsible for the "Holloway Plan," was surprised when he was summoned to Rumsfeld's office one Saturday morning in early 1976 to discuss the proposed Naval Reserve end strength for fiscal 1977. Holloway's staff proposed maintaining the status quo. Rumsfeld vehemently disagreed, arguing that many of the non-hardware units were a waste of funds and the Navy could make do with half the number of reservists. Holloway recalled that Rumsfeld cited a brother-in-law who wasted his weekends doing maneuvering board problems. Holloway, who appreciated that some of the Navy's most talented people, such as Captain Grace Hopper, resided in non-hardware units, disagreed. A bureaucratic battle was about to commence.

On January 21, 1976, the *New York Times* reported that the president's budget for fiscal 1977 called for a reduction in the Naval Reserve. As copies of the budget were distributed and studied, the magnitude of the cuts garnered immediate attention. Rumsfeld requested funding to support only 52,000 SelRes, arguing the Navy only needed reservists to man hardware units such as aircraft squadrons and reserve ships. Among those targeted for elimination were nine Naval Reserve construction battalions.

Testifying before Congress in early March, Joseph T. McCullen Jr., the Assistant Secretary of the Navy for Manpower and Reserve Affairs, defended the administration's position, admitting that while the cuts would impact the reserves, the Navy could depend on the reserves "can-do" spirit. Vice Admiral Charbonnet was more succinct, explaining that congressional

The Holloways: Father James L. Jr. and son James L. III. The senior Holloway served as Chief of Naval Personnel following World War II and expanded NROTC and implemented other officer commissioning programs.

acceptance of the cuts would result in closing half of the reserve centers as well as many Naval Air Reserve training sites. A week later, the Navy announced plans to close 45 reserve centers. Representative Samuel Stratton reacted by proposing an amendment to the military procurement authorization bill to postpone center closures until Congress had time to thoroughly examine the administration's plans. Meanwhile, the Reserve Officer Association and the Naval Reserve Association mobilized their memberships to contact Congress to oppose the proposed cuts.

By the third week of March the cumulative effect of the democratic process had shred Rumsfeld's proposed cuts to pieces. On March 22, both the House Armed Services Committee and the House Appropriations Committee voted to restore the planned end-strength of the Naval Reserve to 102,000. A week later the House Armed Services Committee voted to block the proposed closure of 45 Naval Reserve centers.

Frigate *O'Callahan* underway, named for World War II Medal of Honor Recipient Naval Reserve Chaplain Joseph Timothy O'Callahan.

Before the matter could be addressed in the Senate chambers, a Defense Manpower Commission reported to Congress in April that in light of the continuing Soviet military buildup, the nation needed to maintain its number of those in uniform at 2.1 million, supported by an additional 1 million Defense Department civil servants. Regarding the Navy, the commission recommended upgrading the role of its reserve as part of the Total Force and that current manning levels be maintained.

Given this context, the Senate Armed Services Committee held its own hearings and came to its own conclusions, suggesting that 79,500 SelRes would suffice. The committee report argued that the administration had not justified cutting such reserve programs as mine warfare, harbor defense, and riverine warfare. Eventually the conference committee would agree to authorize an end-strength of 96,500 for fiscal 1977.

As the Senate reviewed the administration's budget and manpower requests, action was completed by both chambers to pass a modification to the War Powers Resolution. Concerned that the resolution limited the president's ability to mobilize the reserves in situations short of all-out war, Congress amended Title 10 of the U.S. Code to enable the president to recall up to 50,000 reservists for 90 days to augment active forces for any operational mission.

CONTINUING TO SERVE

Debates in Washington about the mission, shape, and size of the Naval Reserve continued and often overshadowed the actual work being done by reserve Sailors to contribute to the Navy's combat capabilities. One of Admiral Holloway's ship-manning initiatives was to take five ASW ships that did not routinely deploy overseas and man them with an 80 percent active-duty/20 percent SelRes mix. The designated ships for the two-year program were the San Diego-based frigate *O'Callahan* and destroyer *Agerholm*; the Mayport, Florida-based frigate *Edward McDonnell* and destroyer *Jonas Ingram*; and the destroyer *Richard E. Kraus*, homeported in Charleston.

F-4 Phantom, shown here on the deck of the *America*, and A-7 Corsairs were front-line fighter and attack aircraft in the early 1970s.

Fleet Intelligence Centers reported 30 percent of their work was being completed by reservists. On the air side, the concept of a reserve carrier air wing faced the challenge of an operational readiness examination (ORE) on board the aircraft carrier *Ranger*. Operating seventy-five aircraft including more modern F-4 Phantom and A-7 Corsair, some 1,800 reservists proved their mettle as Reserve Carrier Air Wing 30 scored 94+ during the ORE conducted in mid-November 1976. Unfortunately, during the exercise a fatal mishap occurred during a night landing, claiming the life of one of the reserve squadron executive officers—a sobering reminder that naval reservists also make the ultimate sacrifice in defending their country.

A NEW ADMINISTRATION

As Carrier Air Wing 30 demonstrated its combat capability, it did so knowing another former naval officer would soon commander in chief. However, unlike his four predecessors, Jimmy Carter had earned a regular Navy commission, graduating with the Naval Academy Class of 1947. Accepted for the Navy's nuclear

submarine program, Lieutenant Carter left the service in 1953 to manage the family farm after the death of his father. How his Defense Department appointees would view the Naval Reserve would be determined in the New Year. The Ford administration's budget for fiscal 1978 zeroed in on the 79,500 number cited by the Senate Armed Services Committee the previous May.

Despite the change of administration, Congressman Hébert remained concerned. Speaking to members of the Naval Reserve Association at their 23rd annual conference, Hébert warned that "certain elements in the Pentagon want nothing to do with the Naval Reserve" and the Reserve faced "one of the greatest crises since it was organized." He exhorted those in attendance to "fight, fight, fight," arguing "if you don't fight, you are dangerously close to being lost."

There was substance behind Hébert's remarks. Later testifying before Congress on the subject of the Total Force funding issues, Vice Admiral Charbonnet expressed frustration, claiming that budget analysts within the Office of the Secretary of Defense and the Office of Management and Budget "did not understand the message sent from Congress is something they should listen to." He went on to state: "No matter who we have in the appointed positions at defense or OMB, no matter what the administration is, the career budgeteers continue to exert undue influence in defense budget decisions."

During the Carter administration the Pentagon's so-called "bean cutters" would continue to find ways to save funds by cutting reserve end-strength. For the fiscal 1979 budget, Carter's Secretary of the Navy again proposed a drop to 52,000 SelRes. Once again Congress rebuffed the proposal, but reserve headcount was nonetheless dropped to 87,000.

TAR WARS

However, not only did the number of SelRes continue to be a contested issue, the whole Training and Administration of Reserves, or TAR, program came under question. As the "station keepers" for a quarter century, the TAR program created a career path for reserve officers and enlisted Sailors who were assigned primarily to reserve facilities. Their task was to oversee SelRes training and perform such administrative chores such as recording completed drills, preparing orders for annual training, conducting medical screenings, and preparing for the eventuality of mobilization.

With the saga of Luke Skywalker and Darth Vader packing theaters during the summer of 1977, impetus for what became known as "TAR Wars" was the state of the fleet. As CNO, Admiral Zumwalt had pushed for the rapid decommissioning of the Navy's World War II-vintage fleet to recapitalize funds to build a modern fleet to counter an emerging Soviet navy. In 1975, for example, the Soviets demonstrated their developing sea power prowess during the global "Okean 75" exercise, which involved 220 warships conducting simulated strikes on the United States, its Navy, and allied naval forces. To the dismay of Zumwalt and his successor, Congress chose to use the funds saved for other purposes. With fewer ships, the Navy struggled to maintain deployment schedules, stressing the remaining ships and crews with high operational tempos. To fully man ships deployed overseas, the Navy detailed men and spare parts from recently returned vessels to other overseas assignments. As responsible commanders reported their commands were not ready to go to sea,

charges of a hollow Navy emerged in the media.

One proposal to stem the flow of experienced active-duty naval officers from leaving the Navy was to open billets in the Naval Reserve by phasing out the TAR program. Citing Total Force Policy, Assistant Secretary for Personnel and Reserve Affairs Edward Hidalgo argued at the 1977 House Navy Appropriations hearings that TARs were not proficient in the necessary skills to become immediate assets to the fleet.

Representatives from the Naval Reserve Association and the Naval Enlisted Reserve Association vehemently disagreed, arguing the proposal was a veiled move to steal funding from Naval Reserve programs. Congressman Chappell on the committee also defended the program, pointing out that TARs were required to be rotated through fleet billets and if that had failed to happen, the problem rested with Navy detailing. In the end, the proposal to phase out the TAR program died in Congress.

As the decade came to a close, a son of a World War II Marine veteran pursued his college education at the University of Missouri in St. Louis. "It just wasn't getting it for me," Jeffrey Covington recalled. So he decided to visit the local Marine Corps Recruiting Office. With the Marine recruiter preoccupied, Covington chatted with a Navy senior chief in an adjacent office who had just returned from a four-year stint in the Philippines and the tales of the western Pacific tropics caught his attention. The senior chief told him that if the Marines didn't work out, he could make him a hull technician. When the Marines could not guarantee the technical training he desired, Covington walked back over to enlist in the Navy.

His father's reaction was:

You what?

Joining the Navy for a four-year enlistment, Covington trained as a hull technician at Treasure Island across from San Francisco and then headed down to San Diego. Eventually, Covington wound up on the East Coast, assigned to the Norfolk-based repair ship *Vulcan*. Covington's dreams of overseas duty in tropic climes would have to wait.

10 THE MARITIME STRATEGY

(1980-1990)

An air-to-air left side view of a Soviet Tu-95 Bear aircraft as an F-4 Phantom aircraft intercepts it. Operating between Northern Russia and Cuba, these long-range, turbo-propeller-driven, aircraft monitored U.S. Atlantic Fleet operations.

Geopolitical events adversely affecting the United States awakened the Carter administration on the value of more robust armed forces that could rapidly respond to crises in remote areas of the world.

RUDE AWAKENING

In January 1979, an Islamic revolution forced the Shah of Iran into exile, and during the following November, young Iranian militants stormed the U.S. Embassy in Tehran and took 52 Americans hostage. A month later the Soviet army invaded Afghanistan. In Congress, action was taken to increase the number of reservists that the president could call up in an emergency from 50,000 to 100,000.

Four months before the fall of the shah, Rear Admiral Frederick F. Palmer relieved Vice Admiral Charbonnet as Chief of the Naval Reserve. That a three-star position was filled by a two-star was an ominous sign of where the Naval Reserve stood in the Navy's pecking order. In October Palmer's boss in the Pentagon Chief of Naval Operations, Admiral Thomas B. Hayward, addressed the Naval Reserve Association to discuss his strong support for the reserve and outlined a series of goals,

including finally bringing a resolution to the ongoing struggle to determine Naval Reserve end-strength. Speaking to the *Navy Times* in January 1979, Hayward reiterated his preference for a strong Naval Reserve and its importance to the Total Force, noting that many reserve functions such as medical, legal, port security, and intelligence collection and evaluation would be needed early on during any conflict.

That said, a week later, the *Navy Times* reported that the Carter administration wanted to cut the number of drilling SelRes to 48,700. The cuts would be accomplished through the elimination of four ASW and two light attack helicopter squadrons, nine Seabee battalions and 20 Naval Reserve Force destroyers. Called before Congress in mid-February, Rear Admiral Palmer gave a blunt assessment of what the reductions would mean to the Naval Reserve and the Navy. In the House, Congressman Chappell again questioned the administration's commitment to the Total Force policy with its proposals to retire 35-year-old destroyers. Congress again voted to maintain the Naval Reserve end-strength at 87,000, using $83 million in funds that the Department of Defense wanted for its own agencies to pay for the SelRes billets.

On August 1, 1980, Vice Admiral Samuel L. Gravely, USN, retired. With his roots as a Naval Reserve surface warfare officer specializing in communications, it was fitting that his last tour was as Director of the Defense Communications Agency.

A year later, following the seizure of the U.S. Embassy in Tehran and Soviet tanks rolling into Afghanistan, President Carter's fiscal 1981 budget proposed not only to maintain the Naval Reserve's manning level, but it also boosted funds for military construction and travel. Further progress in 1980 addressed the embattled TAR program. Rather than phasing out the program, the Navy announced that women, restricted line (intelligence), and Supply Corps officers could apply.

The additional officers would be needed as the senior leadership in Washington agreed to assign TARs to non-reserve billets in the fleet to create a sea-shore rotation similar to serving USN officers. With about 30 percent of its TAR officers serving in non-TAR billets, the program needed to expand.

The Naval Reserve also received another boost from Congress, which concurred with a 1979 General Accounting Office study that argued for extending active-duty benefits to SelRes to address manpower shortages. The benefits included providing re-enlistment bonuses for critical ratings and enrolling reservists into the Servicemen's Group Life Insurance program. The GAO budget people also argued that Naval Reserve retention and recruitment would improve if some of the aging hardware could be replaced.

To provide realistic training ashore, eight Naval Reserve Centers received advanced shipboard simulators. Reserve Sailors in places such as St. Louis suddenly found themselves completely immersed in damage control training as they entered darkened compartments to shore up leaking bulkheads and cracked pipes. Similarly, reserve units participated in full-scale firefighting training at shore facilities similar to their active-duty counterparts.

A NEW PRESIDENT AND NAVY SECRETARY

With the election of President Ronald Reagan and the appointment of Naval Reserve Lieutenant Commander John Lehman as Secretary of the Navy, the aging hardware problem would be addressed.

Naval Reserve Force destroyers *McKean* and *Hamner* ported in Seattle.

JOHN F. LEHMAN

By Captain Peter Swartz
U.S. Navy (Retired)

From 1981 through 1987, John F. Lehman Jr., was the nation's 65th Secretary of the Navy—one of the youngest, most energetic and most colorful personalities to hold that office. Brash, combative, abrasive and savvy, Lehman proved from his first day in office to be a powerful, even ruthless, advocate for the Navy and for naval aviation—especially strike aviation. His credentials included a reserve commission as a naval flight officer in the A-6E Intruder, an Ivy League Ph.D. in international relations, a dozen years of experience in a variety of key policy jobs in Washington, and many powerful and loyal friends, mentors and helpers, in both the executive and legislative branches.

Lehman set four major goals: to articulate clearly the need for U.S. naval power; to build a Navy of 600 ships to wield that power; to slash costs wherever possible; and to rekindle a sense of esprit and excitement on the waterfront and at sea. These goals fit comfortably within the "America is back!" agenda of President Ronald Reagan.

The articulation came with the "Maritime Strategy," a wartime strategy of global, forward, offensive operations to bottle up, box in, and kill the Soviet fleet and its land-based air arm in time of war, at the same time defending the NATO flanks in Europe and taking pressure off ground forces battling in Germany.

The fleet that Lehman inherited in 1981 numbered some 479 battle force ships. Reagan, Secretary of Defense Caspar Weinberger, and Lehman thought these numbers were far too low. Lehman fought for more Navy air wings, and worked hard to keep the Navy in the deep-strike and long-range interceptor missions, by improving both the venerable A-6 and the newer F-14 Tomcat fighter. By 1988, a year after he left office, the battle force had grown to 584 ships, including fourteen carriers and fourteen active (and two reserve) air wings, and was well on the way to 600.

Lehman believed the nation would not yield up the required resources for a 600-ship Navy if it believed that its leadership indulged in waste, fraud, and abuse. Consequently, his third major effort was to contain and cut costs. He lowered the unit price of new aircraft—especially the F/A-18—instituted firm fixed-price contracting, reduced overhaul backlogs, blocked expensive "gold-plating" of systems, increased competitive procurements, cut an entire command layer from the Navy's procurement structure, and shifted costs to private industry.

Finally, Lehman sought to boost Navy professionalism, readiness, combat capabilities and morale, especially among naval aviators and most especially among fellow naval reservists. He successfully pushed for a needed "Strike U" to polish the skills of the Navy's attack aviators, and gave full service support to making the movie "Top Gun"—Hollywood's paean to naval aviation. He brought back leather jackets and brown shoes, restructured carrier air wing command, and gave the reserves more first-line ships and aircraft. And he never stopped dropping in on the fleet's ready rooms and mess decks, to find out what was really on the minds of the Navy's seamen and airmen.

John Lehman served as Secretary of the Navy for more than six years—one of the longest terms on record. He has remained a player in debates on America's naval policy through provocative public speeches, articles and books.

Secretary Lehman visiting Marines.

USS *NEW JERSEY* AND RESERVISTS

By Commander Paul Stillwell
U.S. Navy Reserve (Retired)

In December 1982 President Ronald Reagan personally recommissioned the battleship *New Jersey*—forty years to the month after the Philadelphia Navy Yard had launched her hull. The recommissioning symbolized the rebuilding of the nation's defense forces, and the ship also was a substantive addition to the fleet through the capabilities of her gun and missile batteries.

After some preliminary training off the California coast, the ship embarked on June 9, 1983, on a shakedown cruise that was scheduled to last three and a half months and take her to ten ports in seven countries. She stopped at Pearl Harbor en route to the Philippines, Singapore, and Thailand. Then, in late July, the battleship was ordered to take station off Nicaragua as part of a show of naval force following the approach to that country by Soviet and Communist-bloc merchant ships presumably carrying supplies to rebel Sandinistas.

After a period of watchful waiting off the Central American coast, the *New Jersey* was scheduled to return to her homeport of Long Beach for a change of command. Instead, she was diverted once again, this time for a

trip through the Panama Canal and into the Atlantic. U.S. forces had been sent to Lebanon as peacekeepers, but peace had become a rare commodity. Marines stationed in Beirut had come under fire. The frigate *Bowen* provided shore bombardment on behalf of Lebanese forces. The Joint Chiefs of Staff assessed the *New Jersey*'s much greater firepower potential and sent her to the Mediterranean, where she arrived in late September.

The battleship's arrival led to a cease-fire, but only a temporary one. In late October a terrorist drove a truck bomb into the Marine compound at Beirut; the resulting explosion killed 241, including a *New Jersey* chief petty officer who had gone ashore to help the Marines with their radars. The ship's deployment should have ended already, but now there was no end in sight. Representatives from the Naval Military Personnel Command showed up to find relief for crew members whose separation from families was growing longer by the day.

The solution came through the Naval Reserve. The ship would send crewmen home on leave in relays, and reservists would show up to take their places. The first group to go home included a few on humanitarian leave, and the rest of the slots were decided by lottery. The

Four days after Lehman took office, the *New York Times* reported that the Reagan administration would be asking for an additional $7 billion for the current year's budget and an additional $25 billion in 1982 for new initiatives.

As new ships and aircraft entered the Navy's inventory, Lehman called for the "Horizontal Integration" of the Naval Reserve to keep its Sailors current with the skill levels of active-duty Sailors. To do so, the Naval Reserve needed to retain trained Sailors who came into the reserve from the fleet.

Lehman also sought to provide the Naval Reserve with front line ships and equipment.

With the expansion of the active-duty Navy towards a 600-ship fleet, the Naval Reserve needed additional personnel. With regard to manpower, during the eight-year Reagan presidency the number of SelRes increased from under 90,000 to over 151,000. The percentage of reserve Sailors in the overall Navy manning end-strength increased from 17 to 21 percent. Most impressive was the growth of the Naval Reserve's portion of the overall first group of replacements arrived aboard on December 13, 1983, the day before the battleship fired her first bombardment of Lebanon. The new men didn't necessarily fill billets one for one to replace the men who had gone. Instead, those on the voluntary recall to active duty went where their rating specialties and training dictated. Journalist Second Class Lance Johnson was particularly impressed by the greeting he received as he set foot on the *New Jersey*'s deck. One of the regular crewmen extended a hand and said, "Welcome aboard, shipmate."

On December 29 the battleship pulled in for a port visit at Haifa, Israel. It was the ship's first full day in port in 111 days. In January the second group of reservists reported for duty and the first group departed about the same time. One hundred four more of the regular crew members began their leave. Included in the new arrivals were some men who had orders to report to the *New Jersey*'s sister ship *Iowa*, which was then in the process of reactivation and modernization. The time on board the *New Jersey* would speed their training process. A frequently seen television commercial of the time asked the question, "How do you spell relief?" The answer in the commercials was "R O-L-A-I-D-S." When the same question was posed on board the *New Jersey*, the reply was, "I-O-W-A."

In February 1984, President Reagan changed the ship's mission dramatically when he announced that he would be withdrawing most of the Marine Corps forces from Lebanon. Before they went, however, the *New Jersey* had a dramatic day of firing her 16-inch guns. On February 8 she unleashed 288 projectiles at Syrian and Druze gun positions ashore. The firing silenced the guns. The watchful waiting resumed, and the homeward-bound flights continued. All told, there were seven flights, and 727 crewmen made it back to the States. Only one seat had gone unfilled in that time — a crewman who showed up not ready to travel. For the reservists it was an opportunity to experience action firsthand and to provide respite for deployment-weary officers and men of the *New Jersey*.

On April 2 the battleship was relieved of her assignment and began heading to Long Beach. She arrived to a raucous welcome on May 5, which was fifteen years to the day after her arrival in the same port after a stint of firing off Vietnam. Just short of eleven months after her departure, she brought her crew home.

Navy budget, nearly doubling from 1.4 to 2.7 percent. The TAR program more than doubled, with the number of officers and enlisted TARs increasing from 10,066 to 22,987.

Not only did the Naval Reserve keep in step, it also shouldered a greater share of the Navy's mission. As new carriers, cruisers, frigates, and other units entered the fleet, the availability of skilled mid-level petty officers became a challenge for the Naval Reserve. In response to requests for voluntary recall, SelRes joined the fleet to provide the needed manpower and skill sets. The most significant example of a response to a voluntary recall request was the reactivation of the *Iowa*-class battleships. The first of the four World War II-era dreadnoughts would be *New Jersey*. About 375 applications from SelRes and retired Fleet Reservists petitioned for active-duty recall to serve on this historic warship. Eventually, thirteen SelRes and four Fleet Reservists were recalled to serve as part of the recommissioning plank owner crew. Another fifty-one applicants accepted other critical billet assignments in the fleet.

Naval Reserve Center Watertown, New York, which also served as a training facility for the near-century-old New York Naval Militia.

In 1982, the Naval Reserve contributed nearly 3,000 reservists to serve in active-duty billets. To reacquaint reserve Sailors with the ways of the sea, a refresher program was established on the repair ship *Hector*, where SelRes underwent two weeks of intensive training. Nearly 42 percent of the petty officers who underwent the training elected to remain on active duty or join the TAR program.

NEW RESERVE FORCE SHIPS

In addition to filling billets on fleet units, SelRes were beginning to report aboard more modern warships and fly first-line aircraft. The World War II *Gearing*-class destroyers that were approaching four decades of service were phased out in favor of *Knox*-class frigates that entered the inventory in the late 1960s. In 1985, the Navy transferred the lead ship of the *Oliver Hazard Perry*-class along with the *Clifton Sprague* to the Naval Reserve. By the end of the decade the Naval Reserve Force order of battle included fifteen *Perry*- and nine *Knox*-class frigates. To maintain proficiency in the latest tactics, a mid-grade Reserve Surface Warfare Officers course was established at Newport, Rhode Island.

Gray (FF 1054).

Estocin (FFG 15).

As a naval flight officer, Secretary Lehman not only pushed for upgrades in fighter and attack aircraft but sought to establish two reserve tanker squadrons, and two reserve search and rescue helicopter squadrons, and add four C-9 aircraft to enable the Naval Air Reserve to provide reliable, cost-effective ongoing contributory support. One ambitious initiative was to enhance the Navy's Top Gun pilot training program by creating two reserve adversary squadrons. Meanwhile, Helicopter Light Attack Squadrons 4 and 5 based in Norfolk, Virginia, and Point Mugu,

Robert F. Dunn had a relatively short tour as Chief of Naval Reserve and would be assigned to command all Naval Air Forces of the U.S. Atlantic Fleet with a promotion to Vice Admiral. Rear Admiral Cecil J. Kempf, USN, relieved him as Chief of Naval Reserve.

One junior officer stationed on the ammunition ship *Suribachi* in 1983 remembered duty weekends at Naval Station Earle, New Jersey, when the reservists would arrive late on a Friday evening.

> *The morale of a weekend duty section is not always the best, given these guys busted their butts all week and then had to stay behind as their shipmates left for weekend liberty. Then you had these reserves show up who wanted to do things and train. We had to berth and feed them, conduct damage control and other drills and assign them chores that needed proper supervision. Perhaps we were less than sincere when we told them 'We are so glad you are here!'*

Dunn credited Lehman for helping to change attitudes.

> *Traditionally, the air reserve components would get the hand-me-down airplanes, certainly not the newest. Lehman aimed to change this. He insisted that the third F/A-18 squadron be a reserve squadron. It was strongly resisted by the active Navy, but with a firm-handed secretary behind the move it worked out fine.*

Lehman's actions spoke louder than words as he continued to spend his summer two- week active duty for training periods in the cockpit of an A-6 Intruder, maintaining his proficiency as a naval flight officer bombardier. This did much to promote the reserve component and the reserves repeatedly answered the call.

NAVAL RESERVES RESPOND

Within 40 minutes of the suicide bombing of the Marine installation at the Beirut Airport on October 23, 1983, a Naval Reserve C-9B transport from VR-56 lifted off from Sigonella, Sicily, en route to Lebanon with a medical team embarked. Crewed by reservists doing their two weeks of annual training, the C-9B returned to Beirut two days later to provide additional supplies and conduct medical evacuation services.

California, focused much of their training on working with special boat squadrons and Navy SEAL teams to provide air cover and diversion fire to aid insertion and extraction operations.

Relieving Rear Admiral Palmer during this period of rapid of Naval Reserve growth was Rear Admiral Robert F. Dunn. Dunn, a 1951 graduate of the Naval Academy, had a successful career in the attack aircraft community and had been previously stationed in Washington. He quickly discovered that all of the initiatives that moved assets into the Naval Reserve were not fully embraced by the entire Navy establishment. Settling into his new job, Dunn recalled he had two tasks at hand: "One was to convince the regular Navy that the reserves were more than a drain on their time and pocketbook. The other was to convince the reserves themselves they were valuable to the Navy." Of the two, Dunn found the first to be the much harder challenge. "[T]he problem started at the very top," he said. "The CNO Admiral [James] Watkins just didn't want to be bothered with reserve issues—in fact, he didn't want to be bothered with reserves." Dunn found the regulars in the fleet equally skeptical.

Loading sonar buoys prior to a
maritime patrol on a VP-64 P-3 Orion.

NAVAL RESERVE RECRUITING

A demand on Naval Reserve management in the 1980s was recruiting. It had been the responsibility of individual air stations and readiness commands to fill manpower requirements of units under their command. Meeting the reserve manpower requirements of Navy's Cold War Maritime Strategy—establishing fleet hospitals to support the Marine Corps, standing up additional Seabee construction battalions, and forming cargo handling battalions—meant recruiting several thousand people, including medical professionals and those with special skills, but the task was beyond the capability of the surface and air reserve commands. In 1988, the Naval Reserve Recruiting Command was established, reporting directly to Commander, Naval Reserve Force. The new command solved the recruiting problem. The commanding officer, Captain R.A. Perrault, USNR, reported:

For FY 89, The Naval Reserve exceeded all recruiting goals for the first time in history and was the only service component to succeed in medical programs. The combined nurse and physician attainment was 141 percent of the goal. Overall, the officer recruiters produced 102 percent of the goal.

Not only did naval reservists lend operational help, they continued to provide the Navy innovative expertise. In June 1985 the *Navy Times* reported that reservists from Naval Reserve Maintenance Training Facility 110 from Orange, Texas, developed a device to inspect boilers for accumulated fuel oil—the cause of a series of boiler explosions that had occurred in the 1970s and early 1980s.

One of those reservists who contributed his skills was Hull Technician Jeff Covington. As the end of his four-year enlistment in the Navy approached, Covington sought orders to go to diving school as an incentive to re-enlist. When the leading chief in his division could not guarantee those orders, Covington looked at civilian employment back in St. Louis as a welder with McDonnell Douglas. With an offer tended, Covington left active duty, but he decided not to leave the Navy. Joining the Naval Reserve, he brought his civilian employer enhanced skills to work for the Navy as a member Submarine Base Pearl Harbor Detachment 618. Alas, Covington would finally have the opportunity to travel to tropic climes in the Pacific.

Another area where the Navy entrusted the Naval Reserve with critical combat capability was mine warfare. By the 1980s, the majority of some thirty minesweepers constructed during the 1950s were approaching the end of their service life. Countering arguments that helicopters could be employed to perform the mission, the Naval Reserve Association provided testimony to the House Appropriations Committee in 1981 that because of their long-term training, reserve Sailors could sweep mines faster and at less expense than their active-duty counterparts. Subsequently, the Navy elected to keep and upgrade about half of the reserve minesweeping force.

A TRADITIONAL MISSION RETURNS

In addition to maintaining and upgrading fourteen of the venerable minesweepers, the Naval Reserve took on a mine-countermeasures program for twenty-three harbors where the Navy had little presence but for the nearby reserve center. Harkening to the days of the Spanish-American War, the Navy created twenty-two Craft of Opportunity (COOP) units to react to potential mining attempts by Soviet clandestine forces or terrorist groups. The first unit to deploy began operations at Savannah, Georgia, using a former Naval Academy training ship. Crewed full-time by four TARs, the unit trained four nine-man crews to perform mine-countermeasure operations. In a March 1985

Rear Admiral Grace Hopper retired in 1986 on board the USS *Constitution*.

Commissioned in 1956, the minesweeper *Gallant* saw service in Vietnam and would be based in Oakland in the 1980s.

agreement between the Department of Transportation and the Navy, the Maritime Defense Zone concept was formalized, which teamed Naval Reserve and Coast Guard personnel to coordinate coastal defense.

Added to the Naval Reserve mine-countermeasures capacity were five RH-35D Sea Stallion helicopters. Commissioned at Norfolk Naval Air Station in October 1986, the squadron would include 120 TARs who would train 200 SelRes.

WAR IN THE GULF

As the Naval Reserve improved its mine warfare capability, a bitter war between Iran and Iraq threatened oil shipments in the Gulf, especially at the narrow Strait of Hormuz. When Iraqi initial advances into Iran were reversed, the Iraqis started to launch air attacks against tankers approaching and leaving Iranian ports. In March 1984, the Iraqis began attacking Iranian loading facilities at Kharg Island. With Iraqi ports closed by the war, Kuwait served as a surrogate port for the export of Iraqi oil. In response to attacks on its facilities, Iran began targeting Kuwaiti

ships. For the next two years "the tanker wars" took a toll on commercial shipping. The impact of the war began to affect the world economy. By late 1986 the Iranians stepped up their campaign against the Kuwaitis. Seeking a way to preserve its valuable tanker fleet, on December 10, 1986, the Kuwaitis approached the U.S. Coast Guard on how to register their ships under the American flag. Once reflagged, the tankers could come under the protection of the U.S. Navy.

After months of debate in Washington during a period that included damage to the frigate *Stark* by an Iraqi air-launched Exocet missile, President Reagan approved the reflagging under the name of Operation Earnest Will. On July 24, 1987, during the initial operation involving two naval escorts, the former Kuwaiti tanker *Al Rekkah*, now the *Bridgeton*, hit a mine that opened a ten-by-five meter hole up forward. The convoy proceeded, now with *Bridgeton* in the lead to protect the two American warships against potential mine damage. Earnest Will operations came to a halt as the Americans scrambled to consolidate mine warfare assets.

If ever there was reason to mobilize Naval Reserve assets to support an ongoing naval operation, Earnest Will provided it. All but three of Navy's twenty-one minesweepers were in the Naval Reserve Force (NRF). The crews on the NRF ships were trained, eager and ready to go. However, about a third of the NRF crews were SelRes, in billets essential for carrying out the ships mission. Under Title 10 of the U.S. Code, the president had the authority to call up to 100,000 reservists in an emergency, which would have allowed any NRF ship, reserve unit, or individual reservist to be called into active service. The minesweepers

Divers of Naval Reserve Mobile Diving and Salvage Unit 813 (MDSU-813) assigned to Readiness Center Great Lakes brave below zero temperatures during a cold weather diving exercise, February 1988.

could have deployed with their SelRes crew members. However, congressional politics interfered. There was opposition in the Senate to further involvement in the Gulf. The Reagan administration feared that a reserve call-up would be seen as obligating the president to abide by the War Powers Act, which would have made operations in the Gulf subject to congressional approval. As a result, there was no mobilization of naval reservists. When the Naval Reserve called for volunteers to fill the SelRes billets, the number of volunteers far exceeded the requirement, but most were not qualified in the required rates. The Navy had to cross deck Sailors from other fleet ships to fill those billets, and those lacking the billet qualification had to be trained, delaying deployment.

CHANGES AT THE HELM

During this period there were two significant changes in Navy/Naval Reserve leadership. In April 1987, Secretary Lehman resigned and returned to the private sector. His successor was James H. Webb Jr., a 41-year-old Naval Academy graduate and highly decorated Marine Corps Vietnam veteran, who was serving in the Pentagon as the first Assistant Secretary of Defense for Reserve Affairs. The other

Secretary of the Navy James H. Webb Jr.

change was the relief of Vice Admiral Cecil J. Kempf as Chief of Naval Reserve. On his first day as secretary, Webb surprised everyone by naming Rear Admiral F. Neale Smith, a recalled reserve flag officer and Kempf's deputy, to the top position. The selection was not the CNO's choice and was not well received by a Navy establishment that coveted its precious flag billets. Following the change of command at New Orleans, a reporter for *The Times Picayune* asked Chase Untermeyer, Assistant Secretary of the Navy for Manpower and Reserve Affairs, about the appointment of a reservist. He said "James H. Webb, Jr., the new Secretary of the Navy, personally chose Smith." Untermeyer said "two-star [reserve] Generals serve as head of the Army and Air Force Reserves and Webb wanted to bring the Navy into line with the other services."

Taking the helm as the sixth Chief of Naval Reserve two months before the *Bridgeton* mine strike, Smith, as not only the first reserve officer but also first surface warfare officer to take command, represented a sea change in leadership at the top. Having earned his commission in the Naval Reserve through the eighth class to graduate from Officer Candidate School during the Korean War, Smith left active duty to become an oil company executive. In 1984, the Navy brought him on active duty to serve as the Deputy Director of Naval Reserve. Operation Earnest Will continued in the Gulf as Iranian activity increased. Mines and small boats were being used to harass the convoys. Rear Admiral Harold J. Bernsen, Commander of the Middle East Force, requested special warfare assets. Two oil servicing barges, moored in the northern Gulf, were converted into mobile sea bases. More reservists were needed. The reserve volunteer manning process of inviting reservists to come on active duty without being involuntarily recalled, originally intended for the mine sweepers, had been extended to frigates, intelligence personnel, and many other support roles requested by Bernsen. Hundreds of volunteer naval reservists were serving in the Gulf. Smith, concerned about whether the Reserve volunteer process was satisfying the needs of the force commander, flew to Bahrain with his aide and force master chief for a two day visit to observe first hand. After a briefing by the new Middle East Force Commander Rear Admiral Anthony Less, aboard the flagship *Coronado*, the threesome started out to the NRF frigate *Sides* at anchor. En route they met with four reserve naval liaison officers (NLOs) who were going aboard escorted reflagged tankers. This was their twenty-fourth convoy. A normal transit in the Gulf is roughly the distance between Washington and Chicago. None of these officers had merchant marine experience. They learned to carry out their missions in the Gulf as members of Naval Control of Shipping units back home. Aboard *Sides*, Smith's team met with the commanding officer and crew. The same routine was followed aboard minesweeper *Fearless*, on the mobile sea base *Wimbrown VII* and with the small boat units. The feedback clearly indicated the system was working: "The SelRes volunteers are good Sailors, good people and they are doing the job expected of them."

In a 1989 retirement interview with *Navy Times*, Smith expressed his frustration with the politics which caused the administration not to use the presidential authority to call up reserve forces in Operation Earnest Will. He asked rhetorically why the services should put any forces, aircraft, or ships into the reserve if it is possible that in the event of an emergency they may not have access to them.

THE COLLAPSE OF THE SOVIET EMPIRE

Away from the Middle East, events were occurring that would have profound impact on the future of the Navy. Concluding a speech at the Brandenburg Gate in West Berlin on June 12, 1987, President Reagan issued a challenge to the Soviet General Secretary:

"Mr. Gorbachev, tear down this wall!"

Rear Admiral F. Neale Smith, Lieutenant Clay Fearnow, USNR, and Reserve Force Master Chief Larry Sorenson, USNR.

Soviet General Secretary Mikhail Gorbachev and President Ronald Reagan.

Left: The Berlin Wall would be opened in November 1989.

159

Few at the time could have predicted that less than three years later, on November 9, 1989, that barrier between East and West would be opened as the people of Eastern Europe rose to remove the yoke of Communist governments. With the American presidential election of 1988, yet another former Naval Reserve officer occupied the Oval Office—George H.W. Bush.

As the nation's new commander in chief, Bush was not hesitant to use military force when confronting a challenge to national security. With growing tensions between the United States and Panamanian dictator of Manuel Noriega threatening the neutrality of the Panama Canal, on December 19, 1989, Bush sent forces into Panama in Operation Just Cause to oust the Panamanian strong man.

George H.W. Bush earned his commission as an ensign in the Naval Reserve on June 9, 1943, following preflight training at the University of North Carolina, where one of the instructors was Lieutenant (j.g.) Gerald R. Ford. Bush eventually became a torpedo plane pilot. Flying off the *San Jacinto*, Bush attacked Japanese installations on Chichi Jima on September 2, 1944, when his plane was hit and he was forced to bail out. The only member of his three-man aircrew to survive, Bush was rescued by the submarine *Finback*. Rejoining his squadron, he would complete fifty-eight combat missions during the war. Discharged in September 1945, Bush began his academic education at Yale.

However, when the Commander of U.S. Southern Command requested the mobilization of the reserves to help manage civil affairs following the military operation, his request was denied as the administration feared involuntary call-ups could spur congressional opposition in conjunction with the War Powers Resolution.

By the end of the decade, the end-strength of the Naval Reserve had grown to 153,400. The Naval Surface Reserve force contained nearly fifty vessels, including frigates, landing ships, minesweepers, and salvage vessels. The Naval Air Reserve maintained fifty-one squadrons, including fighter and attack aircraft, patrol planes, transports, and helicopters. SelRes drilled at 226 reserve centers around the nation that were divided among sixteen readiness regions.

Testifying at his CNO confirmation hearing before the Senate Armed Services Committee in July 1990, Admiral Frank B. Kelso stated: "Our Reserves will continue to play an important role as the cornerstone of our Nation's Navy mobilization capability."

At the time Kelso spoke, Hull Technician First Class Covington was receiving his orders for annual training at Submarine Base Pearl Harbor. For Covington, it would be his last annual training in the Aloha State. He had been recruited to a new unit based in St. Louis—Mobile Inshore Undersea Warfare Unit 112, commanded by Captain J. Stanton Thompson. Commissioned the previous fall at a local high school with Congressman Ike Skelton as the featured speaker, MIUWU 112 Sailors worked hard to perfect their warfighting skills, taking their portable radar van down to the edge of the Mississippi River to track barge traffic. Donning woodland battle dress uniforms with a triangular patch featuring a shark wearing a set of headphones, members of Thompson's unit gained confidence in their abilities and began to conduct themselves with a bit swagger.

On August 2, 1990, as Petty Officer Covington was requalified at a rifle range on Oahu, Iraq invaded Kuwait. In the Navy Command Center the flag watch officer, Deputy Chief of the Naval Reserve Rear Admiral Wallace Guthrie, monitored the situation. He was soon joined by Admiral Kelso. In the coming weeks, the Naval Reserve would validate the CNO's Senate testimony.

In honor of Rear Admiral Grace Hopper, who died on January 1, 1992, the Navy would christen, and later commission, the destroyer *Hopper*.

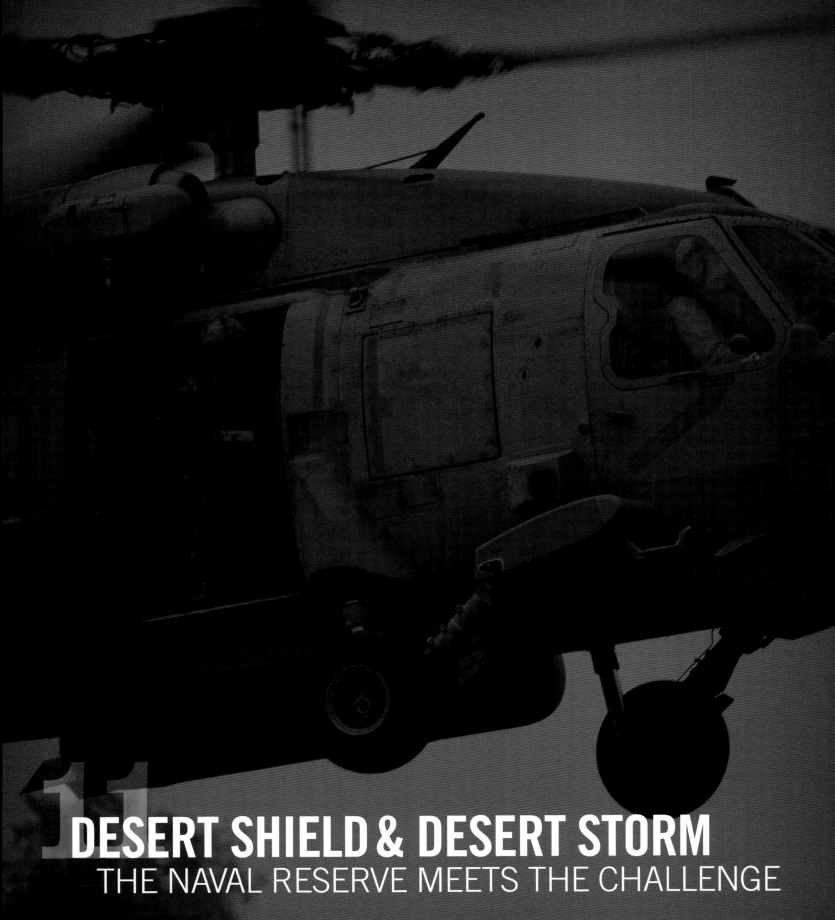

DESERT SHIELD & DESERT STORM
THE NAVAL RESERVE MEETS THE CHALLENGE

(1991-2000)

During a turnover process in 1988 between two TAR officers, the following discussion ensued:

So what's the deal with the safe?

Oh! That's the mobilization safe. You will not need to worry about that during your XO tour here in St. Louis. We haven't really mobilized the Naval Reserve since the Korean War!

Two years later, the executive officer of Naval Reserve Readiness Center, St. Louis, found himself scrambling to find the combination to the safe in the wake of Saddam Hussein's decision to seize Kuwait on August 2, 1990. Concerned that Iraqi forces could continue to roll into Saudi Arabia, the United States and a coalition of allied nations sent forces into the region to support what would be dubbed "Operation Desert Shield."

The Navy rushed ships from the Pacific and Atlantic Fleets to the region to augment its token presence, known as the Middle East Force. By the end of the month some forty American warships crewed by approximately 35,000 Sailors were in the region. To support the manning needs of the afloat force, Rear Admiral Salvatore Gallo, the commander of the Naval Manpower Personnel Center, stood up a "crisis center" that operated around the clock thanks to the influx of naval reservists who volunteered to meet the staffing requirements.

MOBILIZATION FOR DESERT SHIELD

To provide combat support and combat service support, it became clear early on that the nation's reserve forces would have to be called upon. On August 22, President Bush issued Executive Order 12727, invoking Title 10 of the U.S. Code, section 673b, enabling him to recall Selected Reservists from the four service reserve components. The next day, Secretary of Defense Richard Cheney called for the mobilization of 48,800 Selected Reservists, of which 6,300 would come from the Naval Reserve.

In many cases, reservists backfilled billets in the United States that were vacated by the rush of active-duty personnel to the Middle East. Otherwise,

With many active-duty medical personnel pulled from shore billets to staff the deploying hospital ships, like the *Mercy* shown here, naval reservists backfilled ashore and would eventually deploy into the theater.

the recalled Sailors were sent to the Middle East, where they came under the operational command of U.S. Central Command (CentCom), led by General H. Norman Schwarzkopf. CentCom's naval component commander would be Vice Admiral Henry H. Mauz Jr., embarked in Bahrain-based command ship *LaSalle*. Ashore in Bahrain, Rear Admiral Robert Sutton took charge as Commander, U.S. Naval Logistics Support Force.

Active-duty medical personnel from various naval hospitals were reassigned to the hospital ships *Mercy* and *Comfort* so that these ships could immediately put to sea. Thus many of the initial recalls, such as the call-up of 2,500 naval reservists from medical units in late September, helped replenish the wards of the stateside facilities. Not only were these reservists up to the challenge of providing top-notch care for military personnel, but they brought many best-practices with them from the civilian sector. Lieutenant Agnes Burkhart, a reserve nurse who had just given birth to her second child, reported for duty at Naval Hospital Oakland and observed that many Navy doctors and nurses had been recruited into the service right out of medical school and were not networked into various professional societies. "The influx of naval reservists to various facilities truly brought a needed professional depth to Navy medicine," recalled Burkhart.

While aircraft could fly in units such as the 82nd Airborne Division to blunt an Iraqi attack, the heavy armored forces needed to counterattack would have to arrive from sea, with much equipment stored in maritime prepositioning ships based in Diego Garcia. To assure the safe arrival of critical cargoes, Sutton needed minesweepers, port security units, naval control of shipping specialists, cargo handling teams, and medical personnel—capabilities that all resided in the Naval Reserve. The three critical debarkation ports were Al Jubayl and Ad Dammam in Saudi Arabia, and Manama in Bahrain. Sutton requested the activation of three Mobile Inshore Underwater Warfare Units as well as three Coast Guard Reserve Port Security Units to protect his three entry ports from Iraqi saboteurs. Initially, the San Diego-based Commander, Naval Inshore Undersea Warfare Group 1, Captain Dennis Vaughan, USNR, and his staff arrived to deploy and set up MIUWUs 103 and 105 to protect the Saudi ports.

Back in St. Louis, the executive officer oversaw the mobilization of numerous individuals who were specifically requested for their skill sets. One of those individuals was Petty Officer Covington, whose "fix-it" talents were considered a must-have on Captain Vaughan's staff. Following a long-flight on an Air Force C-5 transport to an airfield in the Saudi desert, Covington found transportation to Al Jubayl. There

Naval reservists deplaning in Saudi Arabia.

he found a familiar face. His commanding officer from MIUWU 112 in St. Louis, Captain Thompson, had been brought over to serve as the Port Security Harbor Defense Commander for that critical Saudi port.

Saudi Arabia and Bahrain also hosted three Navy fleet hospitals, of which two were staffed by naval reservists. Some 431 containers housing the contents of Fleet Hospital 5 arrived in the Gulf on August 21 on the MV *Noble Star*, a cargo ship that had been prepositioned at Diego Garcia. The Marine commander, General Walter E. Boomer, insisted that this fleet hospital be placed at Al Jubayl, a short distance from the front lines. As the portable hospital arrived, the naval reservists who would staff the facility departed from Norfolk in Military Airlift Command transports.

ON TO DESERT STORM

As the summer turned to autumn, Saddam Hussein disregarded international calls for his army to vacate Kuwait. Thus, General Schwarzkopf moved forward with plans to dislodge the Iraqis by force. With mines a potential obstacle to any seaborne assault, on October 1 the Dutch heavy-lift ship *Super Servant III* delivered four minesweepers, of which *Adroit* and *Impervious* were Naval Reserve Force ships.

On November 5, President Bush ordered more than 150,000 military personnel to reinforce the forces already in the region—a clear signal that the United States-led coalition was contemplating offensive operations to dislodge the Iraqi army from Kuwait.

Subsequently, on November 14 and on December 1, Secretary Cheney expanded the number of reservists subject to mobilization to 125,000 and then to 188,000. At Naval Reserve centers and air facilities around the nation, the Navy mobilized additional medical and logistical support units as well as air squadrons and ship augmentation units. Included among the units deploying was the New Hampshire-based MIUWU 202, which set up its position at the end of the Mina Sulman pier at Manama.

Seabees from Reserve Naval Mobile Construction Battalions 74 and 24 were part of this wave of reservists who arrived as part of the pre-offensive operations. RNMCB 74 relieved NMCB 4 in Bahrain and performed construction work to enhance the tarmac at Shaikh Isa Air Base and build new facilities for the Navy's Administrative Support

Reserve Naval Mobile Construction Battalions 24 and 74 supported Fleet Hospitals that were placed in Saudi Arabia and Bahrain.

Unit that had been based there for decades. RNMCB 24 relieved NMCB 7 at Al Jubayl and worked to construct defensive positions and extend air strips.

One of the projects RNMCB 74 would help with was to set up Fleet Hospital 15, which arrived in Bahrain in December. Seabees and Bahrainis unpacked and set up the medical tent city adjacent to an oil refinery in less than a week. Meanwhile at Fort Dix, New Jersey, more Naval Reserve medical and support staff completed two weeks of training that emphasized the treatment of chemical and biological warfare-caused injuries. These personnel would deploy to the Bahrain-based hospital and to Fleet Hospital 6, which was built near Fleet Hospital 5 at Al Jubayl.

Although ground combat was weeks away, Fleet Hospital staff did not lack for work. Sailors and Marines had to operate in a harsh environment and shared the desert with cobras, puff adders, vipers, scorpions, poisonous spiders, lice, wasps, mosquitoes, and flies. Navy corpsmen found themselves treating Marines who had maggots deposited in their eyes by the loathsome sheep bot fly.

As part of the combat forces build-up, the Navy began recalling reserve air squadrons. In mid-December, members of Helicopter Combat Support Special Squadrons 4 and 5 arrived in the Middle East, giving the new naval component commander, Vice Admiral Stan Arthur, a combat search and rescue capability.

A Kuwaiti A-4KU Skyhawk aircraft sits parked on the fringes of a crowd that gathered to listen to a speech by President George H.W. Bush on Nov. 22, 1990. The president paid Thanksgiving Day visits to U.S. troops who were in Saudi Arabia for Operation Desert Shield.

During Desert Shield/Desert Storm most Reserve Sailors served on the ground on the Arabian Peninsula.

The day after Christmas, the Navy mobilized four VR transport squadrons based in California, Texas, and Florida. Before New Year's Day the squadrons were operating from Sembach and Bitburg in Germany, and Sigonella in Sicily. During their three-month operation, Naval Reserve C-9 aircraft carried some 18,000 passengers and 4,000 tons of cargo, ranging from replacement parts to bombs and fuses for B-52 aircraft.

WAR BEGINS

At 0141 on January 17, 1991, the destroyer *Paul Foster* unleashed the first barrage of Tomahawk missiles from American warships stationed in the Gulf. With the Tomahawks removing much of Iraq's air defense network, the coalition air assault began and Operation Desert Storm was underway. With the ground war still a month away, on January 18, 1991, President Bush issued Executive Order 12743, authorizing the mobilization of up to 360,000 Ready Reservists. He also extended the activation of recalled Selected Reservists for up to a year. For the Navy, the number authorized for activation climbed to 44,000.

In all, 21,114 naval reservists were recalled, of which over a third deployed to the region. Anticipating heavier casualties in the ground war, the majority of those recalled were from medical units. Besides providing enough men and women to staff Fleet Hospitals 6 and 15, Naval Reserve doctors, nurses, corpsmen, and other medical professionals helped to backfill eighteen major stateside medical facilities as active-duty personnel were rushed to the theater. Naval reservists would eventually provide staffing for the hospital ships and corpsmen who would cross enemy lines with the Marine expeditionary forces. Among those who went into combat with the Marines were many of the 140 chaplains and 85 enlisted religious program specialists, who provided spiritual support not only to Sailors and Marines, but also to Royal Marines.

For logistical support, over 240 reserve weapon handlers augmented personnel at stateside naval weapon stations to prepare ammunition for shipment. On the receiving end, cargo handling battalions offloaded ships and aircraft. Construction battalions (the Seabees), besides constructing the aforementioned three fleet hospitals as well as an Army hospital, built defensive berms and two 6,000-foot runways, set up seven million square feet for aircraft parking, constructed twelve hangars, maintained 200 miles of unpaved roads and built fourteen galleys capable of feeding 75,000 personnel.

At sea, 1,800 naval reservists augmented the crews of more than sixty Navy ships that deployed to the region, including the battleships *Wisconsin* and *Missouri*, which provided devastating gunfire against Iraqi defenses. One of the lessons of the war was that the afloat commands were picky about the billets they needed filled. Rear Admiral Wallace Guthrie, the Deputy Director Naval Reserve during this period, recalled that rather than request the recall of a complete Naval Reserve ship augmentation unit, a command might ask for only those ratings where it had critical shortfalls.

Overhead, Naval Reserve combat support helicopters flew search and rescue missions over Kuwait and Iraq. Further out to sea, Naval Reserve anti-submarine helicopters flew search and rescue missions from Diego Garcia and recovered three members of a B-52 crew from the Indian Ocean.

Also playing important roles were over 350 intelligence and cryptologic specialists who augmented their active-duty counterparts at ashore and afloat command centers. Included were fifteen linguists who had been non-drillers within the Individual Ready Reserve. Their ability to speak Arabic and serve as translators was critical.

With Iraqi forces poised to defend against an amphibious assault from the sea or a direct assault from Saudi Arabia, Schwarzkopf executed his end-sweep flanking movement of armored forces through Southern Iraq to isolate the Iraqis in Kuwait. With Iraqi forces grasping the futility of remaining in place, a huge caravan of military and commandeered civilian vehicles headed north in the night, to be decimated by allied airstrikes. Schwarzkopf held a memorable press conference describing the tactical moves that led to the ground victory. Staging the press conference and handling the questions were Naval Reserve public affairs personnel. Schwarzkopf, a veteran of the Vietnam War, understood that a war won on the battlefield could be lost in the court of public opinion. Given

that most of the recalled Navy public affairs officers worked for various media outlets, Schwarzkopf had a higher comfort level with their expertise than with his career Army public affairs people. Naval Reserve PAOs served Schwarzkopf well. He emerged from the Gulf War as perhaps the most popular American general since Dwight D. Eisenhower.

While gunfire had ceased in the northern gulf, the work of the naval reserves continued. The minesweepers *Adroit* and *Imperious* swept the approaches to Kuwait, and much of the material

7-color desert camouflage uniforms worn during Operation Desert Storm were popularly known as "Chocolate Chips." The uniform was made of a heavy weight material and not suited for hot arid climate conditions.

Naval Reserve Medical personal consult in Saudi Arabia.

that had been sealifted to Bahrain and Saudi Arabia needed to be shipped home. Military Sealift Command's Vice Admiral Francis R. Donovan boasted that his command had delivered the city of Louisville to the region and now Louisville had to come back.

The Navy appreciated the contribution made by its reservists, so much so that in March, offers were made to many recalled reservists to stay on active duty as members of the regular Navy. The Navy extended this offer particularly to the medical reservists, of whom some 589 would request to remain in uniform. For others who looked forward to being released, it would take some time. By the summer of 1991, however, most SelRes who had been activated had returned to rousing welcome home ceremonies that featured hometown parades and yellow-ribbon displays. Petty Officer Covington recalled flying back to San Diego to receive his release from active duty and then flying home to St. Louis to be reunited with his wife and son.

Above: Held on June 8, 1991, the nation welcomed back returning Desert Storm veterans during a National Victory Parade in on Constitution Avenue in Washington, D.C.

THE AFTERMATH

In the aftermath of the war, concerns were raised by the General Accounting Office that many of the recalled reservists would resign after their release from active duty, noting that some reservists, such as pilots and doctors, had lost upwards of 35 percent of their income while activated. Some doctors saw their private practices deteriorate because patients found other caregivers. Yet a survey of naval medical reservists in the autumn of 1992 indicated that 76 percent planned to continue to drill. Of those who intended to leave the Naval Reserve, family separation was cited as the predominate reason.

Noteworthy were those who did not get mobilized for Operation Desert Shield and Storm. One military capability that Saddam Hussein did not possess was submarines. Consequently, the anti-submarine warfare assets of the Naval Reserve that were embedded in Naval Reserve Force frigates and P-3 Orion reserve squadrons remained mostly on the sidelines. As with the active Navy ASW capabilities, these reserve assets would be reduced as the Cold War Soviet Union collapsed and abandoned hundreds of its conventional and nuclear powered submarines.

Taking account of the disintegrating Soviet empire, the 1990 National Security Strategy anticipated that the United States would no longer need to prepare for global conflict but instead should anticipate regional conflicts—a new reality that was validated by Saddam Hussein.

Recognizing the inevitable draw down from the near 600-ship Navy that had been built to fight the Soviets on a global scale, the Navy sought to initially preserve its ASW capability within the Naval Reserve. Much of that capability had been built into the *Knox*-class frigates that began entering service in the late 1960s. Under what became dubbed the Innovative Naval Reserve Concept, the Navy transferred forty *Knox* frigates to the Naval Reserve. Eventually, thirty-two of the frigates were decommissioned and placed in unmanned reserve status. The remaining eight were designated as training frigates (FFTs), with each having the mission of training their own crews as well as four others, which could be assigned to reactivate the mothballed frigates.

The innovative FFT program lasted two years until base closures and budget constraints forced the

The tank landing ship *Frederick* (LST 1184) was transferred to the Naval Reserve Force in January 1995 and changed homeport to Pearl Harbor, Hawaii. From there she conducted bilateral exercises with Southeast Asian armed forces, continuous training exercises with the United States Marine Corps and was on standby to conduct humanitarian assistance and disaster relief missions throughout the Pacific. She would be transferred to Mexico in 2002.

Navy to decommission the remaining *Knox* frigates. By mid-decade the Naval Reserve Force inventory included fourteen *Perry*-class frigates, six of the 1950s vintage minesweepers, two salvage recovery ships, and three tank landing ships (LSTs). Finally, the old sweepers were taken out of service along with the LSTs. However, the Naval Reserve began to add newly commissioned coastal mine hunters (MHCs) to its inventory. More significant, with the emergence of *John F. Kennedy* from an extensive overhaul at the Philadelphia Naval Shipyard in September 1995, the Mayport-based conventional aircraft carrier joined the Naval Reserve Force with a primary mission of providing training services to NAS Pensacola. *John F. Kennedy* would continue as a Naval Reserve Force ship until 2000, when overseas operational commitments forced the Navy to place her back in service with the fleet. In 1996, the Navy converted the amphibious assault ship *Inchon* into a mine-warfare command ship and placed the ship in the Naval Reserve Force.

While the *John F. Kennedy* and *Inchon* were big additions to the Naval Surface Reserve Force inventory, the overall composition of the order of battle gradually evolved. By the turn of the century, the afloat force consisted of eight *Oliver Hazard Perry*-class frigates, the last *Newport*-class tank landing ship, five modern *Avenger*-class mine-countermeasure ships, and ten *Osprey*-class mine hunters.

Oliver Hazard Perry-class frigates (FFG 7) were
powered by low-maintenance marine gas-turbine

NAVAL RESERVE WARSHIPS

Fittingly, the two largest warships ever placed in the Naval Reserve Force had names with strong Naval Reserve connections. *John F. Kennedy* was named for the 35th president of the United States, who served in the Navy during World War II and survived the loss of his *PT-109* in the South Pacific. *Inchon* was named for the bold amphibious assault early in the Korean War, an operation that involved thousands of naval reservists.

Upon returning to Naval Station Mayport, Florida following her extensive overhaul in Philadelphia, *John F. Kennedy* began workups in November 1995 with the assignment of reserve fighter squadron VFA-204. Although a Naval Reserve Force ship, the majority of her crew were active-duty Sailors, with reserve Sailors augmenting the crew. When operating from Mayport, *John F. Kennedy* provided support services to NAS Pensacola to help recently commissioned naval aviators earn their carrier qualifications. However, she also deployed as an NRF ship, first to the North Atlantic in the summer of 1996 with festive port calls at Dublin, Ireland and Portsmouth, England. The carrier also made a summer Mediterranean deployment in 1997 and a fall-winter deployment to the Mediterranean in late 1999, where her aircraft supported no-fly-zone operations over southern Iraq. Before her return to the active fleet in October 2000, she participated in the International Naval Review in New York Harbor and made a port call at Boston. The veteran aircraft carrier was decommissioned on August 1, 2007. In 2011, Caroline Kennedy joined Navy Secretary Ray Mabus in announcing the second aircraft carrier of the *Gerald R. Ford*-class would be named *John F. Kennedy* (CVN 79).

Commissioned in 1970 as a helicopter landing platform (LPH), the Navy converted *Inchon* as a mine countermeasures command (MCS) and support ship in March 1995 and placed her under the command of the Naval Reserve Force on September 30, 1996, homeported at Ingleside, Texas. During in-port steaming trials on October 19, 2001, the ship suffered a fuel oil fire in the bilge of the main boiler room. Petty Officer Third Class Ronnie Joe Palm Jr., 21, of Houston, remained trapped in the space and succumbed to smoke inhalation after helping fellow Sailors escape. Petty Officer Palm was posthumously awarded the Navy and Marine Corps Medal for his heroism. As a result of the damage the Navy decided to decommission the 31-year-old ship.

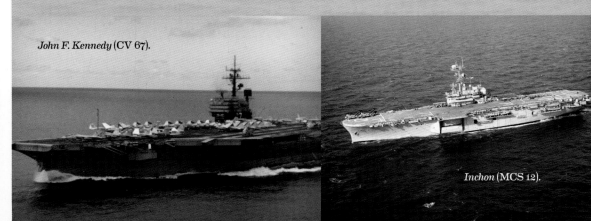

John F. Kennedy (CV 67).

Inchon (MCS 12).

The F-5 Tiger II had many of the flight characteristics of potential adversary aircraft. As foreign air forces modernized, so did the Navy's adversarial squadron.

The Naval Air Reserve Force boasted thirty-five squadrons, including forty-nine F/A-18 Hornet strike fighters and forty-eight P-3C Orion maritime patrol aircraft. The Naval Reserve continued to provide the Navy all of its organic airlift capability with its twenty-seven C-9 Skytrain and twenty C-130 Hercules transports. Naval Reserve aviators continued to play the bad guys, flying F-5 Tiger II jets against fleet pilots enrolled at the Naval Strike and Air Warfare Center at NAS Fallon, Nevada. During the next decade, Naval Reserve adversary pilots transitioned to F-16 Fighting Falcons.

The Naval Reserve continued to provide the Navy with all of its inshore undersea warfare assets, 99 percent of its naval control of shipping assets, 93 percent of its cargo handling capability, and 65 percent of construction battalion forces.

THE PARADIGM SHIFT

But what truly had changed in the years following Desert Shield and Desert Storm was the Navy's mindset about how to effectively use its citizen Sailors. In the 1980s, the reasoning behind naming many of the large drilling facilities as "Naval Reserve Readiness Centers" was rooted in the requirements to prepare an individual to be mobilization ready. Training reserve Sailors to achieve 100 percent readiness was the end-all that unit commanding officers strived for—and fitness reports reflected this.

Over the course of the war, the recall process became more efficient and responsive to the specific needs of the supported gaining commands. Rear Admiral Guthrie recalled that gaining command

recall requests evolved from activating entire units for augmentation—an action that often exceeded gaining command requirements—to requests tailored to specific rates and ratings where critical active personnel shortfalls existed. The experience of Desert Shield and Desert Storm had changed the traditional paradigm of reserve support.

Following Desert Shield/Desert Storm, the post-Cold War period forced the Navy to maintain a high operational tempo. Unfortunately, Saddam Hussein proved resilient and defiant, leading to the declaration of a no-fly zone over southern Iraq to protect that country's Shiite population. Carrier-based aircraft helped enforce the no-fly zone. In the Caribbean, an unstable government led the United States to intervene in Haiti to restore order and democracy. In the Adriatic region, a brutal civil war in the former Yugoslavia led to NATO intervention. In Africa, the Navy helped evacuate foreign nationals in the midst of civil strife in Liberia and provided humanitarian support in the wake of genocide in Rwanda. Over in the Pacific, the United States maintained its forward presence as North Korea continued to threaten its southern neighbor and China made threatening moves against Taiwan.

REAR ADMIRAL THOMAS F. HALL

Rear Admiral Thomas F. Hall, with a background in the fixed-wing patrol squadron community, had a strong appreciation of how Naval Reserve P-3 Orion aircrews had contributed directly to the active forces in hunting Soviet submarines. He was given the task of determining from both an active-duty and reserve perspective what the reductions in end-strength should be following the end of hostilities in the Middle East. As an active-duty flag officer with many connections in the Pentagon's E-ring and well-respected in the Naval Reserve community, Hall was an ideal selection as the Chief of the Naval Reserve. Under his leadership, the Naval Reserve gradually and thoughtfully reduced in end-strength from about 130,000 to 96,000 at the end of Hall's tour of duty. Following his tour as the last active-duty commander of the Naval Reserve, Hall went on to become the president of the Naval Reserve Association and then served as Assistant Secretary of Defense for Reserve Affairs.

Appreciating the contributions made by the Naval Reserve during Desert Shield/Desert Storm, the hard-pressed active forces again turned to the Naval Reserve. Under the leadership of Rear Adm. Thomas F. Hall, innovative changes were made to proactively support operational requirements. Rather than focus on merely meeting mobilization requirements, the Naval Reserve mission began to evolve into providing direct support to the fleet. Ultimately, this mind-set would evolve to such an extent that a decade later, the Naval Reserve Readiness Center moniker was dropped in favor of Navy Operational Support Center.

To give the fleet more reserve manpower, including an increasing number of women, administrative changes enabled reserve Sailors to group drills together and allow them to drill during the week at operational Navy and joint commands. For reserve units that drilled near or at naval installations, the new flexibility gave reservists an opportunity to take on numerous day-to-day operational assignments. For a unit that supported the Deputy CNO for Plans and Policy (N3/5) in the Pentagon, the monthly regimen involved a Saturday morning drill to meet such Navy-wide requirements as physical readiness testing, urinalysis drug screenings, and general military training. Otherwise members of the unit were instructed to coordinate with their active-duty counterparts to

schedule drills during the week. Often unit members could be counted on to fill in at their counterpart's desk when that individual took leave or was sent on special assignment. The new flexible drill rules proved to be a particular boon to the naval medical establishment, which embraced the opportunity to have active and reserve medical specialists working side-by-side. For example, in 1995 Naval Reserve medical personnel provided 68,000 hours of support to Naval Medical Center San Diego. Among the many accomplishments were 1,800 physical examinations.

Unit commanding officers were no longer evaluated solely on readiness but rather on support for the fleet. In addition, the Naval Reserve began to inventory the civilian job skills of its reservists for potential fleet use. For example, with the closure of numerous bases in mid-decade, naval reservists with skills in environmental matters were tapped for their expertise. In another case, when the Commander, Fifth Fleet wanted a history of the U.S. Navy's relationship with the government of Bahrain, the Naval Reserve provided a Ph.D. historian.

Given the scope of tasks assigned to the Navy, both domestic and overseas, the magnitude of the Naval Reserve contribution was quite impressive. Throughout the decade Naval Reserve Force ships

EA-6B Prowler aircraft flown by naval reservists proved to be an invaluable asset during operations in the Adriatic Sea.

MIUWU 206 offloads equipment during Exercise Dynamic Impact in Sardinia in 1994.

and aircraft supported drug-interdiction efforts in the Caribbean Sea and Gulf of Mexico. The Naval Reserve responded to natural disasters such as Hurricane Andrew in southern Florida in August 1992. Seabees were among the reservists who contributed time and equipment to help with the massive clean-up efforts. When the Seabees were not providing disaster relief assistance, they were involved in other military construction projects. Following the influx of Haitian and Cuban refugees to the Navy base at Guantanamo Bay, Cuba, Reserve Seabees worked alongside their active-duty brethren to build shelter, messing, and sanitary facilities.

UPHOLD DEMOCRACY

Every major fleet exercise during the decade depended on naval reservists to provide staffing support.

During Operation Uphold Democracy, which placed American forces on the ground in Haiti in September 1994, the Navy recalled Brooklyn-based MIUWU 203 to active duty to provide port security at Port-au-Prince. Offshore, NRF frigates supported the operation as did reserve P-3C patrol planes, C-9 and C-130 transport aircraft, and search and rescue helicopters.

Not all of the MIUW Sailors were from Brooklyn. Inshore Undersea Warfare Group TWO, based in Little Creek, Virginia, now commanded by Rear Admiral J. Stanton Thompson, was the command responsible for overseeing MIUWU activities in

the eastern half of the country. While Thompson served as the group commodore as a reservist based in western Missouri, the group had a full-time staff of recalled reservists. One of those reservists, Chief Hull Technician Jeffrey Covington, once again found himself in a tropical clime, serving as a Navy liaison to the Army's 10th Mountain Division, which had deployed to restore order in and around Port-au-Prince. With former President Carter and retired General Colin Powell, former chairman of the Joint Chiefs of Staff, negotiating a change of government, Covington recalled the military effort turned to providing humanitarian relief. Amid the harsh poverty, Covington was struck by the sight of a woman with her twin daughters wearing yellow dresses as they made their way around the muck and danger to go to church. "You're like, 'Wow, look at that—the two most precious things among all this.' I'll never ever forget that one."

A year later Naval Reserve EA-6B Prowler aircraft deployed on *Theodore Roosevelt* and from Aviano, Italy, to support Operation Deny Flight operations over the Balkans. These operations were supported by the Naval Air Reserve intelligence program, which not only provided personnel to the Adriatic, but also to commands in Southwest Asia to monitor Iraq as well as the Caribbean to support counternarcotic operations.

In addition to better using the Naval Reserve enlisted and junior officers to support the active forces, CNO Admiral Jay Johnson began tapping the Naval Reserve flag community to draw on their civilian expertise to take command positions. Rear Admiral Martin E. Janczak received orders to Guam to serve as Commander, Naval Forces Marianas. Rear Admiral

Kenneth Fisher served an active-duty tour as deputy commander, U.S. Pacific Fleet. Rear Admiral John B. Totushek found himself in uniform as the Navy's Director of Environmental Programs, Occupational Safety and Health.

RESERVES TAKE CHARGE

Because of the high comfort level between the active Naval Intelligence community and its reserve counterparts, on May 30, 1997, a reserve flag officer, Rear Admiral Larry L. Poe, was selected to assume command of the Office of Naval Intelligence. At the change of command ceremony Poe reflected: "Today is a great day for the Naval Reserve and the one-Navy, Total Force Policy," adding, "the success story is that the entire Naval Reserve Intelligence Command has been included as an integral, indistinguishable part of Naval Intelligence."

One of Poe's inherited challenges was to monitor terrorist activities in the Middle East. On June 25, 1996, a truck exploded near the Khobar Towers, which served as a barracks for U.S. Air Force personnel stationed at Dhahran, Saudi Arabia. The tremendous blast claimed the lives of 19 airmen and could be felt on the nearby island of Bahrain, which hosted the U.S. Fifth Fleet. In addition to tracking the activities of the hostile governments in Iraq and Iran, Poe's active-duty and reserve intelligence collectors and evaluators began to monitor the growing militant movement on the Arabian Peninsula.

To support Fifth Fleet operations in the region, naval reservists performed myriad chores either on voluntary recall orders or during their annual two-week training. Among those commuting back and forth to the region was Jeffrey Covington, who had returned to St. Louis to work for Boeing as a supervisor of the sheet metal riveting process for F-15, F/A-18, and C-17 aircraft. Continuing to drill with MIUWU 112, Covington was promoted to a chief petty officer in 1997. During his stints in the region, Covington conducted maintenance on MIUWU equipment that remained prepositioned in the region.

While Covington worked up in the Gulf, on the southern end of the Arabian Peninsula, Yemen sought American assistance in the struggle against Islamic extremists. Meeting with Yemeni President Ali Abdullah Saleh twice in 1998, the U.S. Central Command commander, Marine General Anthony

Zinni, discussed a wide range of cooperative measures to strengthen Yemeni military, law-enforcement, and anti-terrorism capabilities. In addition, Zinni discussed the use of Aden as a refueling stop for American warships transiting to and from the Fifth Fleet. In March 1999, the first American warship stopped at Yemen to refuel. By October 12, 2000, the pit stop had become routine as the destroyer *Cole* marked the twenty-eighth such arrival. As the destroyer nudged up to the refueling platform, a small boat approached with two Arab men aboard waving at Sailors on deck on sentry duty. The master chief hospital corpsman recalled "there was a huge boom, like an M-80 under a can, but only 100 times louder." The ship lifted up to starboard and rocked to port. In the ensuing minutes and hours, the crew performed magnificently to save the ship. The blast would claim the lives of 17 Sailors.

In Washington Vice Admiral Totushek, who had relieved Rear Admiral Dennis Vaughan as the Chief of Naval Reserve in October 1998, monitored the situation and offered support. Concerned that the attack on the *Cole* could inspire additional suicide attacks on American warships in the region, the Naval Reserve sought volunteers to operate small patrol craft to enhance security. Senior Chief Covington once again answered the call. Following a three-month hitch in the Middle East, Covington again received orders to go on active duty—this time to attend a Senior Enlisted Academy course in New Orleans that had been developed for senior reserve enlisted Sailors. During the course the selection list for Master Chief was released by the Bureau of Personnel with Covington's name on it.

U.S. and Saudi military personnel survey the damage to Khobar Towers caused by the explosion of a fuel truck on June 25, 1996.

12 READY NOW, ANYTIME, ANYWHERE

ANYTIME, ANYWHERE

(2001-2015)

With the United States sustaining near simultaneous blows on September 11, 2001, in Washington, New York, and Pennsylvania, no one could be sure whether additional attacks were pending. "We immediately knew that we were going to need a lot of force protection people," recalled Chief of Naval Reserve Vice Admiral John Totushek, "so the vast majority of the people we brought on very quickly assumed positions guarding gates to support force protection. Again, in a lot of cases people came on before they even were on any kind of a mobilization."

In the Indian Ocean, the homeward-bound aircraft carrier *Enterprise* reversed course. A few days later, President George W. Bush proclaimed a state of national emergency to authorize Secretary of Defense Donald Rumsfeld to mobilize the nation's reserve forces. On September 20, President Bush addressed Congress and the nation and demanded that the Taliban leaders in Afghanistan surrender al-Qaeda leaders, close terrorist training facilities, submit to inspections, and release foreigners who were unjustly being held captive. With the Taliban refusing to meet the American demands, the president ordered the

commencement of Operation Enduring Freedom on October 7. F-14 Tomcats and F/A-18 Hornets roared off the flight decks of *Enterprise* and *Carl Vinson* laden with ordnance and full fuel tanks.

DEFENDING THE HOMELAND AND WAGING WAR

As the president spoke to the nation that September evening, the Navy was in the process of recalling thousands of reservists to active duty. Many of those putting on their uniforms would be assigned to a mission their Naval Militia forebears would have been comfortable with: homeland defense. As the Department of Defense raised force protection levels at facilities across the country, active-duty Sailors found themselves inspecting car trunks and truck cargoes in addition to performing their assigned wartime work. To allow the active-duty Sailors to focus on their real jobs, Totushek was presented with a requirement for some five thousand reservists to man the gates, walk perimeters, and perform other force protection functions. Totushek recalled:

> *We had a thousand people in billets that basically matched that requirement. So we took a lot of people and stuffed them in places they had no idea they'd ever be. We gave them a quick training course on how not to hurt yourself with a shotgun and sent them on—and people did wonderfully well.*

In addition to meeting homeland defense requirements, Totushek responded to requests to support the warfighting commands overseas. For the former drilling reservist, the mobilization process provided a painful education:

> *There was some discussion after 9/11 about who owned the mobilization process. I don't think it was evident to a lot of people, including very senior people in the Navy, that it wasn't the Naval Reserve.*

The responsibility of working with the warfighting commands to respond to manning requests and validate needs fell on the Deputy Chief of Naval Operation for Plans and Policy (N3/N5) in Washington—whose offices had been destroyed in

The American flag, flowing in defiance off the roof of the damaged Pentagon, is draped just to the left of the Chief of Naval Reserve's office on the fourth floor.

Naval reservists in a coastal patrol craft guarding the approaches to the port facilities at Rota, Spain.

the attack on the Pentagon. Whereas the numbers needed to support operational commanders during the Bosnia and Kosovo operations were small enough to individually handle reservists' requests, the demands from Fifth Fleet and other forward commands demonstrated that processes needed to evolve. A mobilization cell, created with staff provided by N3/N5 as well as the Bureau of Naval Personnel and the Naval Reserve Force, worked tirelessly to break bureaucratic logjams. Once the Navy Annex based cell began working on recall requests, naval reservists from around the nation began getting phone calls to report to their local Naval Reserve Center.

With the Fifth Fleet based in Bahrain serving as the pointy end of the spear, many of those recalled received orders to head to this island kingdom. At the time, Capt. Lee Holbrook, held command of the Naval Support Activity that hosted Fifth Fleet and some 50 tenant commands. Reflecting back after he finished his tour in 2003, Holbrook said, "The reserves were a huge, huge, success story in Bahrain. We could not have survived the last two years without our reserves." Overall the Navy population in Bahrain rose

from approximately 2,300 to well over 3,000 Sailors. Holbrook's own command benefited from the arrival of 250 Sailors from ten reserve units that furnished additional security, clerical, and logistical support.

By the end of the year, more than 5,400 naval reservists had been recalled to active duty to support combat operations in Afghanistan and to bolster security at home. Their efforts contributed to the success of the overall campaign as Kabul fell in December to a Northern Alliance of Afghani tribes and Marines were on the ground in southern Afghanistan, home turf for many of the Taliban fighters.

In the wake of the attacks, Master Chief Jeffrey Covington completed anti-terrorism and disaster preparedness training, and chemical warfare courses in San Diego and Fort Leonard Wood, Missouri. He then reported in December to Naval Coastal Warfare Group One Mobile Training Team at San Diego. With the nation at war, training took life or death seriousness. During physical training, push-ups were done with gas masks on.

THE NAVAL MILITIA TODAY!

By Dr. Kenneth W. B. Lightfoot

After World War I, the growth of the Naval Reserve rendered the state naval militias obsolete for U.S. Navy purposes. New, tighter regulations governed the conditions under which states could receive federal assets. In 1938, the Naval Reserve Act stipulated that in order for state naval militias to receive federal support, a minimum of 95 percent of their personnel must also be members of the Naval Reserve who would be relieved of any state duty in times of war and emergency. With the Navy and Coast Guard assuming an ever-greater role for maritime protection during World War II and the Cold War, most states eventually opted not to maintain a naval militia, with New York and New Jersey being notable exceptions. The New York Naval Militia has continuously remained part of its state's military forces to the present time while meeting the 95 five percent federal reservist requirement. New Jersey maintained its Naval Militia status until 1963.

The recent history of the New Jersey Naval Militia provides an instructive case study highlighting what modern naval militia units can accomplish when supported as well as the difficulties they often face. In 1999, Governor Christie Todd Whitman reactivated the New Jersey Naval Militia with the purpose of providing a military waterborne force that could act as a force multiplier for state and federal missions. During the response to the attacks of September 11, 2001, the unit demonstrated the value of a modern naval militia as a force multiplier and the diverse range of services it can offer. Within hours of the attack on the World Trade Center, New Jersey Naval Militia boats were patrolling the Hudson River and for the next two weeks served as one of the primary means of access to lower Manhattan for military and government agency personnel between Ground Zero and the Forward Command Post at Liberty State Park.

The New Jersey Naval Militia garnered widespread praise for its efforts, including letters of commendation from the Navy, the Coast Guard, and the New Jersey State Police. Despite this recognition and record of service, however, the unit was ordered to stand down in April 2002 by a newly appointed adjutant general, citing a need for an organizational review on various grounds. Despite this uncertainty, New Jersey Naval Militia personnel continue to drill every month to refurbish and totally refit a fleet of seven surplus patrol boats obtained from the New Jersey State Police and to participate in extensive emergency management training.

As the Naval Reserve marks its 100th anniversary, the future of the naval militia at both the state and federal level is uncertain. Although the level of support currently varies from state to state, future events could well prove the wisdom of the old adage "you cannot have too many friendlies on the battlefield."

Naval Militia prepare to deploy on harbor patrol.

Naval Reserve F/A-18s from VFA 201 deployed on *Theodore Roosevelt*—the first mobilization of a Naval Reserve fighter/attack squadron since 1968.

Despite the initial success in Afghanistan, Vice Admiral Totushek correctly assessed that the United States would be engaged in a long-term struggle, telling his staff that terrorism "is a cancer that could not be excised with one operation."

OPERATION IRAQI FREEDOM

By the spring of 2002, Northern Alliance and American-led allied forces were completing operations against remaining Taliban and al-Qaeda strongholds in Afghanistan and Washington turned its attention toward Iraq. With senior officials believing the situation in Afghanistan was stabilized, coalition air forces returned in force over southern and northern Iraq to enforce U.N. Security Council Resolution 688, which protected Iraqi minority populations from violent repression from the Baghdad government. By the end of the year coalition aircraft had conducted over 50 airstrikes in response to Iraqi violations.

After debating the issues pertaining to Iraq, on November 8, 2002, the U.N. Security Council adopted

Resolution 1441, giving Iraq thirty days to produce "a currently accurate, full, and complete declaration of all aspects of its programmes to develop chemical, biological, and nuclear weapons, ballistic missiles, and other delivery systems."

As the diplomats pressed for Iraqi compliance to previous agreements on the world stage, President Bush directed the Defense Department to move forward on plans to invade Iraq. Vice Admiral Totushek recalled: "For the first time that I know of, as they were planning for Iraqi Freedom, the reserve force got read into the war plan. So we could advise on almost a real-time basis with N3/5 what units were likely to be called and what kind of individual skills we'd need."

Given the need for operational security, Totushek directed the Naval Reserve Force to hold a stand down to "take all your people and make sure they're ready to go ... and I mean ready to go."

In some cases, the reservists were already gone. On December 12, 2002, Master Chief Covington watched as coastal patrol boats were splashed into Kuwaiti waters.

Included in the mix of Naval Reserve units to be called was Strike Fighter Squadron 201 based out of Naval Air Station Joint Reserve Base Fort Worth, Texas. One carrier deploying to the Middle East ahead of schedule found it could not deploy with one of its fighter squadrons that was undergoing an aircraft transition so the near-term solution simply brought forward a squadron from the next carrier scheduled to deploy, the *Theodore Roosevelt*. Rather than continuing to disrupt active component fighter attack squadron deployment cycles, the Navy mobilized VFA-201 in time to join *Theodore Roosevelt*'s Carrier Air Wing Eight at NAS Fallon in Nevada to conduct pre-deployment workups. As the first tactical Navy reserve squadron to be mobilized since the seizure of the *Pueblo*, the squadron embarked in *Theodore Roosevelt* from January 6 to

May 29, 2003. During the initial phases of what became known as Operation Iraqi Freedom, the squadron delivered over 220,000 pounds of ordnance on enemy targets, earning the unit and its pilots numerous awards for performance.

In addition to VFA-201, the Navy mobilized personnel from numerous VR squadrons to handle logistical requirements. There was caution concerning over-mobilizing the reserves given that no crystal ball existed that could predict the conflict's duration. Other Navy Reserve squadrons also contributed detachments and volunteers to fly over to provide support. As in the previous conflict a dozen years earlier, the Navy rotated Navy Reserve Helicopter Combat Support Special Squadrons 4 and 5 into Kuwait to respond to search and rescue missions. Later, the squadrons operated from bases in Iraq, performing a variety of missions working with special operations forces.

The C-9B Skytrain, the military version of the DC-9 airliner, first entered naval service in 1972 and served for over three decades before being phased out for the C-40 Clipper, the military version of the proven Boeing 737.

Naval Reserve Coastal Warfare assets on patrol in waters off Iraq.

As in Desert Shield/Desert Storm, MIUWUs were mobilized to provide port security, as were medical personnel to backfill stateside hospitals and provide additional medical talent in the region. With American Soldiers and Marines advancing toward Baghdad, coastal warfare craft infiltrated Iraq's network of rivers and waterways. Master Chief Covington had a front-row seat to witness the withdrawal of Saddam's forces.

"And the other large thing we did was staff support, including the ability to help stand up the Joint Task Forces and provide people in the crisis action cells at all the various commands that we support," Vice Admiral Totushek recounted. He added, "and those Sailors again, in a lot of cases, helped win the war."

Naval reservists not only played a role in defeating Saddam Hussein's forces but they also documented the conduct of the war for future analysis. Appointed by the Vice Chief of Naval Operations, Naval Reserve Intelligence Captain David A. Rosenberg led Task Force History, which employed the talents of four mobilized reservists and some two dozen members of Naval Combat

Documentation Detachment 206 who supported the mission during weekend drills and annual training. In the tradition of such Naval Reserve predecessors as Samuel Eliot Morison and James A. Michener, they succeeded in recording Operation Iraqi Freedom better than any other conflict in U.S. Navy history, to include over 650 oral history interviews and forty-three gigabytes of electronic data collected.

DEEP CHANGE

Unfortunately, in both Afghanistan and Iraq, early declarations of the mission being accomplished proved premature as various militant factions rallied to combat coalition efforts to stabilize those nations under democratic rule. Combating insurgencies in Iraq and Afghanistan over the next decade placed additional demands and expectations on those who had traditionally donned a Navy uniform on monthly weekends and for two weeks annual training.

The Chief of Naval Operations through this period was Admiral Vern Clark, who had earned bachelor's and master's degrees in business administration

Art has always played an important role in the Naval Reserve, whether it's for a portrait, a recruitment poster or recording an important event. Above, Allen depicts the loading of a C-2 Greyhound aircraft.

before attending Officer Candidate School. Capping a successful career serving in the surface Navy and with joint commands, Clark became CNO on July 21, 2000. Leading the Navy into the twenty-first century, Clark's business education came into play as he challenged his subordinates to think of the Navy as a multi-billion-dollar enterprise competing for quality people and resources.

From 2001 through 2003, Clark focused on realigning the Navy shore installation and training infrastructure to provide better support for the combatant commanders. One organizational change in the American military organization structure occurred in 1999 with the transformation of the U.S. Atlantic Command to become the U.S. Joint Forces Command, which took on a mission of being the primary force provider for the other unified combatant commanders, such as U.S. Central Command. For the Navy, this meant U.S. Atlantic Fleet morphed into the U.S. Fleet Forces Command with a mission of providing well-trained naval forces to support joint exercises, domestic commitments, and overseas deployments. With the Naval Reserve having authority over nearly 20 percent of the Navy's Sailors, it made

Combat artist Commander Monica Allen records history on canvas.

Admiral Vern Clark earned his Naval Reserve commission on August 20, 1968. Following his initial active-duty tour, he served seven months as a selected reservist. Clark would eventually augment to the regular Navy.

Chief of Navy Reserve John G. Cotton aside incoming Force Master Chief David Pennington and outgoing Force Master Chief Tom Mobley.

sense to have a Reserve presence on the Fleet Forces Command staff. Rear Admiral David Anderson would be the first to fill that role. Eventually, Vice Admiral Totushek established a Reserve Forces Command, initially staffed in New Orleans, to support Fleet Forces Command. The Reserve Forces Command would move from New Orleans to Norfolk, Virginia, in 2009 to facilitate further integration of the Reserve Sailors with the active forces.

As Totushek's tour as Chief of Naval Reserve wound down, the CNO, having a corporate outlook for the Navy enterprise, sought to obtain an even better rate of return on one of his major subsidiaries—the Naval Reserve. The man Admiral Clark chose to be the agent of change was Totushek's deputy, Rear Admiral John G. Cotton.

A 1973 graduate of the Naval Academy, Cotton earned his Wings of Gold and flew A-7 Corsairs with fleet attack squadrons and then transitioned

to the Naval Air Reserve, eventually transitioning to the F/A-18 Hornet and commanding the New Orleans-based VFA-204 River Rattlers. His civilian career as a commercial airline pilot for Eastern Air Lines and then American Airlines allowed him tremendous flexibility to pursue a passion for flying frontline Navy jets. For Cotton, the attack on the Pentagon proved particularly distressing. Not only did he lose colleagues in the attack but also a close friend, Naval Reserve Captain Charles "Chic" Burlingame, who was the pilot of American Airlines Flight 77, the hijacked airliner that was flown into the Pentagon. In addition, in the back of Flight 77 sat Retired Rear Admiral Wilson "Bud" Flagg and his wife Dee. Flagg had been a mentor to Cotton and had spoken at his squadron's change of command.

Promoted to vice admiral, Cotton acted with the full support of the CNO to remove what he continued to see as cultural barriers between the active Navy and its reserve component. For openers he directed that naval reservists needed to report to their active duty supported command during the fiscal year. In past years many reservists had met their two-week training obligation by responding to calls to volunteer to support such activities as Fleet Weeks to the point where the local Fleet week organizers depended on this pool of free labor. By obtaining the services of all of the reservists that they, in essence, were paying for, the various regular Navy commands gained a better appreciation for their part-time Sailors.

More dramatic were changes made to branding. Since 1925 the organization had been known as the U.S. Naval Reserve. On April 29, 2005, President Bush signed an order changing the Navy's reserve component name to "Navy Reserve." In a message to all Navy commands, Admiral Clark noted: "This is more than a name change. It more accurately describes our alignment as one Navy, and I want it to influence the integration between our active and reserve components."

In a further step to blur the perceived divide between USN and USNR, Clark then took the added step of removing the "R." Effective on June 3, 2005, Clark directed:

> *We will refer to all of our Sailors, active and Reserve, as United States Navy Sailors. This shared title will strengthen the bond between our active and reserve components, and enhance the culture of integration needed to most effectively deliver decisive power from the sea.*

Clark directed subordinate commands to start by changing all nametags of Sailors to read "USN." Not everyone embraced the erasures of distinction. Many Reservists, particularly those with long service and those in the retired community, saw no need to eliminate the R. As noted by former Chief of Naval Reserve, F. Neale Smith, "They took pride in their Reserve service and were proud to be identified as Reservists. Having received no direction from BuPers to the contrary, they continued to use USNR."

At the time of his retirement from the Navy Reserve, Force Master Chief Tom Mobley observed:

> *The Navy culture is changing because Navy leadership sees the value added in every Sailor. Notice I didn't say Reserve or active—I said every Sailor, especially those going forward, and living and dying and serving in every area. These are the people I have been honored to serve.*

At the groundbreaking for a new Navy Operational Support Center in Pittsburgh, Pennsylvania, Congressman Tim Murphy stands to the left of Chief of Navy Reserve Vice Admiral Robin Braun. Murphy, a Navy Reserve lieutenant commander, was selected for promotion to commander in fiscal 2015. He is one of few serving members of Congress who are active in the National Guard or Reserve.

In 2009 the Naval Reserve Association changed its name to the Association of the United States Navy. As the Navy Reserve became more fully integrated in the fleet, it became apparent to the association's leadership that there was a continuing need for a larger support and lobby group for the entire US Navy. AUSN includes officers, enlisted personnel, and Navy Department civilians in its membership.

Reservists lay a wreath at the gravesite of Loretta Walsh, Yeoman (F) of World War I fame.

enabled the Navy Reserve to better support the active forces. For example, one of Admiral Clark's initiatives was to create the Navy Installations Command to effectively manage the Navy's vast ashore infrastructure. Reminiscent of the Naval District system that was disbanded in the 1970s, the Commander, Navy Installations Command, established six subordinate regional commands. With the Navy Reserve Readiness Command boundaries out of sync with the Regional Command borders, Vice Admiral Cotton aligned the Readiness Commands to marry up with the Regional Commands and initially arranged for those reserve admirals who had sat in the Reserve Readiness Commander billets to serve as the Regional Commander's reserve component commander. Eventually FTS officers at the O-6 captain rank were selected to fill these billets. The alignment produced immediate benefits since Navy Installations Command assumed responsibility for the care and maintenance of all Navy Reserve facilities, which translated to cost savings when contracting for services. In addition, since the Navy Reserve infrastructure was now wired into the mainstream Navy infrastructure, the regular Navy suddenly recognized some of the subtle contributions Reservists were making on behalf of the service. For example, with the Greatest Generation passing on, the Navy Reserve provided Sailors to conduct thousands of burial honors at cemeteries across the country.

SIDE BY SIDE

Under Vice Admiral Cotton, Navy Reservists continued to support operations overseas. In Iraq and Afghanistan, some have made the ultimate sacrifice. For example, in May 2004 five Reserve Naval Mobile Construction Battalion 14 Seabees were killed and several others were wounded in a mortar attack struck on a base near the Iraqi city of Ramadi.

Navy Reserve Seabees honoring members of their reserve battalion who were killed in action in Iraq.

TARS (Training and Administration of Reserves) had been fixed in the Naval Reserve lexicon for a half century. Vice Admiral Cotton changed the moniker to Full-Time Support (FTS). Once again the change was meant to be more than cosmetic. Cotton wanted to emphasize these full-time reservists on active duty had a primary mission of supporting the active forces—a far cry from the days when these individuals were known as station-keepers. In another move to further emphasize who was working for whom, Naval Operational Support Center commanding officers were relieved of the responsibility of writing fitness reports on the commanding officers of the numerous units that mustered at his or her facility. Instead the active component commander which that reserve unit commanding officer supported now had responsibility for this accountability chore.

In addition to changing the identity, or hiding the identity, of Navy Reservists to hammer the one Navy "One Team" concept, additional structural changes

NAVY EXPEDITIONARY MEDICAL UNITS

Captain Laura Wesely (NC)
Master Chief Ron Naida
U.S. Navy Reserve

When casualties from Iraq first started arriving at Landstuhl Regional Medical Center (LRMC) in Germany in 2001, no one could have predicted how drastically the onslaught of incoming trauma patients would transform the normal battle rhythm of the facility and what the impact would be on its staff.

Prior to 9/11, the U.S. Army medical center served as a regional community hospital. Beginning in the fall of 2001, LRMC became the primary receiving facility for casualties of Operation Iraqi Freedom, Operation Enduring Freedom and later, Operation New Dawn, and stood up a Trauma Program to handle the most horrific injuries modern war can inflict. The hospital became a hub of activity for intermediary care for wounded, ill, and injured warriors from "downrange," primarily Afghanistan and Iraq. At that time, the Deployed Warrior Medical Management Center (DWMMC), the hub established to track and triage incoming casualties and coordinate follow-on care, was receiving more than forty patients a day arriving from U.S. Central Command alone.

In 2006, Navy Medicine established Navy Expeditionary Medical Units (NEMUs) comprised of clinical and administrative support staff to augment Army and Air Force staff at LRMC. With over 350 physicians, mid-level providers, nurses, hospital corpsmen and administrative reservists, primarily from Fleet Hospital Great Lakes, NEMU 07 was the first to deploy. Staff worked throughout the hospital alongside their sister services in an Army-commanded, joint service environment. Sailors on one-year, unaccompanied mobilization orders paved the way for eight subsequent NEMUs and established a rapport with permanent staff that continued long after they had departed. Navy Reserve Medicine continued to be the primary source of augmentees, expanding to include reservists from units across the country.

In the interim, LRMC became a training ground for trauma-related specialists, importing trauma surgeons from around the world, establishing a world-class trauma registry and improving downrange survival rates to levels unheard of during prior conflicts. Staff pioneered the concept of a lung team. Specially-trained medical professionals who recovered patients suffering from severe pulmonary trauma in theater and, if necessary, transported them from the war theater back to the medical center on extracorporeal membrane oxygenation machines.

NEMU staff members, from neurosurgeons and certified registered nurse anesthetists to general surgery techs and orthopedic techs, were intricately involved in the care of these patients. While burnout was a constant threat, morale and job satisfaction remained high. Many requested to extend not one but several years, while others returned at the end of their obligation or early due to family or personal issues. All reported an experience like no other, often the highlight of their careers.

When not on duty or on call, members developed a tradition of volunteerism that demonstrated LRMC's motto of "Selfless Service" and provided compassion and assistance that benefited not only the patient and family, but the community as a whole.

The establishment and sustained superior performance of NEMUs from 2006 to 2014 provided a joint learning environment, fostered collegiality among services, and offered the opportunity for reservists from all corners of our nation to contribute to the war effort and know that they made a difference. It was an experience most will not forget.

Navy Reserve medical teams performed superbly in the field in Iraq and Afghanistan.

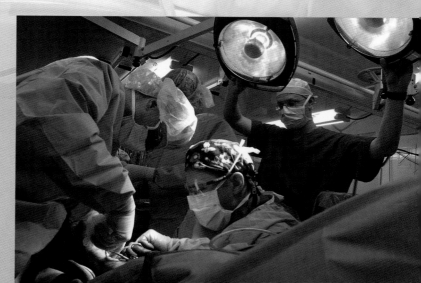

At training facilities such as Fort Dix, New Jersey, and Fort Jackson, South Carolina, Army Soldiers who were combat veterans shared their experience with Sailors who were going to serve on the ground in Iraq and Afghanistan.

While the Navy Reserve mobilized numerous Seabee, medical, MIUW, and aviation units to support the ongoing Global War on Terrorism, a bulk of those recalled—over 50,000 since 9/11—came to the battle not as members of a unit that was involuntarily recalled, but as individuals who volunteered to come on active duty.

The emphasis for what became known as the Individual Augmentee (IA) program came again from the top. Vice Admiral Cotton recalled that Admiral Clark clearly understood the cost benefits of renting manpower instead of owning manpower. To provide the needed people to fill important jobs, the Navy established an Expeditionary Combat Readiness Command as a subset of the Navy Expeditionary Combat Command. The Expeditionary Combat Readiness Command not only recruited talent from the Navy Reserve but also sought volunteers serving in various commands with the active forces.

That so many reservists were willing to voluntarily answer the call to be an IA indicated that Cotton's message that "You're in the Navy and you're going to be deployed and it's not a question of 'if;' it's 'when'" was being taken to heart.

Though Cotton foresaw an increase in involuntary recalls, most reservists came on active duty due to patriotic motivations as well as personal career incentives. During visits to the various Navy Reserve facilities that now were known as Navy Operational Support Centers around the nation, Cotton reminded reservists that future selection boards would consider the location of active duty as well as personal performance.

To increase the talent pool that could be drawn on for IA duty, Cotton pushed to lift age recruitment restrictions from thirty-five to forty-two to obtain the talents of middle-aged Americans. He also pushed for waivers in special cases. Reminiscent of how the Navy brought in many of the nation's best and brightest during World War II to perform non-combat missions, Cotton recalled bringing in William Krissoff, a sixty-one-year-old orthopedic surgeon from Reno, Nevada, as a Navy Reserve lieutenant commander to serve with the Navy Medical Corps in Iraq.

Following the death of his son Nathan, a Marine first lieutenant serving in Iraq, Krissoff applied for a Navy Reserve commission. At a meeting with President Bush during a presidential visit to Nevada, Krissoff reiterated his desire to serve in the Navy Medical Corps. Two days later he had his age waiver. In 2009 he found himself serving at Camp Al Taqaddum in Iraq with the 2nd Marine Logistics Group.

Lieutenant Commander William Krissoff, Navy Reserve Medical Corps, serving in Iraq.

Where Navy Reservists' civilian skills were found most desirable was in areas involving civil affairs. Traditionally an Army Reserve mission, the challenge of rebuilding social and community structures in two separate nations taxed the Army's resources. Hence the Navy stepped up to the challenge to flesh out volunteers to form Provisional Reconstruction Teams. With civilian backgrounds in city management, justice administration, law enforcement, public works, and education, Navy Reservists enthusiastically took on a new mission of rebuilding the infrastructure of broken communities.

While some IAs were building communities, others were saving lives. Volunteer active-duty and Navy Reserve IAs from the EA-6B Prowler community used their electronic warfare skills on the ground in Iraq to support units such as the Army's 10th Mountain Division to detect and counter improvised explosive devices.

As Chief of the Navy Reserve, Vice Admiral Cotton, accompanied by Force Master Chief David Pennington, would travel to the region to check on the morale and needs of the recalled reservists. During one trip to Baghdad they ran into the Command Master Chief for U.S. Naval Forces Iraq, Jeffrey Covington.

Above: Domestically, Navy reservists responded to protect the homeland from such hazards as wildfires on the West Coast to hurricanes pounding the Gulf of Mexico and Atlantic coasts. For example, Navy reservists contributed thousands of man-hours in the wake of Hurricane Katrina in 2005 and Superstorm Sandy in 2012. In the case of Katrina, the storm hit Navy Reserve Headquarters in New Orleans and would factor into considerations to align the command with U.S. Fleet Forces Command in Norfolk, Virginia.

The Navy Reserve's uniqueness as a Navy component that maintains a presence in all 50 states, the District of Columbia and territories provides a strong tradition of community connection that assists in Navy recruiting efforts.

Door gunner on a Navy Reserve helicopter deployed to Iraq.

Since arriving to Kuwait in December 2002, Covington had been selected for the command master chief program and served as Command Master Chief for Naval Coastal Warfare Group ONE, and then served as Command Master Chief for Naval Coastal Warfare Squadron 30 based in San Diego. During that time he met Master Chief Petty Officer of the Navy (MCPON) Joe Campa, who was looking for an outstanding senior enlisted leader for Navy forces serving in Iraq. Covington got the job.

Jeffrey Covington would go on to be the Force Master Chief for Navy Expeditionary Combat Command.

When Covington arrived in Iraq he was stunned. "This is what was unbelievable" he said. "I've seen more people from the reservist side of the house in the strangest, farthest places, most dangerous places, embedded with the Army, embedded with the provisional reconstruction teams, with civil affairs." What impressed Covington was the high morale he encountered among the many Navy Reservists he came across. Covington took exceptional pleasure in introducing his Sailors to visiting flag officers such as Cotton, so their stories could be relayed to audiences back home.

In discussions with the MCPON, Covington expressed interest in relieving Pennington as the Reserve Force Master Chief when Master Chief Pennington retired. However, the commander of the Fifth Fleet, Vice Admiral Kevin Cosgriff, had other plans. After a fifteen-minute interview at Fifth Fleet Headquarters in Bahrain, Covington was selected to be the fleet master chief for the Fifth Fleet. With the job, Covington, who had been on active duty for the better part of eight years, was placed on active duty permanently.

Covington's departure from the Navy's reserve component to its active component represented a tiny bit of good news story for Navy Recruiting Command, which now had one less individual it had to recruit.

Multiply Covington by the hundreds and suddenly you had a major good news story as the Navy Recruiting Command could reduce its recruiting goals and thus reduce its recruiting staff, infrastructure, and advertising budget. Further savings were accrued throughout the Navy's ashore training establishment as former reserve component Sailors came aboard with years of training and experience behind them.

Transfers from the reserve component to the active component partially explain the steady decline in the reserve component through the first decade of the twenty-first century. In 2001, there were some 88,900 reservists in "pay billets." By the end of the decade the number stood at approximately 68,000. A major reduction of some 16,000 billets occurred following a 2004 U.S. Fleet Forces Command zero-based review of force structure and active component support needs.

Of this 68,000, some 52,000 had been mobilized for some period during the previous eight years. As of early 2010, nearly 10 percent of the force (6,500) were on active duty. At that time Navy Reserve Sailors were providing about half of the Navy's ground forces serving with U.S. Central Command. To quote Force Master Chief Covington: "There are more reserves in the fight than people will ever understand." In addition, when a devastating earthquake struck Haiti in January 2010, Navy Reservists played key roles in Operation Unified

Loading relief materials for Haiti.

This bumper sticker was distributed widely to announce the Navy Reserve's new motto.

Response and Joint Task Force Haiti. Aircraft from fifteen Navy Reserve VR squadrons, including C-40 Clippers, C-9 Skytrains, C-20 Gulfstreams, C-130 Hercules, and C-12 Hurons, flew humanitarian assistance flights to bring in food, water, and badly needed medical supplies. When the hospital ship *Comfort* arrived at Port-au-Prince, Navy Reserve doctors, nurses, and hospital corpsmen were embarked to render assistance. Ashore, Navy Reserve Seabees cleared debris to help to begin the rebuilding process.

For the other 90 percent who were not mobilized at this time, they continued to support and participate in Navy exercises and respond to real-world situations. Such is the extent of Reserve Force integration with active component activities that *The Navy Reservist* magazine has emerged as perhaps the best chronicle of ongoing naval operations in print. For some future naval historian doctoral candidate writing a dissertation on U.S. Navy operations in the early twenty-first century, *The Navy Reservist* will serve as an invaluable resource. By documenting the activities of Navy Reservists, the journal is invariably capturing the history of the U.S. Navy.

Assuming command of this leaner operational force in 2008 from Vice Admiral Cotton, newly promoted Vice Admiral Dirk Debbink provided Chief of Naval Operations Admiral Gary Roughead his assessment of the Navy Reserve after a few months at the helm. He noted the five years of "deep change" initiated by his predecessor but also placed those changes in the context of an ongoing evolution that had its roots in the 1990s.

Citing Michael Watkins, author of *The First 90 Days*, who described four types of organizations, Debbink wrote, "the Navy Reserve is clearly a 'sustaining success' organization."

Debbink reflected: "I am of the opinion that your Navy Reserve is more integrated and valued by Navy as a whole than at any other time in my 31 years of service." From Debbink's perspective, his objective would be to "institutionalize the change where appropriate."

Debbink's Force Master Chief Ronney Wright made similar observations based on continuing discussions with his active component peers:

> *During leadership conferences with Senior Enlisted they would tell the story how the Navy Reserve made a major impact and they wanted more of what we had to offer.*

As for institutionalizing the change, the Navy Reserve adopted a new motto: "Ready Now. Anytime, Anywhere." and refined the Navy Reserve mission statement:

The mission of the Navy Reserve is to provide strategic depth and deliver operational capabilities to the Navy and Marine Corps team, and Joint Forces, from peace to war.

Force Master Chief Ronney Wright (left) presents Vice Admiral Dirk Debbink with an Honorary Master Chief certificate in the Pentagon Hall of Heroes at a ceremony honoring the previous Force Master Chiefs of the Navy Reserve and their efforts to establish a Continuum of Service.

VICE ADMIRAL ROBIN BRAUN

Vice Admiral Robin Braun relieved Vice Admiral Dirk Debbink as the Chief of Navy Reserve on August 13, 2012. The daughter of a career naval aviator, Braun graduated from Northern Arizona University and was commissioned in 1980. Designated a naval aviator in February 1981, her first assignment was to Training Squadron (VT) 31, NAS Corpus Christi, Texas, where she served as an instructor pilot in the T-44 aircraft.

Braun served as commanding officer of VR-48, NAF Washington, D.C. Subsequent command tours include Navy Air Logistics Office (NALO); Navy Reserve Carrier Strike Group 10 supporting the aircraft carrier *Harry S. Truman* and Joint Task Force Katrina; and Tactical Support Center 0793 supporting Patrol and Reconnaissance Wing Five.

Her flag officer assignments include deputy commander, Navy Recruiting Command; director, Total Force Management for the Deputy Chief of Naval Operations for Information Dominance (OPNAV N2/N6), and deputy director, European Plans and Operations Center (ECJ-3), Stuttgart, Germany.

FTS MEANS FULL TIME SUPPORT

As the focus of the Navy Reserve Selected Reserves shifted from Readiness to Operational Support, so did the focus of reservists who were on active duty to handle the training and administration of our citizen Sailors. The transition from the acronym TAR to FTS was a clear signal that these officers and enlisted reserve Sailors were also expected to provide operational support.

A good example of one such reserve officer is Jon Kreitz who enlisted in the Navy in May 1982 as a Machinist's Mate where he served in the amphibious assault ship *Nassau* (LHA 4). Eventually receiving his commission through the NROTC program at the Georgia Institute of Technology, Kreitz began a successful Surface Warfare career which included tours in the cruiser *Bunker Hill* (CG 52), destroyer *Mitscher* (DDG 57), and aircraft carrier *Enterprise* (CVN 65). However, it was a shore tour with Headquarters U.S. Pacific Command (HQ USPACOM) that influenced his decision to become a full-time reserve Sailor.

> *I reported there [in Hawaii] on orders to the J3. I was met at the airport by a USAFR Colonel and a SWO TAR commander. They welcomed me with several traditional lei's, and informed me that I wasn't going to the J3. Instead, I was going to be a branch head in the Reserve Forces Division. Needless to say, after a year on the staff I realized how important the Reserve Component was to the day-to-day functioning of the HQ USPACOM staff and the ability of the Department of Defense to meet its missions. From meaningful follow-on Reserve management jobs on the Navy Staff to continued opportunities to serve at sea, it's been an awesome experience all along the way.*

Kreitz went on to command the frigate *Stephen W. Groves* (FFG 29) from 2006 to 2007, where his crew interdicted nearly 20 metric tons of cocaine during two counter narco-terrorism operations deployments. He also commanded the landing platform dock ship *New York* (LPD 21) from 2012 to 2014, leading her through her nine-month maiden deployment and earning the 2013 Battle 'E' Award and the Atlantic Fleet Marjorie Sterrett Battleship Fund Award as the most battle ready ship in the Atlantic Fleet.

Along the way Kreitz earned a Master of Science Degree in Physics from the Naval Postgraduate School and a Master of Military Art and Science Degree in Strategy from the U.S. Army Command and General Staff College. He is a graduate of the Armed Forces Staff College and is a past fellow of the Massachusetts Institute of Technology (MIT) Seminar XXI program.

At his change of command on February 14, 2014, Captain Jon Kreitz is flanked by his relief, Captain Chris 'Bruno' Brunnett and Vice Admiral Carol Pottenger, the first FTS officer to achieve that rank.

Right: Clarence J. (C.J.) Mitchell, Navy Reserve FTS Sailor, became the 15th Reserve Force Master Chief in 2012.

Perhaps if a little additional thought had been given, the end of the statement might have been changed to "from war to peace." As the national leadership under President Barrack Obama slowly extracted American combat forces from the ground in Iraq and then in Afghanistan, the Navy's leadership continued to cement the integration that had been achieved over the past decade as active and reserve component Sailors fought side-by-side. Following months of crafting, in January 2010, the Chief of Naval Operations Admiral Gary Roughead, Chief of Naval Personnel Vice Admiral Mark Ferguson, and Chief of Navy Reserve Vice Admiral Debbink signed and released the *Navy's Total Force Vision for the 21st Century,* a document that reaffirmed that the Navy's most important resource remains its people, whether they be active or reserve component Sailors, civil servants, or contractors. The document also recognized the constant need for the Navy to evolve and innovate to address emerging challenges.

With the reaffirmation of people as the Navy's most valuable resource, Debbink saw the Navy Reserve complementing the active component in a "continuum of service" that allowed Sailors to "stay Navy" while achieving lifelong balance. Conceptually logical, the idea that Sailors could transition between the

On June 7, 2014, NOSC Buffalo dedicated the refurbished Frank Bailey Boathouse featuring this painting of Captain Bailey.

Dr. Phil Lundeberg (right) receiving the Commodore Dudley W. Knox Lifetime Achievement Medal for naval history at a Naval Academy ceremony in 2013. Lundeberg earned his BA in history through the V-12 program at Duke University in 1944.

active and reserve components to pursue a Navy career while also pursuing personal initiatives such as attending college full-time or taking a few years sabbatical to raise a family could enhance the overall capability of the total force. A continuum of service career path addresses this lifelong balance need. By enabling its Sailors the option to transfer back and forth between the components, the Navy's overall capabilities would be enhanced by retaining trained and experienced Sailors for life.

In 2012, the Chief of Naval Operations Admiral Jonathan Greenert released his "Sailing Directions" emphasizing his three tenets of Warfighting First, Operating Forward, and Be Ready with a focus on sustaining core maritime missions, fleet modernization and innovation. At the same time, with the drawdown of U.S. military personnel and expeditionary forces in Afghanistan, the Navy began a reduction of both active and reserve personnel within the Navy Expeditionary Combat Command. As a result, many reserve units were decommissioned including Seabee and Cargo Handling battalions,

Explosive Ordnance Disposal units, Maritime Civil Affairs teams, and Maritime Security Squadrons. Some of these units traced their history back to World War II, and all were critical to supporting missions in Iraq, Afghanistan, and the Horn of Africa. Despite these reductions, there is no doubt that should the need arise for future expeditionary capability, these combat-proven reservists and their "Can Do!" spirit will be ready to answer the call.

As the Navy Reserve approached its centennial, Vice Admiral Robin R. Braun, the 13th Chief of Navy Reserve, continued to evolve the reserve force into new mission areas and platforms. Reserve Sailors who mobilized overseas to support unmanned aerial systems missions are leading the integration of emerging technologies into the fleet. As the Littoral Combat Ship enters the fleet, reservists are augmenting the Active Component to assume maintenance, watchstanding, training, and security responsibilities on the waterfront. In 2014, the first of the Navy's Joint High Speed Vessels, USNS *Spearhead*, made her maiden deployment manned with a Military Detachment of Reserve Sailors. With a modular design that allows it to be rapidly refitted, *Spearhead*'s first mission was conducted to West Africa to assist coastal nations in fostering maritime security to protect their maritime economies. Another rapidly expanding area includes support to U. S. Fleet Cyber Command, where reservists bring both military and civilian expertise to help achieve war fighting superiority in the maritime, cyberspace and information domains.

As the Navy Reserve embarks upon a second century of service, it remains deeply rooted in America's defense strategy through its ongoing mission of support to the Navy. Indeed, a new and diverse generation of highly-trained "Citizen-Sailors" stands ready to answer the nation's call. With their Navy experience and unique civilian skillsets, these men and women are the embodiment of those first patriotic Americans who, at a moment's notice, went selflessly into harm's way for the preservation of liberty.

More than half a century ago, President John F. Kennedy captured the spirit of the "Citizen Sailor" when he said:

> *Today we need a nation of minute men; citizens who are not only prepared to take up arms, but citizens who regard the preservation of freedom as a basic purpose of their daily life and who are willing to consciously work and sacrifice for that freedom.*

Whether mobilizing for overseas contingency operations, providing humanitarian assistance and disaster relief, or contributing to this nation's security, United States Navy Reserve Sailors stand trained and prepared. They were ***Ready Then***. They are ***Ready Now***. They will be ***Ready Always***.

Operated by a civilian crew working for the Navy's Military Sealift Command, USNS *Spearhead* deployed to West Africa with a military detachment consisting of Reserve Sailors.

Named for a stellar Sailor who was Always Ready, the destroyer *Gravely* (DDG 107) honors the Navy's first black flag officer, whose career began in the Naval Reserve.

CONTRIBUTORS/AUTHORS

We humbly thank everyone who had a hand in making this book a reality. This book would not have been possible if not for the contributions and efforts of the following extraordinary people.

AUTHORS

Mrs. Henry F. Butler
I was a Yeoman (F)

Estelle Kemper (Mrs. Butler) served in the Navy as a Yeoman (F) during the First World War following the completion of her college degree (June 1918). She worked within the Supply Section of the Division of Aeronautics of the Bureau of Steam Engineering to help maintain the supply chain of airplane parts moving to factories and air stations/bases. She was honorably discharged in 1919, and looked back on her time in the Navy as a positive experience that allowed her to serve her country in its time of need.

Rear Admiral Joseph F. Callo
U.S. Navy Reserve (Retired)

The First Yale Unit

Besides his 32 years of reserve service, Callo had careers in advertising and television. His body of work includes an award-winning biography of John Paul Jones. He has written extensively about the sea and those who venture forth upon the two-thirds of the earth that is covered with salt water.

Commander Randy Groegen
U.S. Navy Reserve (Retired)

The Admirals' Advantage

A historian for the Office of Naval Intelligence (ONI), she retired with 32 years' enlisted and commissioned service in the Marine Corps and Navy Reserve, having served 23 years as a naval intelligence officer. She volunteered for active duty to support Operation JOINT ENDEAVOR in 1995, and was mobilized in 2001 and served in the command operations staff element at ONI. She earned a Ph.D. in diplomatic and military history from Temple University in 2007.

Captain Wilbur D. Jones, Jr.
U.S. Navy Reserve (Retired)

How the Navy Saved College Football

Jones served with the Department of Defense for 41 years, including 12 as a professor and associate dean at the Defense Acquisition University. The author of 17 books, he is vice chairman of the USS *North Carolina* Battleship Commission and chairman of the World War II Wilmington (N.C.) Home Front Heritage Coalition.

Master Chief James L. Leuci
U.S. Navy Reserve

Sidebar Author and Photo Research

Master Chief Information Systems Technician James L. Leuci II, USN, is assigned to the Naval Reserve Forces Command and is working as the lead historian for the Navy Reserve Centennial Commemoration. For thirty years, he worked at NASA Langley Research Center in Hampton, Va., before retiring in January 2014. He holds a bachelor's degree in Computer Engineering from Christopher Newport University. He is the author of several articles and papers on naval history that have been published in *All Hands, The Navy Reserve Magazine,* and the *Chief Petty Officer 365 Development Guide.*

Dr. Kenneth W.B. Lightfoot
New Jersey Naval Militia

The Militia Today

Lightfoot earned his Ph.D. in English Medieval history from the University of Wales. He has conducted numerous interviews for the Naval Historical Foundation's Oral History Program. He is the historian for the cruiser *Portland.* He has served in the New Jersey Naval Militia for the past fifteen years and stood numerous watches as Officer-in-Charge of the New Jersey National Guard Joint Operation Center during Operation Noble Eagle in the aftermath of the 9/11 attacks.

Commander Jourden Travis Moger (CHC)
U.S. Navy Reserve

History of the Chaplain Corps

Moger (A minister of the Prince of Peace serving in the host of the God of War) holds the rank of Commander. He earned a Ph.D. in history from the University of California, Santa Barbara, and has taught history at the U.S. Naval Academy. He currently serves as Commanding Officer of MEFREL 106 in Washington, D.C.

Captain Alexander G. Monroe
U.S. Navy Reserve (Retired)

NROTC

Commissioned through the NROTC program at the University of Virginia, Monroe served in the oiler *Aucilla.* Following active duty, he earned an M.A. in Government from the College of William & Mary and was employed with the City Manager's Staff in Richmond, Va. A SelRes with various commands, he deployed to the Arabian Gulf during Operation Earnest Will and to the Naval Base at Guantanamo Bay, Cuba, during humanitarian care operations involving Haitian migrants.

Command Master Chief (FMF) Ronald C. Naida
U.S. Navy Reserve

Navy Expeditionary Medical Units

Command Master Chief Ron Naida enlisted in the U.S. Navy in 1984 and trained as a Hull Technician and served afloat and ashore, leaving active duty in 1987. Naida continued his service in the Navy Reserve. He was assigned to various units before changing rates to Hospital Corpsman and served with a USMC artillery battery and then an infantry battalion deploying to Iraq in 2005. CMDCM Naida reported for duty as Senior Enlisted Leader for Navy Expeditionary Medical Unit (NEMU) 14 at Landstuhl Regional Medical Center, Landstuhl, Germany, in February 2013 and continued his position with NEMU 15 to close out the Navy's mission at LRMC in September 2014.

Captain John Lynn Shanton
U.S. Navy Reserve (Retired)

Eagle Boats

Shanton earned a degree in Biology & Chemistry from Western Kentucky University, and received his commission in 1957 through OCS in Newport, R.I. He commanded reserve units in Indiana, Kentucky, Ohio, Maryland, and Virginia, primarily amphibious Atlantic and Mediterranean operations, plus technical writing support. He developed and taught Better Navy Writing for the Naval War College and the Naval Academy.

LISTS

U.S. Navy Reserve Commanders

Apr 1973–Aug 1974	VADM	Damon W. Cooper
Aug 1974–Sep 1978	VADM	Pierre N. Charbonnet, Jr.
Sep 1978–Oct 1982	RADM	Frederick F. Palmer
Oct 1982–Nov 1983	RADM	Robert F. Dunn
Nov 1983–May 1987	RADM	Cecil J. Kempf
Nov 1987–Aug 1989	RADM	Francis N. Smith
Aug 1989–Sep 1992	RADM	James E. Taylor
Sep 1992–Sep 1996	RADM	Thomas F. Hall
Sep 1996–Oct 1998	RADM	G. Dennis Vaughan
Oct 1998–Oct 2003	VADM	John B. Totushek
Oct 2003–Jul 2008	VADM	John G. Cotton
Jul 2008–Aug 2012	VADM	Dirk J. Debbink
Aug 2012–Present	VADM	Robin R. Braun

U.S. Navy Reserve Force Master Chiefs (FORCM)

Aug 1973–Aug 1975	FORCM 1	Richard P. Johnson
Aug 1975–Aug 1976	FORCM 2	Joseph Lalley
Aug 1976–Jun 1979	FORCM 3	Harvey L. Murphy
Jun 1979–Jul 1981	FORCM 4	Don W. McDow
Aug 1981–Jun 1985	FORCM 5	Kenneth L. Gallaher
Jul 1985–Sep 1988	FORCM 6	Larry L. Sorenson
Aug 1988–Oct 1992	FORCM 7	Jeffrey A. Brody
Oct 1992–Jun 1995	FORCM 8	Paul R. Gauthe
Jun 1995–Apr 1998	FORCM 9	Michael Krbec
Apr 1998–Jul 2001	FORCM 10	Christopher C. Glennon
Jul 2001–Jun 2005	FORCM 11	Tom W. Mobley
Jun 2005–Jun 2008	FORCM 12	David R. Pennington
Jun 2008–Jun 2011	FORCM 13	Ronnie A. Wright
Jun 2011–Oct 2013	FORCM 14	Chris T. Wheeler
OCT 2013–Present	FORCM 15	Clarence J. "CJ" Mitchell

IMAGE SOURCES AND CREDITS

The majority of the images used were downloaded from online Federal Government image repositories or scanned at the Naval History and Heritage Command (NHHC). For the first third of the book the Library of Congress and NHHC served as the predominant sources. The NHHC was the primary source for the middle chapters. Department of Defense imagery dominates the back third of the book. For uniform items and many of the ID cards and bumper stickers, Master Chief James Leuci offered use of his collection. The uniform display pictures were assembled by Lieutenant Cheryl Collins, U.S. Navy Reserve. Other Federal Government sources include the Senate and House History offices, the U.S. Marine Corps, and the National Archives.

Non-federal images obtained from online repositories include the painting of Thomas Jefferson by Rembrandt Peale on page 11 from White House Historical Association, the clipper ship image on page 13 from the Museum of Fine Arts, Boston, the image of Augustus P. Cooke on page 16 from the Massachusetts Historical Society, and Lieutenant (jg) Bailey on page 24 from a descendent. John Lonnquest provided the image of his grandfather on page 48 and the image of the capsized *Granite State* (the former *New Hampshire*) on the following page came from the New York City Municipal Archive. The football posters on page 74 came from the Bentley Historical Library at the University of Michigan and the image of Bear Bryant came from the Bear Bryant Museum at the University of Alabama. Page 75 and 132 images of Samuel Gravely came from the Gravely family via Paul Stillwell. Dr. Philip K. Lundeberg provided the his image on page 77 and the loss on *Frederick C. Davis* on page 82. Rear Admiral F. Neale Smith provided the image of the three officer candidates on page 105 as well as the shot of him visiting the Gulf on page 159. The images of Neil Armstrong came from the University of Cincinnati Libraries and Captain Ted Bronson, USN (Retired) who assembled the model aircraft display case at the Navy Museum. The Naval Historical Foundation provided images of its former president Vice Admiral Dunn on page 153 and of Dr. Lundeberg receiving his lifetime achievement medal on page 197.

CHAPTER AND COVER IMAGES

1. New York Naval Militia Sailor circa 1890. **2.** A Naval Reserve Force manned sub-chaser during World War I. **3.** A Navy N3N-3 trainer at NAS Anacostia, D.C. **4.** Lieutenant Walter T. Flynn, USNR peering from deckhouse of *PC-565* following June 2, 1943 sinking of *U-521* off Eastern seaboard. **5.** An armada of warships laid-up at Boston in the late 1940s. **6.** An Iowa-class battleship fires a broadside during the Korean War. **7.** Soviet Surface to Air Missile launchers on display **8.** Market Time interdiction operations off Vietnam as seen from the guntub of PCF-3. **9.** Three of the first female pilot candidates. **10.** A Battleship-Carrier Battle Group; **11.** An SH-60 Seahawk helicopter. **12.** The camouflage pattern used in contemporary utility uniforms. **FRONT COVER.** Painting by Lieutenant McClelland Barclay, USNR, who received a commission in the Naval Reserve in 1938. Two years later, he reported for active duty. Barclay served on shore duty creating recruiting posters and portraits of senior naval officers. In 1940, at his request, Barclay transferred to sea duty as a Combat Artist. In 1943, his ship, *LST-432*, was torpedoed by the Japanese submarine RO-16 in the Solomon Islands. Barclay and most of the crew perished.

SELECTED BIBLIOGRAPHY

Bigelow, Cdr. Rick; Capt. (Sel) Mel Chaloupka; LCdr. Andy Rockett. *United States Naval Reserve: Chronology* 1992. Newport, RI: United States Naval War College Center for Naval Warfare Studies, 1992

Bureau of Navigation *Naval Reserve Multiple Address and Circular Letters, 1940.* Washington, DC: Naval Reserve Division, Bureau of Navigation, Navy Department, 1941.

Bureau of Navigation *Naval Reserve Multiple Address and Circular Letters, 1941.* Washington, DC: Naval Reserve Division, Bureau of Navigation, Navy Department, 1942.

Davis, John Alexander Jr. *Organization and Administration of Naval Reserve Training.* M.A. Thesis, George Washington University, 1950.

Ford, Christopher, and David Rosenberg. *The Admirals' Advantage: U.S. Operational Intelligence in World War II and the Cold War.* Annapolis, MD: Naval Institute Press, 2005.

Gimblett, Richard H., and Michael L. Hadley; Ed. *Citizen Sailors: Chronicles of Canada's Naval Reserve, 1910-2010.* Toronto, Canada: Dunburn Press, 2010.

Goergen, Daniel F. *The Impetus Behind the Creation of the United States Naval Reserve.* M.A. Thesis, U.S. Army Command and General Staff College, 2005.

Heiser, Wayne H. *U.S. Naval and Marine Corps Reserve Aviation, Vol. I: 1916-1942 Chronology.* Manhattan KS: Sunflower University Press, 1991

Holland, William J. Ed. *The Navy.* Washington DC: Naval Historical Foundation, 2000.

Howarth, Stephen. *The Royal Navy's Reserves in War & Peace: 1903-2003.* South Yorkshire, England: Leo Cooper, 2003.

Isenberg, Michael T. *Shield of the Republic: The United States Navy in an Era of Cold War and Violent Peace, 1945-1962.* New York, NY: St. Martins Press, 1993.

Kreh, William R. *Citizen Sailors: The U.S. Naval Reserve in War and Peace.* New York, NY: David McKay Company, Inc., 1969.

Knox, Commo. Dudley W. *A History of the United States Navy.* New York, NY: G.P. Putnam's Sons, 1948.

Manthorpe, William H.J. Jr. *A Century of Service: The U.S. Navy on Cape Henlopen, Lewes Delaware: 1898-1996.* Wilmington, DE: Cedar Tree Press. 2014.

Marolda, Edward J. and Robert J. Schneller Jr. *Shield and Sword: The United States Navy and the Persian Gulf War.* Washington, DC: Naval Historical Center, 1998.

Potter, Frank Hunter. *The Naval Reserve.* New York, NY: Henry Holt and Company, 1919

Rassano, Geoffrey L. *Hero of the Angry Sky: The World War 1 Diary and Letters of David S. Ingalls, America's First Naval Ace.* Annapolis, MD: Naval Institute Press, 2013.

Shanton, John Lynn. *Citizen Sailors: The Naval Reserve Story.* Self-published, 2006.

Still, William N. Jr. *Crisis at Sea: The United States Navy in European Waters in World War I.* Gainesville, FL: University Press of Florida, 2007.

Watters, Cdr. James E; Cdr. Walt Johanson and Capt. (Sel.) Mel Chaloupka, *U.S. Naval Reserve: The First 75 Years.* Newport, RI: United States Naval War College Center for Naval Warfare Studies, 1992.

Wieland, Harold Thomas. *The History of the Development of the United States Naval Reserve, 1889-1941.* Ph.D. dissertation, University of Pittsburgh, 1953.

Williams, Kathleen Broome. *Grace Hopper: Admiral of the Cyber Sea.* Annapolis, MD: Naval Institute Press. 2004.

Winkler, David F. *Cold War at Sea.* Annapolis, MD: Naval Institute Press. 2000. *Amirs, Admirals & Desert Sailors.* Annapolis, MD: Naval Institute Press, 2007.

Zumwalt, Elmo R. Jr. *On Watch: A Memoir.* New York, NY: Quadrangle Books. 1976.

Note on sources: The introduction was extracted from an End of Tour interview of Vice Admiral Totushek conducted by Naval Reserve Volunteer Training Unit 615R in 2003. Up until 1992, the Naval War College studies served as the fundamental background source documents for the narrative that was strongly enhanced by the Wieland dissertation. William Kreh's book helped to tell the 1960s story. The U.S. Naval Institute Oral History with Vice Admiral Robert F. Dunn conducted by Paul Stillwell and various notes provided by Rear Admiral F. Neale Smith helped flesh out the 1980s. From 1992 to present, the Navy League's annual *Almanac of Seapower*, the Navy Reserve Force's *The Navy Reservist*, Captain Shanton's unpublished *Citizen Sailors*, and surveys conducted with recent Chiefs of Naval Reserve and their Force Master Chiefs were critical for chapters 11 and 12. Of note, *The Navy Reservist*, given the active and reserve component integration, has emerged as the Navy's best overall chronicle of contemporary operations. Thanks to Commander Phil Lundeberg and Master Chief Jeff Covington for being allowed to be interviewed for this book. Special thanks to the Centennial Book Committee and numerous others who provided ideas, images, and snippets.

INDEX

A

A-1 Skyraider aircraft, 125
A-4/A-4U Skyhawk aircraft, 122, 124, 125, 166–67
A-6/A-6E Intruder aircraft, 149, 153
A-7 Corsair aircraft, 143, 186
Abel, Kent M., 82
actors and movie stars, 78, 123
AD-1 Skyraider aircraft, 93
Adenauer, Konrad, 116
Adroit, 164, 169–170
aeroplane branch, 27
Afghanistan
    contributions of reservists in, 188
    Enduring Freedom operation, 140, 179–180, 189
    insurgencies in, 179–180, 184
    Seabee service during war in, 109
    Soviet invasion of, 147, 148
    success of operations in, 182
African Americans
    commissions for women, 79
    enlisted force during Civil War, 14
    first black officer to command a ship, 131
    first black pilot, 101
    Golden Thirteen, 76
    in the Navy, 14
    officer training and duty assignments, 76
    V-12 program enrollment, 75, 76
Agerholm, 142
Agnes, Hurricane, 135
aircraft carriers
    aircraft for, 122
    air wings for, training pilots for, 63
    force strength, 88
    funding for, 90
    introduction of, 48
    Korean War service of, 100, 101, 103
    landing on by Will Rogers, 57
    pilots for, 48
    supercarrier program, 90
Air Defense Command, 111
Air Force, U.S., 89, 90, 108
air stations
    closures, 111
    establishment of, 51, 55, 56
Alabama (battleship), 24
Alabama (*New Hampshire, Granite State*), 19, 49
Allen, Barbara, 133
Allen, Monica, 185
Allen, Walter H., 109
ALNAV 67, 49
Alvarez, Everett, Jr., 125
AM-1 Maulers aircraft, 93
America, 143
Ames, Alan W., 38
Anacostia Naval Reserve Air Station, 111, 141
Anacostia Naval Reserve Aviation Training Unit, 112
Anderson, David, 186
Anderson, George, 116
Andrew, Hurricane, 176
Andrews, Adolphus, 59
Andrews Air Force Base, 111
Antares, 67
Antietam, 103
anti-war movement, 128
Antonio Lopez (Spain), 21
Aphrodite, Operation, 129
Arban (Soviet Union), 127
Arbor, Jesse, 76
Arizona, 25, 81
Arkansas, 70
Armed Forces Reserve Act (1952), 107–8
Armstrong, Neil, 131
Army Specialized Training Program, 73
art, 185
Arthur, Stan, 165
Association of Naval Militias of the United States, 18, 51

Association of the United States Navy (AUSN), 187
Atlanta, 18
Atlantic, Battle of the, 69
atomic weapons, 88, 89
Augmentation Board, 87
Automatic Sequence Controlled Calculator, 79
aviation
    aircraft for, 51, 57, 152–53, 160, 174
    birth of, 27, 38
    budgets and funding for, 56
    contributions of aviators during WW II, 56
    growth of, 57
    officers assigned to, 48
    organization of, 60
    overseas training of squadrons, 110
    pilots, need for, 48
    post–WW II reserve force and infrastructure, 91, 111
    readiness of, 121, 143
    rebuilding of, 51
    recruitment of pilots for WW II, 72
    reorganization of reserve force and, 55–56
    training of aviators, 55–56, 92, 121–22
    WW II casualties, 81
    WW II contributions of naval aviators, 56, 64
    See also Naval Air Reserve, U.S.; Naval Reserve Flying Corps

B

B-52 aircraft, 168
Bailey, Frank J., 24, 33, 51, 53, 56, 59, 77–78, 197
Bakret, E.J., 67
Balkans operations, 176
Baltimore, 18
Baltimore Naval Reserve Training Center, 68
Barbary Wars, 11–12
Barber, Michael C., 126
Barclay, McClelland, 202
Barnes, Phillip, 76
Barnes, Samuel, 76
Barney, 68
Bassett, Frederic B., Jr., 25, 27
Batfish, 136
Battle "E" award, 119
battleships
    "in commission in reserve" status of older ships, 24
    construction program for, 29
    first steel ship, 16
    force strength, 88
    influenza infection rate on, 45
    Korean War service of, 100
    naval militia training on, 24
Baugh, Dalton, 76
Baxter, James P., 54
Bayly, Lewis, 32
Bayne, Marmaduke Gresham "Duke," 87
Beach Jumpers, U.S. Navy, 78
Becuna, 87
Beirut, Lebanon, 150–51, 153
Belmont, August, Jr., 38
Benevolence, 104, 133
Berlin Airlift, 115
Berlin Crisis, 114, 115–16, 119, 120
Berlin Wall, opening of, 159–160
Bernard, John H., 18
Bernsen, Harold J., 158
Biddle, 68
Bigelow, Elmer Charles, 84
Blakely, 68
Blandy, William H.P., 110
Blandy Board (Naval Reserve Evaluation Board), 110, 111, 112
blimp operations, 92
Blue, Victor, 25, 29
Boeing 737 aircraft, 183
Boeing F4B-1 aircraft, 63
Bogart, Humphrey, 36

Bogue, 82
boiler inspections and explosion prevention, 155
Bon Homme Richard, 101
Boomer, Walter E., 164
Boston, 18
Bowen, 150
Bowfin, 136
Boxer, 101
Brannon, 127
Braun, Robin, 187, 195
Breckenridge, 68
Brewer, David, 54
Bridgeton (*Al Rekkah*), 156, 158
Briggs, Zeno E., 51
Bristol, 127
Britain, Battle of, 68
Brown, Jesse L., 101
Brown, Paul, 74
Brown, Wellesley Laud, 38
Brunnett, Chris "Bruno," 196
Bryant, Bear, 74
Buckley, 82
Bunker Hill, 196
Burgess-Dunne Flying Boat, 28
Burke, Arleigh, 112
Burke, Edward R., 70
Burkhart, Agnes, 163
Burlingame, Charles "Chic," 186
Bush, George H.W., 160, 163, 164, 166, 168
Bush, George W., 179, 182, 191
Bush, Robert Eugene, 84
Butler, Mrs. Henry F. (Estelle Kemper), 34
Byrd, Richard E., 51

C

C-2 Greyhound aircraft, 185
C-9/C-9B Skytrain transport aircraft, 152, 153, 168, 174, 176, 183, 194
C-12 Huron aircraft, 194
C-17 aircraft, 177
C-20 Gulfstream aircraft, 194
C-40 Clipper aircraft, 183, 194
C-47 cargo aircraft, 108
C-118 cargo aircraft, 122–23
C-130 Hercules transport aircraft, 174, 176, 194
California, 85
California Naval Militia, 17
Campa, Joe, 193
Cann, Tedford H., 41
Capodanno, Vincent, 126, 129
Carl Vinson, 179
Carney, Robert B., 110
Carrier Air Group 8, 103
Carrier Air Group 15, 103
Carrier Air Group 101, 101
Carrier Air Group 102, 101
Carrier Air Wing 30, 143
Carson, Johnny, 78
Carter, Jimmy, 143–44, 147, 148, 176
Cassady, John H., 101
Cavalla, 136
Chambers, Washington, 27
chaplains, 104, 126, 129, 168
Chappell, Bill, 139, 145
Charbonnet, Pierre N., 139, 141, 143–44, 147
Charleston, 18
Cheney, Richard, 163, 164
Chesapeake, 12
Chicago, 18
Chicago Naval Reserve, 53
Chief of Naval Operations, Office of
    creation of, 25
    naval militia oversight by, 28
    Naval Reserve Policy Division, 60
Chief of Naval Reserve, 137–38, 139
Churchill, Winston, 73
Citizen Sailors (Kreh), 123, 125, 128
Civil Engineer Corps (CEC), 109
Civil Engineering Corps Volunteer Reserve, 109
Civil War, 14–15
Clark, Vern, 9, 184–86, 187, 188, 191
Cleveland, Grover, 17
Clifford, Clark, 122
Clifton Sprague, 152

Coast Guard, U.S.
    Coast Guard Reserve, 139
    coordination of coastal defense with, 156
    tanker wars and reflagging of Kuwaiti ships, 156, 158–59
Cobia, 136
COBOL (COmmon Business-Oriented Language), 132
Cod, 136
Cold War
    Berlin Crisis, 114, 115–16, 119, 120
    contributions of reservists, 151–53, 155–56
    Cuban missile crisis, 116, 127
    Maritime Strategy for, 149, 155
    service of reservists to counter Soviet threat, 127
Cole, 177
college football, 74
Comfort, 163, 194
commerce and trade
    attacks on US commercial vessels, 11
    foreign hulls carrying exported US goods, 15
    overseas trade handled by American-flagged hulls, 13, 15
    tanker wars and reflagging of Kuwaiti ships, 156, 158–59
Connecticut Naval Militia, 17
Consolation, 104
Constellation, 11, 123, 125
Constitution, 156
Continental Navy, 64
Continuum of Service career path, 197–98
convoy and escort system
    tanker wars and reflagging of Kuwaiti ships, 156, 158–59
    WW II role, 75, 81–83
    WW I role, 40, 61
Conway, Edwin Francis, 55
Cooke, Augustus P., 16–17
Cooper, Damon W., 137–38, 139
Cooper, George, 76
Cooper, Jackie, 78
Copeland, Robert W., 77
Coronado, 158
Cotton, John G., 186, 188, 191, 193, 194
Counihan, J.L., 110
Courtney, Charles E., 51
Covington, Jeffrey "Jeff," 9, 145, 155, 160, 164, 170, 176, 177, 180, 182–83, 184, 191, 193–94
Craft of Opportunity (COOP) units, 155–56
Cravelie, 92
Crosby, James, 81, 82
Crosgriff, Kevin, 193
cruisers
    construction program for, 29
    force strength, 88
    influenza infection rate on, 45
    Vietnam War service, 121
Cuba
    refugees from, assistance to, 176
    Soviet missiles in, 116, 127
    Spanish-American War, 20–22, 23, 24, 155
Curtiss biplanes, 27
Cushing, 18

D

Dale, 18
Dallas Naval Air Station, 101
Daniels, Josephus
    letter about commission for Daisy Erd, 35
    naval reserve, support for, 25, 49
    naval reserve legislation, amendments to, 29
    uniform modifications, 31
    value of reserve force, 43
    Victory Medal award ceremony, 34
Davis, John Alexander, 72
Davison, F. Trubee, 38, 57
Davison, Henry P., 38

DC-9 aircraft, 183
Debbink, Dirk, 194–95, 197
De Demagall, A.A., 67
Defense, Department of
    amalgamation of Navy and War Departments into, 89
    budgets and funding for, 143–44, 147–48
    renaming of National Military Establishment as, 107
    Soviet threat and force strength of US military, 142
Deferment Board and discharge and deferment requests, 70
Delaney, John, 58
Denby, Edwin, 49
Denfeld, Louis E., 90, 91, 93
Dental Reserve Corps, 25, 40, 62
Deny Flight, Operation, 176
Deployed Warrior Medical Management Center (DWMMC), 189
Depression-era budgets, 56, 58
Desert Shield/Desert Storm, Operation
    contributions of reservists, 164–170, 174, 175
    deployments during, 9
    mobilization for, 163–68, 174
    parades to welcome returning veterans, 170
    Seabee service during, 109
    start of, 160, 163
destroyer escorts
    Berlin Crisis service of, 115, 119
    Cold War service of, 127
    decommissioned "in-service" status, 112
    decommissioning of, 135
    deteriorating condition of and readiness, 121
    Korean War service of, 100, 119
    Southeast Asia service to combat Communist threat, 119–120
    training aboard, 119
    WW II service of, 81–83, 119
    See also *Frederick C. Davis*
destroyers
    aging ships, replacement of, 152
    Berlin Crisis service of, 115
    Cold War service of, 127
    construction program for, 29
    decommissioning of, 135
    deteriorating condition of and readiness, 121
    Fleet Naval Reserve training vessels, 53
    force strength, 88
    influenza infection rate on, 45
    Southeast Asia service to combat Communist threat, 119–120
    Vietnam War service, 121
Destroyers for Bases Agreement, 69
Dewey, George, 20, 21, 23
disaster-relief and humanitarian assistance, 135, 174, 176, 192, 194
Ditman, Albert J., 38
Dixie, 21
Donovan, Francis R., 170
Douglas, Lewis, 56
Douglas A-4/A-4U Skyhawk aircraft, 122, 124, 125, 166–67
Douglas AD-1 Skyraider aircraft, 93
Douglas C-118 aircraft, 122–23
draft (Selective Service program)
    Civil War draft, 14
    extension of for Korean War, 97
    peacetime draft before WW II, 70
    re-establishment of, 94
    reserve enlistments and exemption from, 94
    Selective Training and Service Act (1940), 70, 72–73
    Vietnam War draft, 120–21
    WW II draft, 72–73
Driver, Randolph S., 127
drug-interdiction operations, 175–76
Drum, 136
Dubuque, 58
Dudley, Bill, 74
Duerk, Alene B., 133

INDEX

Dunn, Robert F., 153
Dunwoody Institute, 36

E

EA-6B Prowler aircraft, 176, 177, 191
Eagle boats, 50, 51, 53
Earle Naval Station, 153
Earnest Will, Operation, 156, 158–59
Edmunds, 119
Edward McDonnell, 142
Eisenhower, Dwight D., 108, 169
Ellicott, J.M., 22
Elmer, Horace, 20, 21
employment
    legal protection of jobs of reservists, 107
    repeated recalls of reservists and job security, 116
Enduring Freedom, Operation, 140, 179–180, 189
English, 91
enrollment card, 29
Enterprise, 63
Enterprise (nuclear-powered aircraft carrier), 121, 137, 179, 196
Epperson, 135
Erben, Henry, 20–21
Erd, Daisy M.P., 35
Essex, 131, 138
Estocin, 152
Eurich, Alvin C., 75
Ewen, Edward, 92
Expeditionary Combat Readiness Command, 191

F

F4B-1 aircraft, 63
F-4/F-4B Phantom fighter aircraft, 127, 143
F4U Corsair aircraft, 101
F-8 Crusader aircraft, 122, 123, 127
F9F/F9F-2/F9F-5 Panther aircraft, 98–99, 101, 103, 131
F-14 Tomcat fighter aircraft, 147, 149, 179
F-15 aircraft, 177
F-16 Fighting Falcon aircraft, 174
F/A-18 Hornet fighter aircraft, 149, 153, 174, 177, 179, 182, 186
Fairbanks, Douglas, Jr., 78
Falgout, 131
Fallon Naval Air Station, 174, 183
Farragut, David, 15
Farwell, John V., 38
Faurot, Don, 74
Fearless, 159
Fearnow, Clay, 159
Fenton, C.W., 67
Ferguson, Mark, 197
FFT program, 171
Finback, 160
Fisher, Kenneth, 176–77
Flagg, Dee, 186
Flagg, Wilson "Bud," 186
Flaherty, 83
Flaherty, Francis Charles, 83, 84
Flanagan, H.P., 67
Fleet Hospital 5, 165
Fleet Hospital 6, 165, 168
Fleet Hospital 15, 165, 168
Fleet Naval Reserve
    characteristics and organization of, 29, 52
    inspection board to determine readiness, 55
    organization of, 53
    pay for officers and enlisted men, 52
    recall of reservists, 151–52
    training of, 53
    training requirements, 52, 59
    transfer to after retirement of Sailors, 51, 59
    WW II mobilization, 68, 70
Fleet Naval Reserve (Aviation), 52
Fleet Reserve Association (FRA), 51
Fleet Weeks, 186
Fletcher, 84
Flexible Response, 115
flying boats, 28
Fonda, Henry, 78

football, 74
Foote, Andrew H., 14
Ford, Gerald R., 120, 138, 143, 160
Ford, Glenn, 123
Ford, Henry, 50
Ford, John, 78
Forrestal, James, 87–88, 89, 90, 91, 107, 108
Forrest Sherman–class destroyer, 120
Fort Dix training facility, 190
Fort Jackson training facility, 190
Fort Worth Naval Air Station Joint Reserve Base, 183
France
    convoy and escort system for supplies for, 40
    naval reserve, report on strength of, 15
    Quasi-War with France, 11, 12
    sea power of, 88
    warship development in, 15
    WW I role, 25
Frank Bailey Boathouse, 197
Franklin, 85, 126
Franklin, William B., 35
Frederick (LST 1184), 171
Frederick C. Davis, 77, 81–83
frigates, 152, 160, 171, 172, 176, 197
Fry, Alfred B., 51
Full-Time Support (FTS) program, 188, 196

G

Gallant, 156
Gallivan, James, 35
Gallo, Salvatore, 163
Game Warden, Operation, 125
Gates, Artemus L., 38
Gearing-class destroyers, 152
Georgia Naval Militia, 17
Gerald R. Ford–class aircraft carriers, 173
Germany
    Battle of Jutland, 30
    Berlin, division of into occupation zones, 115
    Berlin Airlift, 115
    Berlin Crisis, 114, 115–16, 119, 120
    Berlin Wall, opening of, 159–160
    declaration of war against by US, 32, 68
    Poland invasion by, 61, 68
    sea power of, 88
    WW I role, 25
    See also U-boats
GI Bill, 104–5
Glenview Naval Air Station, 92, 101, 138
Global War on Terror, 191
Godt, Eberhard, 81
Goodwin, Reginald, 76
Gorbachev, Mikhail, 159
Gordon, Nathan Green, 84
Gorshkov, Sergei, 110
Gould, Erl C.B., 38
Graham, Otto, 74
Granite State (*New Hampshire, Alabama*), 19, 49
Gravely, 198–99
Gravely, Samuel L., Jr. "Sam," 75, 77, 95, 100, 131–32, 133, 148, 199
Gray, 152
Gray, William B.D., 29
Great Britain
    Battle of Britain, 68
    Battle of Jutland, 30
    convoy and escort system for supplies for, 40
    Q-ship deployment by, 32
    U-boat campaign against, 69
    War of 1812, 12–13
    warship development in, 15
    WW I role, 25
Great Depression, 56, 58
Great Lakes Fleet Hospital, 189
Great Lakes Naval Reserve Air Station, 63
Great Lakes Naval Reserve Readiness Center, 157
Great Lakes Naval Training Station,

33, 109
Great Lakes Recruit Training Center, 36, 75, 76
Great White Fleet, 23
Greenwood, 127
Greer, Howard E., 135
Gruening, D.W., 67
Guantanamo Bay, Cuba, 176
Gulfport Naval Training Camp, 36, 46, 122
gunboats, 12, 14, 45
Guthrie, Wallace, 160, 169, 174
Gygax, Felix, 59, 60

H

Haifa, Israel, 151
Hair, James, 76
Haiti, 174, 176, 194
Hall, Thomas F., 175
Hall, William Edward, 84
Halsey, William, Jr., 81
Halyburton, William David, Jr., 84
Hambleton, Iceal, 129
Hamilton, Thomas J., 74
Hammann, Charles Hazeltine, 40, 41
Hamner, 148
Hancock, Joy Bright, 93
Hancock, Levi, 82, 83
Harding, Warren G., 49
Harry S. Truman, 195
Haven, 104
Hawk (*Hermione*), 24
Hayden, Joseph Ralson, 42
Haynesworth, 91
Hayter, 83
Hayward, Thomas B., 147
Headquarters Construction Companies, 109
Hébert, F. Edward, 127, 137, 138, 143
Hector, 152
Helicopter Combat Support Special Squadron 4, 165, 183
Helicopter Combat Support Special Squadron 5, 165, 183
Helicopter Light Attack Squadron 4, 152–53
Helicopter Light Attack Squadron 5, 152–53
Helldiver aircraft, 64
Hermione (*Hawk*), 24
Herring, Rufus Geddie, 84
Hidalgo, Edward, 145
Hirsch, Elroy, 74
Holbrook, Lee, 180
Holloway, James L., III, 141, 142
Holloway, James L., Jr., 54, 94, 141
Holloway Plan, 94, 131, 141
Hoover, Herbert, 57
Hopper, 161
Hopper, Grace Murray, 79, 113, 132, 133, 141, 156, 161
Horizontal Integration of reservists, 150
Horne, Frederick J., 64
hospital ships, 104, 133, 163, 194
Howarth, Stephen, 79
Hudnet, Thomas, 101
humanitarian and disaster-relief assistance, 135, 174, 176, 192, 194
Hummel, Paul L., 139
Humphrey, Hubert H., 129
Hunchback, 14
Hunt, 115
Hussein, Saddam, 163, 164, 171, 174, 184
Hutchins, Johnnie David, 84

I

Illinois, 19
Illinois (*Prairie State*), 70
Illinois Naval Militia, 17, 28, 33
Impervious, 164, 169–170
Inchon, 171, 173
Individual Augmentee (IA) program, 191
Individual Ready Reserve, 141, 169
influenza pandemic, 45–46
Information Dominance Corps (IDC), 140
Ingalls, David S., 38, 39, 40, 57, 78
Ingram, Jonas, 81–82

Innovative Naval Reserve Concept, 171
Inshore Undersea Warfare Group TWO, 176
Insurgente (France), 11
intelligence operations
    Cold War and Soviet operations, 127
    contributions of reservists, 62, 140, 143, 177
    Desert Shield/Desert Storm operations, 169
    post–WW II force strength, 92
International Naval Review, 173
Iowa, 100, 101, 151
Iran
    embassy hostage crisis in, 147, 148
    revolution in, 147
Iran-Iraq War, 156, 158–59
Iraq
    contributions of reservists in, 188, 191, 193
    insurgencies in, 184
    invasion of Kuwait by, 160, 163
    Iraqi Freedom operation, 140, 182–84, 189
    no-fly zone over, 174
    Seabee service in, 109, 188
Iron Curtain, 115

J

Jacksonville Naval Reserve Training Unit, 110
Janczak, Martin E., 176
Japan
    attack on Japanese sub by crew of *Ward*, 67, 68
    bombing of Hiroshima and Nagasaki, 88
    sea power of, 88
    surrender of and end of WW II, 83, 89
Jefferson, Thomas, 11–12
jet aircraft, 101
John F. Kennedy, 171, 173
John F. Kennedy (*Gerald R. Ford*–class aircraft carrier), 173
Johnson, Jay, 64, 176
Johnson, John B., 136
Johnson, Lance, 151
Johnson, Louis, 90
Johnson, Lyndon B., 120, 121, 122, 125, 127
Johnson, Richard P., 137
Joint Reserve Intelligence Centers (JRICs), 140
Jonas Ingram, 142
Jones, Herbert Charpiot, 85
Joseph P. Kennedy Jr., 129
Jouett, 131–32
Juneau, 83
Jupiter (*Langley*), 48, 57
Just, Paul, 82, 83
Just Cause, Operation, 160
Justice, Charlie, 74
Jutland, Battle of, 30

K

Katrina, Hurricane, 192
Kearsarge, 24
Kelly, Gene, 78
Kelso, Frank B., 160
Kemper, Estelle (Mrs. Henry F. Butler), 34
Kempf, Cecil J., 153, 158
Kennedy, Caroline, 173
Kennedy, Edward, 129
Kennedy, Eunice, 129
Kennedy, Jean, 129
Kennedy, John F.
    aircraft carriers named for, 171, 173
    assassination of, 120
    Berlin Crisis, 115–16, 119
    moon challenge by, 113, 115, 131
    readiness statement by, 198
    WW II service of, 112, 115
Kennedy, Joseph P., Jr, 129
Kennedy, Joseph P., Sr., 129

Kennedy, Pat, 129
Kennedy, Robert F. "Bobby," 128–29
Kennedy, Rose P., 129
Kent State University, 128
Kerrey, Joseph Robert, 129
Khobar Towers truck bomb attack, 177
Khrushchev, Nikita, 110, 116
Kimmel, Husband, 72
King, Ernest J., 58, 63, 81, 90
King, Martin Luther, Jr., 128
Knapp, R.H., 67
Knox, Dudley W., 23, 40, 46, 197
Knox, Frank, 68, 70
Knox-class frigates, 152, 171
Korean War
    amphibious attack and minesweeping operations, 112
    awards and honors earned during, 101
    Blue Beach landing, 102
    coalition military response to, 97
    combat support services, 103–4
    cost of, 108
    experience of reservists for, 105, 107
    naval aviation role in, 101, 103, 110
    officers for, 104–5, 108
    recall of reservists for, 97, 100, 105, 107
    recommissioning of ships for, 97, 100
    recruitment for, 95
    Seabee service during, 103–4, 109
    start of, 97
    truce and end of combat, 108
    weather and flight operations, 101
Korn, Bertram W., 126
Kreh, William R., 123, 125, 128
Kreitz, Jon, 196
Krissoff, Nathan, 191
Krissoff, William, 191
Kuwait
    Iraqi invasion of, 160, 163
    tanker wars and reflagging of Kuwaiti ships, 156, 158–59

L

LaBarge, Charles L., 108
Laird, Melvin R., 120, 135
Lake Erie, Ballet of, 13
Lake St. John, 127
landing ship medium (rocket) (LSM[R]s), 125
landing ship tanks (LSTs), 102, 171
Landstuhl Regional Medical Center (LRMC), 189
Langley (*Jupiter*), 48, 57
LaSalle, 163
Lasch, K.C.J., 67
Latimer, Julian, 51, 52
LCI(G)-449, 84
LCS (Littoral Combat Ship), 12, 197
Leahy, William D., 62, 81
Lear, Charles, 76
LeBreton, David W., 77
Lehman, John F., Jr., 148–150, 152, 153, 158
Lemmon, Jack, 78
Lend-Lease Act, 69
Leopard (Great Britain), 12
Less, Anthony, 158
Lester, Fred Faulkner, 85
letters of marque, 12–13, 14
Leviathan, 36
Lexington, 48, 63
Leyte, 100, 101
Leyte Gulf, Battle of, 77
Liberia, 174
Ling, 136
Lionfish, 136
Littoral Combat Ship (LCS), 12, 197
Long, John D., 21
Lonnquest, Theodore C., 48
Louisiana Naval Militia, 17
Lovett, Robert A., 38
LSM(R)s (landing ship medium [rocket]), 125

INDEX

LST-375, 85
LST-473, 84
LST 1184 (*Frederick*), 171
LSTs (landing ship tanks), 102
Luce, Stephen B., 15
Ludlow, George, 40, 41
Lujack, Johnny, 74
Lundeberg, Philip K. "Phil," 77, 82–83, 95, 197
Lusitania (Great Britain), 27, 32

M

Maas, Melvin J., 58, 59, 60, 63, 79
Mabus, Ray, 173
MacArthur, Douglas, 97, 100, 103
MacKenzie, John, 41
Macklin, Charles F., 51
Maddox, 123
Madison, James, 12
Madison, James Jonas, 41
Magic Carpet, Operation, 89
Mahan, Alfred Thayer, 15, 17, 21
Maine, 20
Manpower and Reserve Affairs, Assistant Secretary of the Navy for, 127, 141
Marine Corps Reserve, U.S., 29
Maritime Defense Zone, 155–56
Maritime Strategy, 149, 155
Market Time, Operation, 125
Marshall, George C., 97, 107
Marshall Plan, 97
Martin, Graham, 76
Martin, Harold M., 103
Martin AM-1 Mauler aircraft, 93
Maryland Naval Militia, 17
Mary Luckenbach, 104
Massachusetts Institute of Technology, 36
Massachusetts Naval Militia of Volunteers, 17, 18–19
Matthews, Francis, 90
Mauz, Henry H., Jr., 163
Mayport Naval Station, 171, 173
McAdoo, William, 19
McAfee, Mildred H., 79, 93
McCullen, Joseph T., Jr., 141
McCulloch, Dave, 38
McGinty, 119
McKean, 148
McKinley, William, 21
McNamara, Robert S., 116, 119, 120, 121, 122
McNary, Kathleen L., 133
McQuiston, Irving M., 62–63
McWhorter, John, 82
medical and hospital facilities
    Desert Shield/Desert Storm operations, 163, 164, 165, 168
    Fleet Hospitals, 165, 168, 189
    hospital ships, 104, 133, 163, 194
    Korean War operations, 104
    Landstuhl Regional Medical Center (LRMC), 189
medical personnel
    concerns about resignation of, 171
    flexible drill rules and contributions of, 175
    Iraqi Freedom operation, 184
    recruitment of, 191
medical units
    Medical Corps Volunteer Reserve, 55
    Medical Reserve Corps, 25, 40, 41
    Naval Reserve Medical Corps, 61–62
    Navy Expeditionary Medical Units (NEMUs), 189
Medicine and Surgery, Bureau of, 61–62
Memphis Naval Air Station, 101
merchant marine
    government support to strengthen, 16–17
    impact of Civil War on, 15
    letters of marque, 12–13, 14
    overseas trade handled by, 13, 15
    pool of seamen from during time

of war, 12, 13, 14, 15, 16–17, 25, 35
    training of seamen, 15
Merchant Marine Naval Reserve
    budgets and funding for, 55, 62
    characteristics and organization of, 52, 59
    Depression-era budgets, 58
    flag of, 55
    implementation of, 55
    recruitment for, 55, 62
    WW II mobilization, 69–70
Merchant Marine Training Center, 61
Mercy, 163
Mero, Everett B., 18
Meyerkord, Harold D., 125
Miami, 14
Michener, James A., 184
Michigan Naval Militia, 17, 21, 23
Midway, Battle of, 64
MiG-15 fighter aircraft, 103
Militia Act (1792), 11, 14
militias
    Civil War and, 14
    exemption of seamen from land militias, 12
    legislation to establish, 11
    naval militia for national emergencies, 11
    See also naval militias
Miller, 115
Miller, Jacob W., 16, 17, 22
Minerd, Bob, 82
mine warfare, minesweeping, and mine-countermeasure operations
    coastal defense mission, 155–56
    Desert Shield/Desert Storm operations, 164, 169–170
    Iran-Iraq War operations, 156, 158–59
    Korean War operations, 112
    vessels for, 171, 173
    WW I operations, 43
Minnesota, 18
Missouri, 100, 101, 169
Mitchell, Clarence J. "C.J.," 196
Mitscher, 196
Mobile Diving and Salvage Unit 813 (MDSU-813), 157
Mobile Inshore Undersea Warfare Unit 103 (MIUWU 103), 164
Mobile Inshore Undersea Warfare Unit 105 (MIUWU 105), 164
Mobile Inshore Undersea Warfare Unit 112 (MIUWU 112), 160, 164, 177
Mobile Inshore Undersea Warfare Unit 202 (MIUWU 202), 164
Mobile Inshore Undersea Warfare Unit 203 (MIUWU 203), 176
Mobile Inshore Undersea Warfare Unit 206 (MIUWU 206), 176
Mobley, Tom, 186, 187
Moffett, William, 57, 62
Monia, Charles S., 125
Monitor, 15
Monterey, 138
moon land and the space race, 113, 115, 131
Moorer, Thomas H., 121
Morison, Samuel Eliot, 78, 95, 184
Motley, Marion, 74
movie stars, 78, 123
Murphy, Tim, 187

N

N2S trainer aircraft, 101
Nassau, 196
National Military Establishment, 107
National Naval Volunteers, 30
    amalgamation of Naval Reserve Force and, 37, 40
    deployment of, 32, 33
    force strength of, 33
    status of compared to Naval Reserve Force, 37, 40
    training of, 30, 33
Nautilus, 110
Naval Academy, U.S.
    commissioned officers from for fleet, 48

elitism among graduates, 87, 88
    expansion of, proposal for, 52
    legislation to abolish, 60
    NROTC program compared to, 54
    training and orientation programs at, 33, 36, 40, 62
Naval Affairs Committee, 25
Naval Air Reserve, U.S.
    aircraft for, 92, 93, 121–22, 160, 174
    anti-submarine operations, 110–12, 135
    birth of, 38
    budgets and funding for, 121
    force strength of, 160
    Korean War service of, 101, 103, 110
    post–WW II reserve force and infrastructure, 92, 93
    Pueblo seizure, response to, 121–22, 183
    readiness of, 113, 121–22
Naval Air Reserve Intelligence Unit 861, 123
Naval and Marine Corps Reserve Act, 107
Naval Auxiliary Reserve, 29
Naval Aviation Cadet program, 62–64, 87
Naval Aviation College Program, 131
Naval Aviation Personnel Act (1940), 64
Naval Aviation Reserve Act (1938), 64
Naval Coastal Warfare Group ONE, 180, 193
Naval Coastal Warfare Squadron 30, 193
Naval Coast Defense Reserve
    characteristics and organization of, 29
    recruitment of women, 31–32
Naval Combat Documentation Detachment 206, 184
Naval Enlisted Reserve Association, 108, 110, 145
Naval Institute, U.S.
    first meeting of, 15
    maritime education role of, 15
    Proceedings from annual meetings, 15
Naval Intelligence, Office of (ONI), 140
    foreign naval reserve organizations, study of, 16
    French naval reserve, report on, 15
Naval Militia, Division of, 25
Naval Militia, Office of, 24, 25
Naval Militia Act, 25
Naval Militia Affairs, Division of, 28
Naval Militia Association, 19, 25, 37, 40
Naval Militiaman's Guide (Bernard), 18
Naval Militiamen's Handbook (Slayton), 18
naval militias
    aeronautical reserve, establishment of, 27–28
    aircraft loan program, 28
    duties and mission of, 17–20, 179, 181
    eligibility requirements, 12
    federal control over, 30, 33, 181
    force strength of, 19, 23–24
    funding for, 18, 24, 25
    future of, 181
    growth of, 23–24
    legislation to establish, 11, 12, 25
    organization of, 18
    retention of by states, 91, 181
    role in national reserve force, 22–25, 181
    skills of men in, 19
    social position of enlisted men, 18–19
    Spanish-American War role, 20–22
    state-based system for, 17–19
    supervision of state militias, 25

training of, 12, 18, 19, 24, 25
    training of, compensation for, 25
    value of during Spanish-American War, 22
    White Squadron training cruise, 18
Naval Mobile Construction Battalions 74, 165
Naval Preparedness Act, 29, 30, 31–32
Naval Railway Battery, U.S., 42
naval reserve
    centralized armed force, opposition to, 17
    during Civil War, 14
    former Sailors as reserve force, 25, 29
    importance of during time of war, 15
    legislation to establish, 15–17, 19, 22–23
    national reserve force, need for, 22–23
    organization of, 16
    role in naval militias, 22–25, 181
Naval Reserve, U.S.
    branding and name change of, 187
    budgets and funding for, 52, 56, 58, 91, 139, 141, 143–44, 145, 147–48, 150–51
    career advancements, 131–34
    classes of reservists, 52, 59, 90
    Depression-era budgets, 56, 58
    flexible drill rules, 175
    force strength of, 91, 147–48, 160
    identification cards, 89
    inspection board to determine readiness, 55
    interwar year training and preparedness, 60–64
    leadership structure of, 137–38
    legislation to reform policies, funding , and organization, 58–59
    mission of, 110, 135–37, 139, 151, 155–56, 171, 174–77
    morale in, 60
    morale of regular Sailors about working with reservists, 153
    organization of, 60
    pay for officers and enlisted men, 52
    poster for, 134
    post–Korean War officer terminations, 108
    post–Korean War reorganization, 110, 111
    post–WW II reserve force and infrastructure, 90–95
    post–WW II training, 91–92
    ratio of regular Sailors to reservists, 79, 150
    readiness of, 112–13, 121, 142–43
    recall of reservists, 68, 97, 100, 105, 107, 116, 142, 151, 174, 179–180
    recruitment for, 135, 155
    reduction in force strength, 138–39, 141–42, 144, 175
    reorganization of reserve force as, 51–52
    reorganization under Naval Reserve Training Command, 111–12
    selection board and promotion examination procedures, 53
    Soviet threat and force strength of, 142
    training of, 95, 148, 174, 175
    training requirements, 52
    value of to the Navy, 153
    War Powers Resolution and recall of reservists, 142
    See also Navy Reserve, U.S.
Naval Reserve Act (1925), 51–52, 55, 64
Naval Reserve Act (1938)
    amendment to establish WAVES program, 79
    classes of reservists, 59, 90

passage of, 59
    provisions of, 59–60, 61, 62, 64, 181
Naval Reserve Advisory Board, 58
Naval Reserve Appropriations Act, 38
Naval Reserve Association
    formation of, 18, 108
    minesweeping capabilities of reservists, support for, 155
    name change of, 187
    purpose and mission of, 108, 110
    readiness and the deteriorating condition of equipment, opinions about, 121
    reduction in reserve force, opinions about, 138, 139, 141, 143
    TAR program, opinions about, 145
Naval Reserve Bulletin, 55
Naval Reserve Emergency Communications Van, 94
Naval Reserve Evaluation Board (Blandy Board), 110, 111, 112
Naval Reserve Flying Corps
    characteristics and organization of, 29
    commissions for officers in, 48, 49
    number of aviators trained through, 37
    training of, 36–37
    WW I role, 38
Naval Reserve Force, U.S.
    amalgamation of National Naval Volunteers and, 37, 40
    appeal for men for cruise to Europe, 49
    budgets and funding for, 49, 51, 55
    classes of reservists, 29, 52, 55
    commissions for officers in, 49
    creation of, 29–30
    drill requirements, 48
    force strength of, 32, 37, 43
    rank and precedence of recalled officers, 37
    readiness of, 55
    reorganization of, 49, 51
    retainer pay for, 48, 51
    status of compared to National Naval Volunteers, 37, 40
    training of, 35–37, 40, 48, 51
    transfer of reservists to Voluntary Naval Reserve, 49
    value of to Navy, 43, 51
    WW I role, 32–43, 105
    WW I uniforms, 30–31
Naval Reserve Medical Corps, 61–62
Naval Reserve Officers Association (NROA)
    Depression-era budgets, 56, 58
    legislation to reform policies, funding , and organization, 58–59
    merger with RONS, 108
    naval reserve legislation, opinions about, 51, 60
    organization of, 51
Naval Reserve Officer Training Corps (NROTC)
    anti-war movement and protests against, 128
    changes in program, 54
    expansion of, 94
    father of, 54
    implementation of program, 52, 54
    legislation to establish, 52, 54, 64
    Nurse Corps option, 54
    societal changes and changes to program, 54
    source of naval officers through, 60, 70, 72, 73, 77
    stipends for students in, 52, 54
    success of program, 54
    V-7 program, 70, 72, 73, 74, 77
    women enrollment in, 54
Naval Reserve Personnel Center, 138
Naval Reserve Policy Board, 59
Naval Reserve Policy Division, 60

INDEX

Naval Reserve Readiness Centers, 148, 157, 163, 174, 175

Naval Reserve Recruiting Command, 155

Naval Reserve Surface Warfare Officers course, 152

Naval Reserve Training Command, 111

Naval Surface Reserve force, 160, 171

Naval War College, 15, 17, 22

Navigation, Bureau of
  Deferment Board, 70
  Division of Naval Militias, 25
  Naval Reserve Affairs meeting, 58
  Naval Reserve Division director, 59
  Naval Reserve Force Division, 46
  Office of Naval Militias, 24
  recruitment of women by, 31
  Regulations Governing the Organization and Administration of the Naval Reserve Force, 48
  replacement of by Bureau of Personnel, 90
  selection board and promotion examination procedures, 53, 55

Navy, U.S.
  aircraft for, increase in, 149
  all-volunteer force, 133
  augmentation of reservists following WW II, 87–88
  budgets and funding for, 56, 58, 89–90, 91, 150–51
  commissions for reserve force officers, 49
  cultural barriers between reservists and regular Sailors, removal of, 186–88
  Depression-era budgets, 56, 58
  draft inductees for WW II, 73
  force strength of, 12, 22, 33, 43, 88
  Great White Fleet power-projection and diplomacy cruise, 23
  mission of, 151
  morale about working with reservists, 153
  pay for crew during Civil War, 14
  peacetime diplomacy role of, 23
  post–WW II budgets, 89–90
  professionalism of, 149
  ratio of reservists to regular Sailors, 79, 150
  readiness of, 144–45, 149
  realignment of organization and infrastructure, 184–88
  recruitment for, 193–94
  Soviet threat and force strength of, 142
  transfer between active and reserve components, 193–94, 197–98
  two-ocean Navy, creation of, 69
  value of reserve force to, 43, 51, 153
  volunteer enlistments for WW II, 73
  years since establishment of, 9

Navy Expeditionary Combat Command, 191

Navy Expeditionary Medical Units (NEMUs), 189

Navy Installations Command, 188

Navy League of the United States, 18

Navy Operational Support Centers, 175, 191

Navy Reserve, U.S.
  branding and name change of Naval Reserve, 187
  centennial anniversary of, 9, 181
  contributions of reservists, 188, 191–98
  cultural barriers between regular Sailors and reservists, removal of, 186–88
  events and activities leading to establishment of, 11–25
  evolution of, 194–95
  father of, 11
  force strength of, 194
  former Sailors as reserve force, 25, 29
  legislation to establish, 25
  mission statement, 195
  mobilization for Global War on Terror, 191
  morale of reservists, 193
  motto of, 194
  readiness of, 198
  tradition of service of, 9
  transfer between active and reserve components, 193–94, 197–98
  uniqueness of and recruitment efforts, 192
  See also Naval Reserve, U.S.

Navy Reserve Readiness Command, 188

Navy's Total Force Vision for the 21st Century, 197

Nebraska, 24, 33, 51

Nelson, Dennis, 76

Netherlands, 88

Neuffer, Judith A., 133

Nevada, 77

Newberry, Truman H., 23

New Dawn, Operation, 189

New Hampshire (Alabama, Granite State), 19, 49

New Hampshire (battleship), 19

New Jersey, 24, 101, 150–51

New Jersey Naval Militia, 17, 181

New Look national security strategy, 108

Newport-class tank landing ships, 171

New York, 70, 196

New York Naval Militia, 17, 19, 21–22, 23, 24, 28, 32, 181

Nguyen Van Kiet, 129

Nichols, Neil E., 58

Nimitz, Chester W., 70, 72, 81, 90, 117

Nitze, Paul, 123

Nixon, Richard M.
  divided nation during administration of, 131
  election of, 129
  investigation of administration, 139
  Naval Reserve service of, 108, 120
  postal worker strike, 135
  resignation of, 138
  Rumsfeld appointment under, 141
  War Powers Resolution passage under, 139
  Zumwalt appointment under, 133

Noble Eagle, Operation, 140

Noble Star, 164

Nolde, R.B., 67

Noriega, Manuel, 160

Norris, Thomas R., 129

North Atlantic Treaty Organization (NATO), 97

North Carolina Naval Militia, 17

Northern Pacific, 51

North Korea
  Pueblo seizure by and US response to, 121–22, 183
  threat to South Korea, 174
  See also Korean War

O

Obama, Barrack, 197

O'Brien, Clifford Gregory, 83

O'Callahan, 142

O'Callahan, Joseph Timothy, 85, 126, 142

Officer Candidate School (OCS), 104–5

Ohio Naval Militia, 24

Okean 75 exercise, 144

Oklahoma, 83, 84

Olathe Naval Air Station, 101

Oliver Hazard Perry–class frigate, 152, 171, 172

One Navy concept, 135–37, 177, 188

Organized Reserves
  characteristics and organization of, 59
  intelligence operations by, 92
  post–WW II reserve force and infrastructure, 91, 95–96
  Seabees in, 109
  WW II mobilization, 68

Oriskany, 103

Osprey-class mine hunters, 171

Outerbridge, William W., 67

P

P-2/P2V-3 Neptune aircraft, 110, 127

P-3/P-3C Orion aircraft, 153, 171, 174, 175, 176

Paick, J.A., 67

Pakanowski, Eugene, 82

Palm, Ronnie Joe, Jr., 173

Palmer, Frederick F., 147, 153

Palmer, Jean, 93

Palmer, Leigh C., 36

Pampanito, 136

Panama and the Panama Canal, 160

Parle, John Joseph, 85

Passaic, 19

patrol boat riverine (PBRs), 125

Patten, Thomas, 108

Paul Foster, 168

PC-1264, 75

Pelham Bay Naval Training Station, 33, 35, 46

Pennington, David, 186, 191, 193

Pennsylvania, 25

Pennsylvania Naval Militia, 17

Pensacola
  flight training at, 64
  Pensacola Naval Air Station, 131, 171, 173

Pentagon, attack on, 9, 179–180, 186

Pepper, George, 52

Perrault, R.A., 155

Perry, Oliver Hazard, 13

Personnel, Bureau of, 90, 97, 133, 177

Petrel, 18

Petty, Orlando Henderson, 41

Philadelphia, 18

Philippines, 23

Philippine Sea, 100, 138

Pierce, Henry Clay, 46

Pierce, Samuel S., 28

Pittsburgh Navy Operational Support Center, 187

Plunkett, Charles P., 42

Poe, Larry L., 177

Pohlman, Dianna, 126

Poland, 61, 68

Pontiac Naval Reserve Training Center, 103

postal worker strike, 135

Pottenger, Carol, 196

Powell, Colin, 176

Prairie, 21, 24

Prairie State (Illinois), 70

Preston, Arthur Murray, 85

Princeton, 100, 101

PT-109, 112, 115, 173

PT-363, 85

PT-489, 85

Pueblo, 121–22, 183

Purple Heart, 31

Q

Q-ships, 27

Quasi-War with France, 11, 12

Quigley, Robin, 132, 133

R

radio operations
  Korean War operations, 100
  training radiomen, 92
  Volunteer Communications Reserve, 55, 60, 61

Ramage, James D., 137

Ranger, 143

Ready Reserves
  categories of, 107
  circumstances for recall of, 107
  creation of, 107
  Desert Storm, mobilization for, 168
  force strength of, 110
  training requirements, 107, 110
  2x6 program, 110

Reagan, John, 76

Reagan, Ronald, 148, 149, 150, 151, 156, 158, 159, 160

recruitment posters, 31, 32, 69, 71, 95, 112

Al Rekkah (Bridgeton), 156, 158

religious program specialists (RPs), 126, 168

Remy, 115

Repose, 104

Requin, 136

Reserve Forces Act (1955), 110

Reserve Forces Bill of Rights and Vitalization Act (1967), 127

Reserve Forces Command, 186

Reserve Naval Mobile Construction Battalions 12, 122

Reserve Naval Mobile Construction Battalions 22, 122

Reserve Naval Mobile Construction Battalions 24, 164–65

Reserve Naval Mobile Construction Battalions 74, 164–65

Reserve Officers Association (ROA), 108, 136, 138, 139, 141

Reserve Officers of the Naval Service (RONS), 108

Reserve Officers of the Naval Service-Naval Reserve Officers Association (RONS-NROA), 108

Reserve Policy Board, 59

Reynard, Elizabeth, 79

RH-35D Sea Stallion helicopters, 156

Rhode Island Naval Militia, 17, 19

Richard E. Kraus, 142

Ridgway, Matthew, 103

Robeson, George M., 15

Robinson, 115

Rodgers, J.L., 42

Roger, Will, 57

Roosevelt, Eleanor, 79

Roosevelt, Franklin D.
  aviation cadet program, approval for, 63
  death of and support for Navy, 88
  Depression-era budgets, 56, 58
  loss of university generation, programs to avoid, 73
  national emergency declaration, 61, 68, 70
  naval reserve, support for creation of, 25
  NROTC legislation, 52
  value of reserve force to Navy, 51

Roosevelt, Theodore, 19, 20, 22, 23, 49

Roper, John, 107

Rosenberg, David A., 184

Roughead, Gary, 194, 197

Royal Navy, 12, 79, 88, 110

Royal Navy Volunteer Reserve, 27, 79

Rumsfeld, Donald H., 139, 141, 179

Russell, Richard, 116

Russia, WW I role of, 25

Rutter, L.R., 56

Rwanda, 174

S

S-2/S2F Tracker aircraft, 110, 127, 141

Sailors/seamen
  education and training of, 15
  former Sailors as reserve force, 25, 29
  maritime education infrastructure, legislation to support, 15
  pay rates during Civil War, 14
  pool of from merchant marine during time of war, 12, 13, 14, 15, 16–17, 25, 35
  retirement options for, 51
  skills of merchant marine and naval militia, 12

Saint Louis, 21–22

Saint Louis Naval Reserve Readiness Center, 148, 163

Saint Paul, 100

Saint Paul Naval Reserve Training Center, 68

Sampson, 30

Samuel B. Roberts, 77

San Diego Naval Air Station, 101

San Diego Naval Training Camp, 46

Sandy, Superstorm, 192

San Francisco Naval Training Station, 45, 46

San Jacinto, 160

Sarasota, 48

Sather, Richard C., 125

Satterlee, Herbert L., 18, 22

SC-144, 53

Schlesinger, James, 135–36

Schwarzkopf, Norman, 163, 164, 169

scout cruisers, 29

Seabees
  Afghanistan War service of, 109
  Desert Shield/Desert Storm service of, 109, 164–65, 168–69
  disaster-relief and humanitarian assistance, 176, 194
  importance of contributions of, 109
  Iraq War service of, 109, 188
  Japanese surrender, celebration of, 83
  Korean War service of, 103–4, 109
  mission and role of, 109
  post–WW II force strength, 92, 109
  recruitment for Maritime Strategy, 155
  Vietnam service of, 109, 122
  WW II service of, 109
  WW I service of, 109

Sea Dragon, Operation, 125

sea power
  decline in, 15
  of Navy compared to navies of other countries, 88
  resolution reaffirming sea power role in national defense, 89
  Soviet sea power, 88, 144
  technology and, 15

Seattle (Washington), 61

Selected Reservists (SelRes)
  benefits for, 148
  Berlin Crisis service of, 115–16, 119, 120
  characteristics and organization of, 112
  Cold War recalls and force strength of, 116
  Desert Shield/Desert Storm recalls, 163–68
  force strength of, 135, 142, 150
  readiness of, 112–13, 121, 142–43
  recall of, 151
  recruitment for, 135
  reduction in force strength, 138–39, 141–42, 144, 147
  Southeast Asia service to combat Communist threat, 119–120
  War Powers Resolution and recall of, 142

Selective Service program. See draft (Selective Service program)

Selective Training and Service Act (1940), 70, 72–73, 97

September 11 attacks
  homeland defense in response to, 179–181
  mobilization of reservists after, 109
  naval intelligence operations following, 140
  naval militia response during, 181
  Pentagon, attack on, 9, 179–180, 186
  World Trade Center, attack on, 9, 181

Sherman, Forrest P., 101

ships
  aging ships, replacement of, 148, 150
  construction program for, 29, 69
  decommissioning of, 144
  development of by Britain and France, 15
  expansion of fleet size, 149, 150
  Fleet Naval Reserve training vessels, 53
  force strength, 88, 160
  influenza infection rates on, 45–46
  modern ships for reservists, 152
  recommissioning of, 97, 100, 150–51
  steel navy, funding for, 16
  suicide attacks against, 177
  warships, 173
  White Squadron training cruise, 18
  See also specific types of ships
Sides, 158–59
Silversides, 136
Sims, William S., 32, 38, 40
simulator training, 148
Skelton, Ike, 160
Skiles, Jane M., 133
Slayton, William, 18
Smedberg, William R., III, 116
Smith, F. Neale, 158–59, 187
Solarium, Project, 97
Soley, James Russell, 14, 15, 17
Soley, John Codman, 15, 17, 18–19
sonar buoys, 153
Sorenson, Larry, 159
Sousa, John Philip, 33
South Carolina Naval Militia, 17
Southeast Asia
  active forces for service in, 116
  Communist threat in and role of reservists in, 116, 119–125
  withdrawal of troops from, 133, 135
South Weymouth air base, 111
Soviet Union
  Afghanistan invasion by, 147, 148
  Berlin Crisis and occupation of Berlin, 114, 115–16, 119, 120
  collapse of, 171
  competition for influence between US and, 97
  Cuban missile crisis, 116, 127
  expansion of navy of, 127, 144
  sea power of, 88, 144
  Sputnik launch and race to space, 113
  submarine fleet of, 110, 111, 112, 171
  threat from, growth of, 92
  threat from and force strength of US military, 142
space race and the moon landing, 113, 115, 131
Spanish-American War, 20–22, 23, 24, 155
Spanish influenza pandemic, 45–46
Spears, John, 21
Spears, William O., 59
Spearhead, 198
Spruance, Raymond, 81
Squantum Naval Reserve Air Station, 51, 111
Standby Reserves, 107
Standley, William, 59
Stark, 156
Staunton, Sidney A., 15, 17
Stearman N2S trainer aircraft, 101
Stennis, John, 115
Stephen W. Groves, 196
Stockton, Charles H., 22
Stone, Ellery W., 108
Stratton, Samuel, 141
Sturtevant, Albert D., 38
Sub Chaser 103, 53
Sublett, Frank, 76
submarines
  construction program for, 29
  force strength, 88
  influenza infection rate on, 45
  museum ships, 136, 137
  Soviet submarine fleet, 110, 111, 112, 171
  training on, 92, 136–37

submarine warfare
  anti-submarine operations, 110–12, 135
  anti-submarine vessels, 50
  reduction in ASW capabilities, 171
  reserve ASW capabilities, 171
  WW I, 27, 32, 40, 41, 43
  WW II anti-submarine operations, 69, 77, 81–83
Sullivan, Daniel Augustus Joseph, 41
Sullivan brothers, 83
Super Servant III (Netherlands), 164
Supply Corps Reserve, 92
Surface Reserve Division, 92, 160, 171
Surface Warfare Officers course, 152
Suribachi, 153
Sutton, Robert, 163, 164
Swanson, Claude, 52, 56
Swift, Operation, 126
Swift Boats, 125

T
T-5 Tiger II aircraft, 174
T-44 aircraft, 195
Taiwan, 174
tanker wars (Iran-Iraq War), 156, 158–59
TAR (Training and Administration of Reserves) program, 144–45, 148, 151, 152, 155–56, 188, 196
Task Force History, 184
Tatum, Jim, 74
Taussig, 131
Taussig, Joseph, 30, 32, 33
Taylor, Robert, 78
Teardrop, Operation, 77, 81–83
technology
  contributions of Hopper to advancements in, 79, 113, 132
  readiness and, 113
  sea power and, 15
Tenadores, 51
Tet Offensive, 121, 122
Texas, 16
The Bluejacket's Manual, 18
The First 90 Days (Watkins), 194
The Influence of Sea Power on History (Mahan), 17
The Navy Reservist, 194
Theodore E. Chandler, 131
Theodore Roosevelt, 176, 182, 183
Thomas, Charles, 110
Thompson, J. Stanton, 160, 164, 176
Ticonderoga (aircraft carrier), 123, 125, 137
Ticonderoga (steamship), 40, 41
Toledo, 100
"Top Gun," 149
Top Gun pilot training program, 152–53
Torsk, 136
Total Force Policy, 135–37, 142, 143–44, 145, 147, 177
Totushek, Jan, 9
Totushek, John B., 9, 177, 179, 182, 184, 186
Tower, John, 137
Tracy, Benjamin, 17, 19
Training and Administration of Reserves (TAR) program, 144–45, 148, 151, 152, 155–56, 188, 196
Tripoli, 11–12
Triumph, 97
Truman, Harry S., 88, 89, 90, 91, 93, 94
Truxtun, Thomas, 11
Tu-95 Bear patrol aircraft, 127, 147
Turner Joy, 123, 125
2x6 program, 110
two-time losers, 107, 120

U
U-boats
  Eagle boat sinking by, 50
  sinking of *Lusitania* by, 27
  threat from during WW I, 32, 40, 41, 43
  threat from during WW II, 69, 77, 81–83
  warnings before attacks by, 32
UMT (universal military training), 107

Ungerland, Bruce, 39
Unified Response, Operation, 194
uniforms
  changes to under Zumwalt, 133
  desert camouflage, 169
  no distinction between regular Sailors and reservists, 81
  for women, 30, 34
  WW I Naval Reserve, 30–31
United Nations Security Council Resolution 1441, 182
United States, 90
United States (US)
  anti-imperialist movement in, 23
  colonial power status of, 23
  competition for influence between Soviets and, 97
  declaration of war against Germany by, 32, 68
  European aid from, 97
  moon land and the space race, 113, 115, 131
  national security strategy for regional conflicts, 171
  projection of power overseas by, opposition to, 23
universal military training (UMT), 107
University of Washington, 36
Untermeyer, Chase, 158
Uphold Democrcy, Operation, 176
Utah, 24

V
V-5 program, 55, 74, 101
V-7 program, 70, 72, 73, 74, 77, 79, 87, 94, 105
V-9 program, 79, 80
V-10 program, 79, 80
V-12 program, 73, 74, 75, 76, 77, 79, 94, 197
Valley Forge, 97, 98–99
Vanderbilt, Aaron, 17
van Dyke, Henry, 126
Vaughan, Dennis, 164, 177
Vermont Naval Militia, 17
Vesuvius, 21
VF-5 squadron, 63
VF-32 squadron, 101
VF-51 squadron, 131
VF-781 squadron, 103
VFA-201 squadron, 182, 183
VFA-204 squadron, 173, 186
Victory Medal, 31, 34
Vietnam War
  active forces for service in, 116
  anti-war movement, 128
  awards and honors earned during, 123, 125, 129
  combat support services, 122–23
  draft during, 120–21
  NROTC program and, 54
  riverine operations, 125
  Seabee service during, 109
  service of reservists during, 116, 119–125
  Tet Offensive, 121, 122
  withdrawal of troops from, 133, 135
Vinson, Carl, 58, 89
Virginia Naval Militia, 17
Volunteer Communications Reserve, 55
Volunteer Naval Reserve
  budgets and funding for, 55, 61
  characteristics and organization of, 29, 52, 59
  Depression-era budgets, 58
  force strength of, 49, 91
  implementation of, 55
  intelligence operations by, 92
  post–WW II reserve force and infrastructure, 95–96
  radio operations and Communications Reserve, 55, 60, 61
  Seabees in, 109
  training requirements, 52
  WW II mobilization, 69–70
Vorys, John M., 38
VP-64 squadron, 153
VP-741 squadron, 110
VP-812 squadron, 103

VP-872 squadron, 116
VP-892 squadron, 103
VR-56 squadron, 153
Vraciu, Alex, 81
VS-872 squadron, 116
VS-873 squadron, 116
VT-31 squadron, 195
Vulcan, 145

W
Wabash, 18
Wadsworth, 32
Wadsworth, James W., 70
Wahlen, George Edward, 85
Walsh, Loretta P., 35, 188
Walton, 119
Wanamaker, John, 38
Ward, 67, 68, 69
War Manpower Commission, 73
Warner, John, 135, 136, 137
War of 1812, 12–13
War Powers Resolution/War Powers Act, 139, 142, 158, 160
war service chevrons, 31
Washington (Seattle), 61
Washington, Thomas, 48, 49
Washington Navy Yard, 9
Wasson, Joe, 108
Watertown Naval Reserve Center, 152
Watkins, James, 153
Watkins, Michael, 194
WAVES (Women Accepted for Volunteer Emergency Service), 79, 80, 93, 133
Webb, James H., Jr., 158
Weinberger, Caspar, 149
Welles, Gideon, 14
Westmoreland, William C., 121, 122
White, Robert W., 51
White, William, 76
Whitehurst, 119
White Squadron training cruise, 18
Whitman, Christie Todd, 181
Whitney, William C., 16, 17
Whitthorne, Washington C., 15–16, 17
Wieand, Harold T., 22, 62–63
Wilkinson, Bud, 74
Williams, Jack, 85
Willy, Wilford, 129
Wilson, H.W., 22
Wilson, Stanton R., 126
Wilson, Woodrow, 50, 68
Wiman, Charles D., 38
Wimbrown VII, 159
Wisconsin, 101, 169
Wolverine, 81
women
  career advancements and barriers to advancement, 132–33
  commissions for African Americans, 79
  duty assignments for, 79, 94
  first female officer, 79
  Navy uniforms, 30
  NROTC program enrollment, 54
  officer commissions, 79, 80, 113
  post–WW II reserve force, 93–94
  recruitment for Naval Coast Defense Reserve, 31–32
  training of, 80
  WAVES (Women Accepted for Volunteer Emergency Service), 79, 80, 93, 133
  WW I role, 33–35
Women's Armed Services Integration Act (1948), 93–94, 113, 132–33
Women's Reserve, 80
Worden, John, 15
World Trade Center, attack on, 9, 181
World War I (WW I)
  armistice signing and end of, 42, 43, 46
  awards and honors earned during, 31, 34, 38, 40, 41
  Battle of Jutland, 30
  convoy and escort system during, 40, 61
  demobilization at end of, 46, 48–49, 90
  Lusitania, attack on, 27, 32
  mine-laying operations, 43

  Naval Reserve Force role in, 32–43, 105
  Naval Reserve uniforms, 30–31
  Seabee service during, 109
  start of, 25
  submarine warfare, 27, 32, 40, 41, 43
  US entrance into, 32, 68
  Western Front naval railway battery crew role, 42
  women's role during, 33–35
  women's uniforms during, 34
World War II (WW II)
  anti-submarine operations, 77, 81–83
  attack on Japanese sub by crew of *Ward*, 67, 68
  awards and honors earned during, 82, 84–85, 126
  Battle of Britain, 68
  Battle of Leyte Gulf, 77
  Battle of Midway, 64
  Battle of the Atlantic, 69
  bombing of Hiroshima and Nagasaki, 88
  call up of reservists in preparation for, 61
  casualties during, 81–85
  contributions of naval aviators during, 56, 64
  convoy and escort system during, 75, 81–83
  demobilization at end of, 87–91
  Destroyers for Bases Agreement, 69
  events leading to, 60
  mobilization for, 68–70, 105
  officers for, 70–72, 73, 74, 75–78, 79–80, 81
  Pacific Fleet role, 72
  Pearl Harbor attack, 67, 68, 77, 84
  recruitment posters, 69, 71
  retirees returning to duty for, 77–78
  Seabee service during, 109
  ship reactivation for, 69
  start of, 61, 68
  surrender of Japan and end of, 83, 89
  voluntary recall of reservists, 68
wound chevrons, 31
Wright, Ronney, 195
Wyandotte, 21
Wyoming, 70

Y
Yacona, 46
Yale Unit, First, 38
Yankee, 21–22
Yemen, 177
yeoman (F), 33–35
yeowomen, 35
Yorktown, 63
Yosemite, 21, 23

Z
Z-Grams, 133
Ziegemeier, Henry J., 48
Zimmerman Telegram and Arthur Zimmerman, 32
Zinni, Anthony, 177
Zumwalt, Elmo R., 133, 144